# MODERN CURRICULUM PRESS
# POETRY WORKS!
## The Idea Book

by Babs Bell Hajdusiewicz

**Modern Curriculum Press**
A Division of Simon & Schuster
13900 Prospect Road
Cleveland, Ohio 44136

**Modern Curriculum Press**
A Division of Simon & Schuster
13900 Prospect Road
Cleveland, Ohio 44136

ISBN 0-8136-0727-2     2 3 4 5 6 7 8 9     94 93 92 91 90

# Table of Contents

Foreword . . . . . . . . . . . . . . . . . . . . . . . . . . . . . . . . . . . 5
Using **Poetry Works!** . . . . . . . . . . . . . . . . . . . . . . . 6
Responding to the Collection . . . . . . . . . . . . . . . . . . 7

## Adventure . . . . . . . . . . . . . . . . . . . . . . . . . . . . 9

Adventures of Isabel . . . Ogden Nash . . . . . . . . . . . 10
Bubbles Popping . . . Deborah Vitello . . . . . . . . . . . . 12
The Dark House . . . Anonymous . . . . . . . . . . . . . . . . 14
Hairy Toe . . . Anonymous . . . . . . . . . . . . . . . . . . . . . 16
Hungry Mungry . . . Shel Silverstein . . . . . . . . . . . . . 18
Mr. Bear . . . Babs Bell Hajdusiewicz . . . . . . . . . . . . 20
The Purple People Eater . . . Sheb Wooley . . . . . . . 22
True Story . . . Shel Silverstein . . . . . . . . . . . . . . . . . 24
Index to Related Poems . . . . . . . . . . . . . . . . . . . . . . 26

## Animals . . . . . . . . . . . . . . . . . . . . . . . . . . . . . . 27

Bird Carpenter . . . Leland B. Jacobs . . . . . . . . . . . . 28
Bunny Rabbit's Predicament . . .
   Babs Bell Hajdusiewicz . . . . . . . . . . . . . . . . . . . . 30
Cat . . . Mary Britton Miller . . . . . . . . . . . . . . . . . . . . 32
Eletelephony . . . Laura Richards . . . . . . . . . . . . . . . . 34
Fourteen Cats . . . Eileen Ellen Murphy . . . . . . . . . . 36
If the Spider Could Talk . . .
   Babs Bell Hajdusiewicz . . . . . . . . . . . . . . . . . . . . 38
If You Should Meet a Crocodile . . . Anonymous . 40
Mother Doesn't Want a Dog . . . Judith Viorst . . . . 42
Sleepy Tiger . . . Babs Bell Hajdusiewicz . . . . . . . . 44
Index to Related Poems . . . . . . . . . . . . . . . . . . . . . . 46

## Feelings . . . . . . . . . . . . . . . . . . . . . . . . . . . . . . 47

Bed in Summer . . . Robert Louis Stevenson . . . . . 48
It's Not Fair! . . . Babs Bell Hajdusiewicz . . . . . . . . . 50
Mumps . . . Elizabeth Madox Roberts . . . . . . . . . . . 52
My Turn to Talk . . . Babs Bell Hajdusiewicz . . . . . . 54
One-Eyed Teddy . . . Robert D. Hoeft . . . . . . . . . . . 56
Solo Sunday . . . Babs Bell Hajdusiewicz . . . . . . . . 58
Stealing Feelings . . . Babs Bell Hajdusiewicz . . . . 60
To Be or Not to Be . . . Anonymous . . . . . . . . . . . . . 62
Wishful Thinking . . . Pearl Bloch Segall . . . . . . . . . . 64
Index to Related Poems . . . . . . . . . . . . . . . . . . . . . . 66

## Me . . . . . . . . . . . . . . . . . . . . . . . . . . . . . . . . . . . 67

Drinking Fountain . . . Marchette Chute . . . . . . . . . . 68
Extraordinary Me . . . Babs Bell Hajdusiewicz . . . . 70
I, Myself, and Me . . . Babs Bell Hajdusiewicz . . . . 72
Me a Mess? . . . Babs Bell Hajdusiewicz . . . . . . . . . 74
Mud Monster . . . Bonnie Kinne . . . . . . . . . . . . . . . . 76
My Loose Tooth . . . Ruth Kanarek . . . . . . . . . . . . . . 78
The Poet Says . . . Babs Bell Hajdusiewicz . . . . . . . 80
The Secret Place . . . Tomie de Paola . . . . . . . . . . . 82
Silly Sleep Sheep . . . Helen C. Smith . . . . . . . . . . . 84
Statue on the Curb . . . Babs Bell Hajdusiewicz . . 86
Whose Face? . . . Lonny Alexander . . . . . . . . . . . . . 88
Index to Related Poems . . . . . . . . . . . . . . . . . . . . . . 90

## Me and Others . . . . . . . . . . . . . . . . . . . . . . . . . 91

Alas! . . . Babs Bell Hajdusiewicz . . . . . . . . . . . . . . . 92
From Mars to Safety . . . Babs Bell Hajdusiewicz . . 94
Goops (Table Manners) . . . Gelett Burgess . . . . . . 96
Hey, Bug! . . . Lilian Moore . . . . . . . . . . . . . . . . . . . . 98
Jonathan Bing . . . Beatrice Curtis Brown . . . . . . . . 100
Moochie . . . Eloise Greenfield . . . . . . . . . . . . . . . . . 102
Nancy Hanks . . . Rosemary Carr and
   Stephen Vincent Benét . . . . . . . . . . . . . . . . . . . . 104
Old Grumbler . . . Oscar Brand . . . . . . . . . . . . . . . . 106
Rudes . . . Babs Bell Hajdusiewicz . . . . . . . . . . . . . 108
Index to Related Poems . . . . . . . . . . . . . . . . . . . . . . 110

# Nature ............................ 111

Dandelion . . . Hilda Conkling ...................... 112

The Family of the Sun . . . Anonymous .......... 114

Fog . . . Carl Sandburg ............................ 116

The Frost Pane . . . David McCord ............... 118

Have You Seen Edgar? . . .
Teresa Lynn Morningstar ...................... 120

Last Word of a Bluebird . . . Robert Frost ........ 122

The Pasture . . . Robert Frost.................... 124

Silly Trees . . . Babs Bell Hajdusiewicz........... 126

Tommy . . . Gwendolyn Brooks ................... 128

Trees . . . Harry Behn............................ 130

When Icicles Hang by the Wall . . .
William Shakespeare........................... 132

Index to Related Poems........................ 134

# Numbers ............................. 135

Arithmetic Pie . . . Babs Bell Hajdusiewicz........ 136

Calendar Rhyme . . . Babs Bell Hajdusiewicz..... 138

Countdown to Recess . . Babs Bell Hajdusiewicz .. 140

Cycles . . . John Schaum......................... 142

I've Figured It Out . . . Babs Bell Hajdusiewicz ... 144

If All the Seas Were One Sea . . . Anonymous ... 146

Lining Up . . . Babs Bell Hajdusiewicz............ 148

Old Noah's Ark . . . Anonymous ................. 150

Index to Related Poems........................ 152

# Word Play ............................ 153

Bad and Good . . . Alexander Resnikoff.......... 154

Glug! Gurgle! Glug! . . . Babs Bell Hajdusiewicz.. 156

Have You Ever Seen? . . . Anonymous .......... 158

In and Out . . . Babs Bell Hajdusiewicz........... 160

Keep a Poem in Your Pocket . . . Beatrice
Schenk de Regniers........................... 162

My Favorite Word . . . Lucia Hymes and
James L. Hymes ............................. 164

Poets and Pigs . . . John Schaum ............... 166

Railroad Reverie . . . E. R. Young .............. 168

Yellow Butter . . . Mary Ann Hoberman........... 170

Yummy Humpty Dumpty . . . Anonymous ........ 172

Index to Related Poems........................ 174

# Adding Music ........................ 175

Cycles . . . John Schaum......................... 176

Fog . . . Carl Sandburg .......................... 177

Index . . . Sue Burkey............................ 178

Old Grumbler . . . Anonymous ................... 179

Poets and Pigs . . . John Schaum ............... 180

Purple People Eater . . . Sheb Wooley ........... 181

# Meet the Poets ...................... 182

Gwendolyn Brooks................................ 183

Tomie de Paola .................................. 184

Robert Frost..................................... 185

Babs Bell Hajdusiewicz........................... 186

Carl Sandburg................................... 187

William Shakespeare ............................. 188

Shel Silverstein ................................. 189

Judith Viorst.................................... 190

Deborah Vitello................................. 191

Anonymous..................................... 192

# Related Poems ...................... 193

# Indexes ............................... 256

Author ......................................... 256

First Line ...................................... 258

Title .......................................... 260

Curriculum Connections .......................... 262

Literature Connections........................... 267

# Acknowledgements ................. 269

# Foreword

Five-year-old Tommy appeared to be practicing what he claimed he would one day be able to do — scale walls like Spiderman. But what was he saying as he leaped in the air? His mother, listening more closely, heard it clearly this time: "When icicles hang by the wall . . ." She questioned Tommy, who knowingly replied, "That's a poem by Shakespeare, Mommy. Look! I got the icicle. Want a lick?" Here was proof that poetry works.

## Poetry in the Classroom

Poetry works in the classroom when the words of poems are meaningful and useful to children, when words and sounds are interesting, informative, humorous, adventurous, or thought-provoking.

Poetry works when we introduce poems that we enjoy. Children listen. They listen because they want to share the experience, to learn, to laugh, to think, and to read, recite, and write those words with us. In short, because of our enjoyment and modeling, children develop their listening, speaking, reading, and writing skills as they strive to make poems their own.

We know poetry works in the classroom when children make meaningful connections, using the words they've learned to express the images, feelings, and wonder of living . .

"Mrs. Hajdusiewicz! Look! The fog comes on little cat feet!" My tension from the long drive to school in foggy morning traffic vanished as the four of us stood huddled under the overhang, looking through Carl Sandburg's eyes, singing the poet's words that were now our own. Yes, indeed, poetry works!

## A Late Start

Ironically, **Poetry Works!** probably had its beginning long ago in a four-room schoolhouse in Burrows, Indiana. Though I loved every other aspect of school, I hated poetry. During my eight years there, I held fast to a dislike of anything resembling a poem, except for Joyce Kilmer's "Trees" because it made sense. A tree was, indeed, lovelier than a poem — or so I believed until my students changed my thinking.

My interest in poetry began with a spontaneous recitation of my old favorite, "Trees," as my sixth graders gathered around to observe a particularly colorful tree in the schoolyard. To my amazement (and theirs, no doubt), they listened in silence — even Randy and Jeremy, who heretofore had little interest in anything but spitballs.

My thinking was challenged again the next year while teaching preadolescents with primary-grade abilities. Early in the year, I noted the children's lack of familiarity with nursery rhymes, so I read aloud and recited a few rhymes. My students were fascinated and wanted more.

Convinced that poetry was a valuable tool for teaching, but having exhausted my repertoire, I scrambled for more poems. I read every children's poem I could find. Here was an opportunity to grow with my students and, hopefully, assure that they didn't miss what I had.

Every few days we read and reread another of my finds, throwing out a few but adding most of the poems to our list of favorites to enjoy in some way every day. As the list grew, so did the students' language skills. Their self-confidence flowered.

Just as children introduced me to the joys of reading and using poetry, they also led me to writing. Watching their interests, their imaginations, and their needs, I wrote and shared, continually encouraged by children's responses and by the conviction that poetry works!

## Writing Poetry Works!

Selecting poems for this collection has been fun and rewarding. Fun because in spite of having read and recited the final selections thousands of times, I never tire of their words. I never read one of them without finding some aspect of newness in it.

During those thousands of recitations, I have had the pleasure of sharing in children's enthusiasm for poetry — a lit up face, a wiggly giggle, a silent expression of wonderment, or a spontaneous "I just love that poem!" I know your children will "just love" these poems, and I am equally confident that you too will enjoy sharing special moments with poetry in your classroom.

*Babs Bell Hajdusiewicz*

# Using Poetry Works!

**Poetry Works!** will help you enrich your curriculum, using poems that have proven to be popular with children in classrooms across the country. It aims to engage you and your children in enjoyment of meaningful poetry all year long.

## Using the Poetry Works! Posters

The collection features 75 posters, grouped by subject matter. The posters are an ideal way to introduce the poems. Colorful and easy to read, they can be used in small groups or with an entire class.
- Use them to facilitate shared language experiences.
- Display favorite Poetry Posters where children can read and reread them on their own.
- Laminate posters so you and children can write on them with non-permanent markers.
- Provide practice in cloze procedures by masking words and phrases and having children supply them as you read.
- Display groups of posters so children can compare poems.
- Use the posters as models for children's art and writing.

## Using the Idea Book

The Idea Book provides material that will help you interest and intrigue your students. Its flexible format recognizes the diversity of classroom organization and teaching styles. The book is divided into these parts:

**Responding to the Collection** This section contains ideas to help you get started and activity suggestions you will want to use over and over with a variety of poems.

**Responding to the Poems** In this section you will find teaching suggestions that are specific to the 75 poems in the core collection. They will help you involve children in meaningful discussion and purposeful reading and writing over a variety of subject areas. The activities contain references to the more than 60 additional poems reprinted in the section entitled "Related Poems."

You will want to choose the activities that best suit your children's needs and your teaching style. You'll also want to adapt the suggestions and jot your own ideas in the margins as you use the various poems in **Poetry Works!**

**Blackline Masters** Each of the 75 poems included in the **Poetry Works!** Posters is printed on a blackline master that can be reproduced. These masters appear opposite the ideas for responding to each poem. They have many uses.
- Cut apart the text of a poem. Tape lines or phrases to sheets of paper and have children illustrate them.
- Make a transparency and display it on an overhead projector.
- Provide children with personal copies of favorite poems to illustrate and compile in a book.

**Adding Music** Reproducible song pages accompany several poems. Once children have become familiar with a poem, they will enjoy adding a tune to the words. The music will emphasize the close relationship between poetry and songs.
- Compile songs to make individual song books. Add other favorite songs if desired.
- Sing a song. Then pretend to take away the music to see what's left. Help children say the words and then write them.

**Meet the Poets** This section includes pictures of selected poets accompanied by brief biographies. These reproducible pages will help children associate poems with the men, women, and children of yesterday and today who have written to share their thoughts with others.
- Laminate the pictures and display them with the corresponding Poetry Posters.
- Insert poet pictures in anthologies of favorite poems compiled by children.
- Display the Anonymous poet frame with a poem by an unknown poet. Children can also draw their own picture inside this empty frame and display it along with the other poet pictures.

**Related Poems** The more than 60 poems in this section will further enrich your study of poetry. All of these poems are included in the indexes at the back of the book for easy reference.

# Responding to the Collection

## Making Time for Poetry

There's never enough time, is there? But aren't you always looking for creative ways to capture and maintain children's interest? Try the following ideas to help you do just that while bringing poetry into your busy days with children.

- Introduce a theme or lesson with a poem. Read "Silly Trees" or "The Frost Pane" to focus attention on a lesson about nature or seasons. Use "True Story" to introduce the theme of real and make-believe.
- Set aside one read-aloud time per week for poetry. Establishing a regular time for poetry each week helps build a repertoire of familiar poems and also sets the stage for the activities for each poem.
- Read or recite one poem every day. Occasionally you may wish to have a student do the daily reading.
- Tape record favorite verses so children can listen to them independently.
- Recite poems during those odd moments when children are regrouping or waiting for the bus. This is a good time to play an identification game in which you quote a line and challenge children to identify the poem and author.

## Beginning With Nursery Rhymes

Nursery rhymes are a good place for children of any age to begin having fun with poetry. There are dozens to choose from, and they are readily available.

Nursery rhymes acquaint children with basic vocabulary and provide them with knowledge of the world, two vital prerequisites for reading. The rhymes are fun to learn and chant out loud. They are also easy to act out, which means children use their new vocabulary and knowledge naturally.

Many children are already familiar with some of the rhymes and — with a little refreshing — so are their parents. Nursery rhymes provide an opportunity for parents and children to enjoy poetry together.

## Reading Aloud

Poems are meant to be read aloud. Children will love listening to you read and very soon they will want to join in.

- Display the Poetry Poster where children can see it easily.
- Introduce the poem by presenting the title and author and then thanking the author: " 'Tommy,' by Gwendolyn Brooks. Thank-you, Gwendolyn Brooks." Children respond favorably to this routine and after a few times, insist on thanking the poet, should you forget!
- Read the poem once so children can enjoy the sound of the words and begin to understand the structure of the poem. Since children frequently follow the model they see and hear during the first reading of a poem, you'll want to read in a lively and animated way.
- Read again, sometimes tracking the words to help children with print-to-speech correspondence. It's helpful to read and then reread each new poem to allow children the opportunity to think about what they first heard. Children can join in on the second reading. They especially enjoy repeating any expressions or gestures you've modeled.
- Vary this routine by reciting a poem before introducing the poster, by displaying the poster a day before reading the poem, or by reading aloud from the Idea Book.
- You can readily identify a "good" poem if children ask eagerly to hear it again. If responses are not what you expected, try reintroducing the poem at a later time, perhaps by reading in a different rhythm, by experimenting with expression and gestures, or after providing for additional introductory discussion.

## Collecting Quotes

Children can expand their spoken and written language with quotes from favorite poems. Many children will, of course, memorize parts of poems as they recite them again and again. Here are some ways to stimulate that process.

- Write favorite lines on sentence strips. Draw a picture clue on each one to help children identify it, and display the sentence strips in the classroom. Read the strips with children and have them identify the poet.
- Display a favorite line and have children write about or draw pictures of the image the line creates. Hang their papers under the quote.

- Encourage children to write favorite quotes on index cards. Challenge them to create a treasure box to hold their quotes. Suggest that they refer to the quotes and use them in their writing.

## Making a Rhyming Dictionary

A rhyming dictionary is an important writing tool for poets. Children enjoy and learn from making and using their own.

All children need to start their dictionary is three-hole-punched paper and metal rings. On each sheet, they can write groups of rhyming words. For example, one page would contain words that end with the *ake* sound, including *lake, take,* and *snake.* Another might list words with the *ar* sound such as *car, far,* and *star.* As the dictionary grows in thickness, children will find that they need to alphabetize it. Commercially available divider pages will help them organize their books.

## Using Reference Books

When you or the children are searching for information in an anthology or other resource book, recite or sing this:

### Index

If I don't know
On which page to look,
I'll use the index
In the back of my book.

In the absence of an index, turn to the front of the book as you say this poem:

### Table of Contents

If there is no index in the back of my book,
I'll turn to the front and take a look.
The table of contents is where I will look
To find out what is in this book.

This poem will help children who are having difficulty selecting a library book.

### Book Search

Since I can't tell a book by its cover,
A page or two helps me discover:
Do I like what I see?
Can I read eaisly?
Or should I go search for another?

## Practicing Punctuation

Display a Poetry Poster that includes a period, comma, question mark, and exclamation mark. These poems all work well: "Nancy Hanks," "My Turn to Talk," "Sleepy Tiger," "Poets and Pigs," and "Whose Face?"

Write a sentence on the chalkboard, leaving out the punctuation. Then use techniques such as these to dramatize the punctuation mark.
**Period** Walk dramatically to the end of the sentence. Stop and stand very still and say:
I'm a period. That's what I am.
I come and stand here at the end.
**Question Mark** Shrug your shoulders and raise your hands in a questioning fashion, while saying:
Am I a question mark? Oh, yes.
I ask you to think, then answer or guess.
**Exclamation Mark** Run excitedly to the end of the sentence. Jump into place with these words:
I'm an exclamation mark!
I'm here to end an exciting remark!
**Comma** Wiggle or sway as you move to the appropriate place. Wiggle continuously as you say:
I'm a wiggly comma 'cause
You need to take a breath and pause.
**Quotes** Display a familiar poster that contains quotes. You might try "When Icicles Hang by the Wall" (Nature: Poster 11), "Bunny Rabbit's Predicament" (Animals: Poster 2); "In and Out" (Word Play: Poster 4); or "Mr. Bear" (Adventure: Poster 6). Write the words of a speaker on the chalkboard without quotes. Then, with a volunteer, stand in the space before the quote. Raise your hand over your head and bend forward from the waist. Have the volunteer stand behind you and do the same thing. Read the words and then dash to the other end to close the quote.

Children enjoy acting out the punctuation marks. Encourage them to think of their own ways to do so.

## Closing a Poetry Session

Many teachers find it helpful to end poetry time with the same poem. Children of all ages delight in reciting "Fog," by Carl Sandburg (Nature: Poster 3), and then softly singing the words while moving quietly — like fog — to the next activity.

# UNIT 1
# ADVENTURE

1. Adventures of Isabel
2. Bubbles Popping
3. The Dark House
4. Hairy Toe
5. Hungry Mungry
6. Mr. Bear
7. The Purple People Eater
8. True Story

# RESPONDING TO
# Adventures of Isabel

BY OGDEN NASH

## Talking About Feelings

Children will enjoy talking about each of the characters Isabel met and how she felt and acted toward each one. Ask children how they would feel and act if they met "an enormous bear," "a wicked old witch," or "a hideous giant."

## Analyzing Characters

Describe each of the poem's characters and have children identify them. List the names on the chalkboard. Ask questions such as, Which character appears in every stanza? or, Who else appears? to help children decide who is the main character and who are supporting characters.

Encourage children to think about reality and fantasy as they talk about each character and his or her actions. Help children realize that some things about a character in a poem or story may be real while other qualities are pretend. For example, bears are real but a talking bear is not. Help children list qualities under headings of Real and Make-believe for each character. Invite children to brainstorm real and make-believe characters from stories, TV shows, cartoons, or comic books.

## Comparing Illustrations

Help children discuss the artist's rendition of the characters in the poem with questions such as, "What do you like or dislike about the way the artist drew the witch?" and "How else do you think Isabel could look?"

If possible, obtain *The Random House Book of Poetry, Sing a Song of Popcorn,* or another anthology to show children how other artists have illustrated this poem. Help children discuss their preferences.

## Illustrating the Poem

Invite children to draw the poem's characters. Have children write each character's words inside a speech bubble for display in the classroom or for fun in sharing the poem with parents at home.

## Using Words Meaningfully

Stimulate children's interest in unfamiliar words from the poem by using those words in your conversation during routine activities. For example, you may comment that a child is "self-reliant" when he or she completes a task independently or that a child "showed no rage and showed no rancor" when you witness self-control. Similarly, you may note how "ravenous" you feel at lunchtime or that since the buses are waiting, everyone will need to "scurry."

## Comparing the Poem to Other Literature

Children may recognize that the giant's words to Isabel are from "Jack and the Beanstalk." You may want to reread that story or other giant stories such as "David and Goliath" or a Greek myth about Odysseus and the Cyclops, a giant with one eye in the middle of his forehead. This would also be a good time to introduce the poem, "Tall and Small" included in the Related Poems.

# Adventures of Isabel

Isabel met an enormous bear,
Isabel, Isabel, didn't care;
The bear was hungry, the bear was ravenous,
The bear's big mouth was cruel and cavernous.
The bear said, Isabel, glad to meet you,
How do, Isabel, now I'll eat you!
Isabel, Isabel, didn't worry,
Isabel didn't scream or scurry.
She washed her hands and she straightened her hair up,
Then Isabel quietly ate the bear up.

Once in a night as black as pitch
Isabel met a wicked old witch.
The witch's face was cross and wrinkled,
The witch's gums with teeth were sprinkled.
Ho ho, Isabel! the old witch crowed,
I'll turn you into an ugly toad!
Isabel, Isabel, didn't worry,
Isabel didn't scream or scurry,
She showed no rage and she showed no rancor,
But she turned the witch into milk and drank her.

Isabel met a hideous giant,
Isabel continued self-reliant.
The giant was hairy, the giant was horrid,
He had one eye in the middle of his forehead.
Good morning, Isabel, the giant said,
I'll grind your bones to make my bread.
Isabel, Isabel, didn't worry,
Isabel didn't scream or scurry.
She nibbled the Zwieback that she always fed off,
And when it was gone, she cut the giant's head off.

*Ogden Nash*

# RESPONDING TO
# Bubbles Popping

BY DEBORAH VITELLO

## Exploring The Meaning

After the second reading, reread the last two lines of the poem. Discuss what children think Deborah Vitello meant by her warning, "be glad you're not a bubble."

Would children like to be a bubble? Before they answer that question, you may want to read about other kinds of bubbles in poems from this collection: "Bubble Gum," by Nina Payne, and "Bubbles," by Babs Bell Hajdusiewicz, in Related Poems, and "Bunny Rabbit's Predicament," by Babs Bell Hajdusiewicz (Animals: Poster 2). Talk about times and places where children have seen bubbles — in boiling water, in sea foam, in dishwater. Then have children write a few sentences telling why they would or would not want to be a bubble.

## Identifying Couplets

This poem is written in couplets — each pair of lines rhymes. Have children find examples of pairs of rhyming words in the poem. Then read other poems that follow the same pattern: "The Last Word of a Bluebird," by Robert Frost (Nature: Poster 6), "The Family of the Sun" (Nature: Poster 2), "Extraordinary Me," by Babs Bell Hajdusiewicz (Me: Poster 2), and "Eletelephony," by Laura Richards (Animals: Poster 4). Children will enjoy finding the rhyming couplets in these poems.

## Writing Couplets

Children like to write their own rhyming couplets. A good way for them to begin is to use a line from the poem as a starter. Try using this line from the last stanza:

Popping, popping! everywhere . . .

Then help students make up new lines:

Over here and over there, or
On my nose but I don't care.

Many words end with the *air* sound. You may want to refer to "Mr. Bear," by Babs Bell Hajdusiewicz (Adventure: Poster 6), for examples of words with this sound.

## Blowing Bubbles

This activity can be conducted indoors, but will be more effective in a large outdoor space. Mix dishwashing liquid and water with a few drops of glycerin, which is available in drug stores. Then provide children with bubble-making instruments, such as wire loops or straws. The straws may be used as is or with their tips fringed and fanned out.

Show children how to make bubbles. Encourage them to observe the colors and shapes of the bubbles.

## Extending Ideas

After blowing bubbles, spend a few minutes talking about other aspects of bubble-blowing the poet could have mentioned, things like the color of bubbles, the various sizes, the difficulty of catching them, and their soapy feel. Some children may wish to compose an additional verse using one or more of these ideas.

## Exploring Bubble Shapes

Have children describe the shape of a bubble. Challenge them to think of as many bubble-shaped objects as they can: balloons, light bulbs, or the moon, for instance. Children can combine their ideas to make a poster called Bubbles, Bubbles Everywhere.

## Looking At Contractions

Challenge children to find all the contractions in the poem. Have them write out the expanded form of each one and substitute it for the contraction. Note how the expanded form changes the rhythm of the line.

See Meet the Poet, page 191.

# Bubbles Popping

Why don't bubbles ever last?
They seem to disappear so fast.
No matter where they go to play,
You can bet they'll go away.

If they fall down on the ground
They just pop without a sound.
If they float up in the sky,
You might as well tell them goodbye.

Popping, popping! everywhere,
On the ground or in the air.
Just be glad you're not a bubble,
Or you'd be in for lots of trouble!

*Deborah Vitello*

# RESPONDING TO
# The Dark House

BY ANONYMOUS

## Enjoying Suspense

Children will enjoy the atmosphere of a dark room as you read with suspense and drama. Try reading the poem in a progressively softer voice as well as a progressively louder one. Ask children which pattern they prefer and why. Help children relate the idea of a progressively softer voice to that of going from a big, dark wood to a tiny box.

## Dramatizing Suspense

As they listen or share in reading the poem, have children use their bodies to be a big forest and then get slightly smaller and continue to shrink to depict each smaller place or item. Children may also want to imagine their school as the wood and the classroom as the room as they act out the poem.

## Building Sight Vocabulary

As you read aloud, children will enjoy identifying and, perhaps, listing such words as *wood, house,* and *room,* that name a location. You may want to have children write these words on cards and show the appropriate card whenever you pause in the reading. You can also mask the location words and have children write them.

## Innovating On The Text

Ask questions such as, How else might a wood look? or, How else might we describe a wood, a house, and the other places? to help children think of words to substitute for *dark* throughout the poem. Have children list all their words, try each, and then circle the ones that make sense in the poem. Invite children to try their leftover words to find a different word to describe each of the locations. In each case, ask children to think of a title for their new text. Help children realize that an adjective or describing word may not always make sense for every use.

Children will also enjoy substituting other words for *GHOST.* You might introduce a surprise ending of a different sort by reading the poem with lots of suspense and ending with the word *nothing.*

## Using Commas

Prior to this activity, you'll want to have children read or recite the poem, substituting other words for *dark.* Talk about the use of a comma to separate the two descriptive words. Then emphasize each comma as you write several lines of the poem using a substituted word.

Challenge children to help write and punctuate other sentences with several consecutive describing words.

## Making Size Comparisons

Provide objects in different sizes for children to arrange in order from largest to smallest as they read or recite the poem with you.

Use containers in varying sizes for children to "nest," or place inside each other, from largest to smallest or the reverse.

Provide or ask children to bring in objects that nest in graduating sizes such as cannisters, baskets, measuring spoons or cups, or speciality hammers with screwdrivers in the handle. Read the poem as they assemble the objects and, for extra fun, try reading the poem backwards as they reassemble the items.

At random times, as children manipulate any items in graduated sizes, ask what poem comes to mind.

See Meet the Poet, page 192.

# The Dark House

In a dark, dark wood there was a dark, dark house,
And in that dark, dark house there was a dark, dark room,
And in that dark, dark room there was a dark, dark cupboard,
And in that dark, dark cupboard there was a dark, dark, shelf,
And on that dark, dark shelf there was a dark, dark box,
And in that dark, dark box there was a GHOST!

*Anonymous*

# RESPONDING TO
# Hairy Toe

BY ANONYMOUS

## Dramatizing The Poem

After hearing this poem once, children will be eager to join in on the repetitive ghost-like phrases "Where's my Hair-r-ry To-o-oe?/Who's got my Hair-r-ry To-o-oe?" Track the words on the poster as they read or recite.

This poem also begs to be dramatized. One child can play the woman, while another group makes creaking, groaning, windy sound effects and a third group says the repeating lines. You or a child can be the narrator.

## Making A Made-For-TV Movie

Discuss the many pictures readers see in their minds while reading this poem. Note that the first line could be drawn, as could the second and third. Make a list of scenes that could be illustrated. Have groups of children draw these pictures on a long roll of adding-machine tape to make a movie.

Demonstrate how to show the movies through a milk carton cut to make a TV set like the one shown below. Children will enjoy looking at each other's movies.

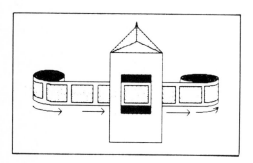

## Writing A New Ending

Encourage children to create an additional ending for "Hairy Toe." Ask questions like these to get them started:

What happened next?
Who was asking for the Hairy Toe?
Did the woman return it?

## Using Special Cues When Reading And Writing

Many words in this poem are elongated with hyphens: *Hair-r-ry To-o-oe, r-r-um-mbled, cr-r-a-ack, cr-e-eak.* Point to these words as you draw out the reading of them. Elicit from children that the effect of this technique is to make the words sound ghostlike, eery, or frightening. Ask volunteers to read lines with and without the drawn-out words and discuss the difference.

You may want to compare this technique to the one used in "If All the Seas Were One Sea" (Numbers: Poster 6) in which words that are to be emphasized are capitalized.

Give children large sheets of paper to make their own poetry posters. Suggest that they write a ghost story using hyphens and capital letters to emphasize words. They will, of course, illustrate these scary stories and read them aloud to classmates.

## Understanding Personification

Note that a weather reporter might describe the wind by saying, "Winds blew at 15 miles an hour." Poets, on the other hand, often use words that make the wind seem like a person or animal. Ask children to point to the words in the poem that make the wind seem alive: *moan, groan, hit, growled.* Work with children to make a list of other lively words that might be used to describe the wind: *whisper, howl, scream, call,* and so on.

See Meet the Poet, page 192.

# Hairy Toe

Once there was a woman who went out to pick beans,
and she found a Hairy Toe.
She took the Hairy Toe home with her,
and that night, when she went to bed,
the wind began to moan and groan.
Away off in the distance
she seemed to hear a voice crying,
"Where's my Hair-r-ry To-o-oe?
Who's got my Hair-r-ry To-o-oe?"

The woman scrooched down,
way down under the covers,
and about that time
the wind appeared to hit the house,

smoosh,

and the old house creaked and cracked
like something was trying to get in.
The voice had come nearer,
almost at the door now,
and it said,
"Where's my Hair-r-ry To-o-oe?
Who's got my Hair-r-ry To-o-oe?"

The woman scrooched further down
under the covers
and pulled them tight around her head.

The wind growled around the house
like some big animal
and r-r-um-mbled
over the chimney.
All at once she heard the door cr-r-a-ack
and Something slipped in
and began to creep over the floor.

The floor went
cre-e-eak, cre-e-eak
at every step that thing took towards her bed.
The woman could almost feel
it bending over her bed.
Then in an awful voice it said:
"Where's my Hair-r-ry To-o-oe?
Who's got my Hair-r-ry To-o-oe?"

*Anonymous*

# RESPONDING TO
# Hungry Mungry

BY SHEL SILVERSTEIN

## Dramatizing The Poem

Dramatizing this poem can be a hilarious experience for children. One person can be Hungry Mungry. Make oak tag signs with the names of the foods he ate and assign these cards to children who will represent the foods. (Use words and/or pictures for the signs.) Other items Hungry Mungry "eats" may also be depicted by children wearing signs. There should be more than enough items so that everyone in the class gets a chance to participate.

## Mapping Locations

Together, you may wish to list all the places that Hungry Mungry ate: Chicago's Water Tower, Pittsburgh, New York, Tennessee, Boston, Mississippi River, Egyptian pyramids, churches in Rome, grass in Africa, ice in Nome, hills in Brazil. Using a world map and a separate map of the United States, have children mark all these places with a map tack or removable stick-on notes. You may wish to discuss the references the poet makes to each place. For example, why does he say "ice in Nome?" (Nome is in Alaska, and Alaska is very cold and full of ice.)

Interested children might draw a world map and illustrate it with pictures of Hungry Mungry eating everything from his neighborhood (it could be in your hometown) to Washington, D.C., to the hills of Brazil.

## Using Colorful Words

Encourage children to make a list of all the words and expressions in the poem that describe the eating process: *ate, eaten, gulped, gobbled, munched, chewed, drank, sipped, nibble*; and "licked his lips," "gnashin' his teeth," "wiped his mouth upon his sleeve," "opened up his mouth." Ask how the poem would be different if the poet restricted himself to "eat, ate and eaten." Count the number of times the poet would have used those words, so children will understand that the poet wanted to vary the way he expressed himself. As an extension, challenge the class to see if they can come up with any eating-related words or expressions *not* used in the poem such as *swallowed, chomped, gnawed, dined, savored, devoured,* and *tasted*.

## Sequencing

Children will be quick to notice that Hungry Mungry started out by eating the food on his table, then moved on to the neighborhood, the nation, the world, and the universe. His actions bring to mind this way of writing an address:

[Child's Name]
[Street Address]
[City, State, and Zip Code]
[Country]
[Continent]
[Earth]
[The Solar System]
[The Milky Way]
[The Universe]

Children can decide what Hungry Mungry would eat in each place.

## Comparing Poems

Children will understand — when you read "Goops," by Gelett Burgess (Me and Others: Poster 3) — that Hungry Mungry could be called a Goop. Have them explain why, using quotes from the text.

See Meet the Poet, page 189.

# Hungry Mungry

Hungry Mungry sat at supper,
Took his knife and spoon and fork,
Ate a bowl of mushroom soup, ate a slice of roasted pork,
Ate a dozen stewed tomatoes, twenty-seven deviled eggs,
Fifteen shrimps, nine baked potatoes,
Thirty-two fried chicken legs,
A shank of lamb, a boiled ham,
Two bowls of grits, some black-eye peas,
Four chocolate shakes, eight angel cakes,
Nine custard pies with Muenster cheese,
Ten pots of tea, and after he
Had eaten all that he was able,
He poured some broth on the tablecloth
And ate the kitchen table.

His parents said, "Oh Hungry Mungry, stop these silly jokes."
Mungry opened up his mouth, and "Gulp," he ate his folks.
And then he went and ate his house, all the bricks and wood,
And then he ate up all the people in the neighborhood.
Up came twenty angry policemen shouting, "Stop and cease."
Mungry opened up his mouth and "Gulp," he ate the police.
Soldiers came with tanks and guns.
Said Mungry, "They can't harm me."
He just smiled and licked his lips and ate the U.S. Army.

The President sent all his bombers — Mungry still was calm,
Put his head back, gulped the planes, and gobbled up the bomb.
He ate his town and ate the city — ate and ate and ate —
And then he said, "I think I'll eat the whole United States."

And so he ate Chicago first and munched the Water Tower,
And then he chewed on Pittsburgh but he found it rather sour.
He ate New York and Tennessee, and all of Boston town,
Then drank the Mississippi River just to wash it down.
And when he'd eaten every state, each puppy, boy and girl,
He wiped his mouth upon his sleeve and went to eat the world.

He ate the Egypt pyramids and every church in Rome,
And all the grass in Africa and all the ice in Nome.
He ate each hill in green Brazil and then to make things worse
He decided for dessert he'd eat the universe.

He started with the moon and stars and soon as he was done
He gulped the clouds, he sipped the wind and gobbled up the sun.
Then sitting there in the cold dark air,
He started to nibble his feet,
Then his legs, then his hips
Then his neck, then his lips
Till he sat there just gnashin' his teeth
'Cause nothin' was nothin' was
Nothin' was nothin' was
Nothin' was left to eat.

*Shel Silverstein*

# RESPONDING TO
# Mr. Bear

BY BABS BELL HAJDUSIEWICZ

## Dramatizing

Children will enjoy seeing and hearing the drama you share as you read aloud. Demonstrate an air of confidence in controlling a bear; make a gesture to "halt!" as you read "abruptly;" point for each "Mr. Bear! Mr. Bear;" pose charmingly for "debonair."

Invite children to pantomime phrases such as "woke himself up with a monstrous scream," or "I nearly froze." Suggest that classmates try to guess the phrases.

## Identifying Real and Make-Believe

Ask children what could be real in the poem and what is pretend. They will no doubt see that a bear is real but a human does not control a bear in its cave. Have children give reasons to support their opinions.

You may want to list the real and pretend ideas and the reasons for each. This is also an excellent opportunity to model the writing of indirect quotations such as this:

Joey says that bears don't wear clothes because bears are wild animals.

## Categorizing Clothing

Children will enjoy listening for the types of clothes Mr. Bear could have worn if he hadn't fallen asleep. Reread the poem and substitute other clothing words children suggest.

Help children list words for kinds of clothing under headings such as Headgear, Body Wear, and Footwear. You'll want to allow for specific styles and brand names as children brainstorm. Invite children to draw an animal or human character wearing an item from each list and then write something about their characters for a display that might be titled We Don't Go Out in Our Underwear!

## Recognizing Rhyming Words

Have children see how many different words rhyme with *bear* as you reread the poem. Write or circle each word. Challenge children to add even more words to the list.

## Analyzing Rhyming Words In Context

Ask children to listen to the words *closed* and *froze* to tell why they are not a perfect pair of rhyming words. Reread the stanza in which the words appear and give children the opportunity to talk about why they think the poet only approximated rhyming sounds. Challenge children to find other poems containing imperfect rhyming pairs and talk about why they think each pair was used.

## Viewing A Poem As A Story

Have children tell why they think the poet began the poem as if telling a story. Help them understand that "Mr. Bear" does in fact tell a story and is therefore called a narrative poem. Children will enjoy other narrative poems — "Old Grumbler" (Me and Others: Poster 8) and "True Story" (Adventure: Poster 10), for example — from this collection.

Tell children that the poet actually began writing a story but changed to the poetic form after playing with rhyming words. Invite children to tell and then write a prose version of "Mr. Bear."

## Capturing Facial Expressions

Ask children to use their faces to show how Mr. Bear's face might have looked as he lazed sleepily or as he growled. Have children show how the narrator's face might look in situations such as when Mr. Bear is being reprimanded.

Encourage children to draw the characters' facial expressions for display under a title such as A Face Says It All. Children might include the character's words in a speech bubble.

See Meet the Poet, page 186.

# Mr. Bear

I'll tell you a story of how old Mr. Bear
Almost went out in his underwear!

Mr. Bear was asleep when he had a bad dream
And woke himself up with a monstrous scream!

He was heading outside of his comfortable cave
When I stopped him abruptly to make him behave!

And I said:
"Mr. Bear! Mr. Bear! Now don't you dare
Go out of this cave in your underwear!
Mr. Bear! Mr. Bear! You must be aware
It's winter outside; there's snow in the air!"

Well, he growled at me as if to say,
"Get out of here! Get out of my way!"

But I said:
"Mr. Bear! Mr. Bear! I know it's unfair
To be rudely awakened in a scary nightmare.
Mr. Bear! Mr. Bear! Please, stay right there!
Don't leave your cave! There's snow everywhere!"

He looked at me with eyes half-closed;
Then G-R-O-W-L-E-D again! I nearly froze!

But I said:
"Mr. Bear! Mr. Bear! You'll have to prepare!
A bear mustn't go out in just underwear!
Mr. Bear! Mr. Bear! Sit down in your chair!
If you want to go out, you'll need something to wear!

"Let's see, Mr. Bear, here's a coat and a pair
Of boots and hat . . . mmmm, you'll look debonair!
Mr. Bear? Mr. Bear? Well, I do declare!
Mr. Bear is snoring in his underwear!"

*Babs Bell Hajdusiewicz*

# RESPONDING TO
# The Purple People Eater

BY SHEB WOOLEY

## Comparing Poems About Strange Creatures

"The Purple People Eater" is one of several poems about strange creatures that can be found in this collection. You may want to present this one at the same time as "Adventures of Isabel," by Ogden Nash (Adventure: Poster 1), "Mud Monster" by Bonnie Kinne (Me: Poster 5), and "Extraordinary Me," by Babs Bell Hajdusiewicz (Me: Poster 2).

Once children are familiar with all four poems, they can debate the relative merits of the creatures by answering questions such as these:

- Which creature is scariest? Funniest?
- How are the creatures alike? Different?
- Which one would you want to make into a stuffed animal?

Children should back up their responses with quotes from the poems.

## Dramatizing The Poem

Children will have fun performing the second stanza of "The Purple People Eater" as a fingerplay, using actions like these:

one-eyed (Hold fist to middle of forehead.)
one-horned (Hold fist to nose.)
flyin' . . . (Flap arms like wings.)

## Singing The Poem

Once children are familiar with the words, it's time to add music to "The Purple People Eater." (See Adding Music, page 175.) Point out that Sheb Wooley is both a poet and songwriter; he shares both words and music with others.

In this connection, read "The Poet Says," by Babs Bell Hajdusiewicz (Me: Poster 7). Then have children change the title to read "The Songwriter Says." Have them read the poem with you, changing *poem* to *song* and *read* to *sing* throughout.

## Remembering Rock 'n Roll

Sheb Wooley's song was a top-of-the-charts hit in the late 1950s. Even now, you may be able to find a recording of it on an oldies album. Children can compare their rendition of the song to the one on the recording. Suggest that they make a recording of their own version.

## Examining Mood

Note that the mood of the poem changes from the beginning, when the purple people eater seems scary, to the end when it is described as "friendly." Ask children what other clues let them know that this is not a terrifying monster. They may point out that Wooley says it is "undergrowed" and "wears short shorts" — not attributes we usually associate with a monster.

## Writing The Way People Talk

Children can look at "The Purple People Eater" to find words or expressions which, while they may not be spelled correctly, accurately mimic the way people talk. Suggest that children substitute correct spellings: *coming* for "a-comin'," *shaking* for "shakin'," and *because* for "'cause." Ask them which sounds better in the poem.

## Creating A Cartoon

Mr. Purple People Eater might make a good Saturday-morning cartoon character. Let children create some buddies for him and decide where he lives. Then they can make up adventures for him and his friends. Once they have decided on characters, setting, and plot, they can draw the pictures.

See Adding Music, page 181.

# The Purple People Eater

Well, I saw the thing
a-comin' out of the sky,
It had one long horn and one big eye.
I commenced to shakin' and I said, "Ooh-wee,
It looks like a purple people eater to me."

It was a one-eyed, one-horned,
flyin' purple people eater,
One-eyed, one-horned,
Flyin' purple people eater,
One-eyed, one-horned,
Flyin' purple people eater,
Sure looked strange to me.

Well, he came down to earth
And he lit in a tree, I said,
"Mister Purple People Eater,
Don't eat me."
I heard him say in a voice so gruff,
"I wouldn't eat you
'cause you're so tough."

Well, bless my soul, Rock 'n Roll,
Flyin' purple people eater
Pigeontoed, undergrowed,
Flyin' purple people eater,
He wears short shorts,
Friendly little people eater,
What a sight to see!

*Sheb Wooley*

# RESPONDING TO
# True Story

BY SHEL SILVERSTEIN

## Listening Critically

Before you read "True Story," tell children to listen carefully to find out if they think the title is a good one: Is this a true story?

After reading, look at the poem again to find reasons why this story could not be true. Children will find plenty of proof in the text: pirates in a cave, a mermaid who cut him loose, a water snake named Clyde who pulled him out of quicksand, and so on. The last line, of course, could not possibly be true, since the author is alive to tell the story.

## Staging Tableaux Vivants

Children will have fun with this old-fashioned technique in which actors present scenes while remaining silent and motionless as in a photograph. Each pair of lines in this poem presents an image that children could depict. Encourage them to make their facial expressions and body postures dramatic — they should really ham it up for this presentation.

## Reading More By And About The Author

Shel Silverstein is a great favorite of children, and they will want to read more of his works. Another of his poems, "Hungry Mungry," appears on Adventure: Poster 5. One of his best books, *Lafcadio, the Lion Who Shot Back*, available in most libraries, is another example of a tall tale. It is fun to read aloud.

This collection also contains a biography and photograph of Silverstein, which children will enjoy reading.

## Thinking With The Poet

Ask children to name words in the poem that rhyme. They will quickly note all the words that rhyme with *ride*. (You may want to write the words and note the different ways of spelling the same sound.)

Have children try to imagine how the poet constructed the story. Did he start with the story and a few lines? Did he write the other lines to fit the rhyming pattern he had started?

## Writing Tall Tales

By improvising on the text of "True Story," children can create their own tall tale. Start by changing only a word or two:

This morning I jumped on my horse
And went out for a ride,
And some crocodiles chased me . . .

Then progress to changing whole lines as new ideas are generated in discussion.

Begin by working with the whole class. Then let interested students make up their own, individual "True Story."

## Reading Related Books

A number of authors have written versions of classic American tall tales. *Paul Bunyan* by Steven Kellogg is one such tale in book form. *John Henry*, by Ezra Jack Keats, is another example of a famous American tall tale. As you read these books, you can call attention to the elements all these heroes have in common — exaggerated strength, bravado, incredible adventures.

James Stevenson explores the form in a somewhat different way. In his books, Grandfather always calms his grandchildren's fears by recounting how life was when he was a boy. His stories always turn out to be very entertaining tall tales.

See Meet the Poet, page 189.

# True Story

This morning I jumped on my horse
And went out for a ride,
And some wild outlaws chased me
And they shot me in the side.
So I crawled into a wildcat's cave
To find a place to hide,
But some pirates found me sleeping there,
And soon they had me tied
To a pole and built a fire
Under me — I almost cried
Till a mermaid came and cut me loose
And begged to be my bride,
So I said I'd come back Wednesday
But I must admit I lied.
Then I ran into a jungle swamp
But I forgot my guide
And I stepped into some quicksand,
And no matter how I tried
I couldn't get out, until I met
A water snake named Clyde,
Who pulled me to some cannibals
Who planned to have me fried.
But an eagle came and swooped me up
And through the air we flied,
But he dropped me in a boiling lake
A thousand miles wide.
And you'll never guess what I did then —
I DIED.

*Shel Silverstein*

 # Index to Related Poems

1. Bubble Gum ...........................................page 201
2. Bubbles .................................................202
3. Tall and Small .........................................241

# UNIT 2
# ANIMALS

1. Bird Carpenter
2. Bunny Rabbit's Predicament
3. Cat
4. Eletelephony
5. Fourteen Cats
6. If the Spider Could Talk
7. If You Should Meet a Crocodile
8. Mother Doesn't Want a Dog
9. Sleepy Tiger

# RESPONDING TO
# Bird Carpenter

BY LELAND B. JACOBS

## Giving A Dramatic Reading

After repeated read-alouds, children will enjoy reciting the poem with you. Divide the class in half. One half can repeat the first stanza. The other half of the class can say the second stanza out loud.

## Viewing Animals As Workers

Explore the idea of birds building their nests by carrying materials in their beaks. Talk about other animals and specific body parts they use for work, for example, the elephant's trunk, the pig's snout, the beaver's tail, the duck's bill and webbed feet, the octopus' suction cups, or an insect's antennae.

Help children think of other "animal carpenters" and the structures they build, such as the beaver's dam, a spider's web, ant hills and tunnels, a burrow made by a gopher or mole, or a caterpillar's cocoon.

In the spring, children may want to lay out sticks, string, and other materials that birds can gather for their nests. A nature walk might offer children a view of animal homes or even the animals at work.

## Learning About a Carpenter's Work

Encourage discussion about carpenters and the work they do. Talk about kinds of houses people might build, such as houses of brick or wood, apartment buildings, tepees, yurts, log cabins, or domes. You may want to use Harvey Weiss' book, *Shelters: from Tepee to Igloo* as a resource. Urge children to think about other kinds of building that carpenters do, such as making furniture, wood toys, or kitchen cabinets.

Ask questions about how carpenters learn to build things, why a level, plane, and rule would be needed, and when a carpenter might work outside or inside. If possible, invite a carpenter to visit your classroom to talk about building and demonstrate tools.

## Identifying Tools And Their Uses

Have children identify the words in the poem that name tools used by carpenters. Elicit the names of additional hand tools a carpenter might use such as pliers, drills, wrenches, screwdrivers, and various power tools. If real tools are not available, you may want to show pictures from catalogs. Invite children to tell about the tools they have seen or used and what each tool is for.

You may want to have children draw tools or cut pictures from catalogs and then write about how to use the tool. In addition, children can describe a tool, telling how it is used, and have classmates try to guess its name.

## Thinking Of Other Occupations And Their Tools

Help children think about people's occupations and the tools of their trades such as a baseball player's bat and cleats, a bricklayer's trowel and mortar, a musician's instrument and music, a gardener's clippers and mower, or a writer's pen and paper. Children enjoy naming an occupation and having classmates guess what tools that person uses.

For an extension, read "The Poet Says" (Me: Poster 7). Then have children innovate on the text by substituting other occupational titles, the tools used, and a product of the work. For example, the *seamstress* says, "A *jacket* is a part of me — so I must *sew* that part of me. I take some *fabric*, a *needle* and *thread*, to *sew* what's in my mind and then you have a *jacket* to *wear* — I've given you a part of me."

## Using Homographs

Call attention to words with the same spelling but different meanings by asking children if carpenters hammer their *fingernails* and use *airplanes* to build things. Then discuss the poem's meaning and other meanings of the words *levels* and *rules*. Have children think of and discuss other examples of homographs.

# Bird Carpenter

Carpenters use nails and hammers,
　Planes and levels.
　Saws and rules.

Birds build houses so much simpler —
　Beaks are all
　They have for tools.

*Leland B. Jacobs*

# RESPONDING TO
# Bunny Rabbit's Predicament    BY BABS BELL HAJDUSIEWICZ

## Enjoying The Poem

Encourage children to talk about what they would do if they had chewing gum stuck to their faces or clothes. Summarize discussion by stating that it "certainly would be a predicament." Before reading the poem, have children predict how the rabbit will get into his predicament and how he will get out of it.

On repeated readings, you may want to chant the poem following its "rap" rhythm.

## Dramatizing

Encourage children to beckon their audience to "come along" for the story at the beginning. For the last stanza, partners may act out pride in accomplishment and join hands, and then, on the last line, lean their heads together.

## Talking About Predicaments

Children will enjoy talking about predicaments that they, their friends, or family members have experienced. Share your own experiences or pose questions such as, Did you ever get stuck in a tree so you couldn't get down? or, What if you lost a boot when you had to go out in the rain? Help children realize that many predicaments can be avoided through forethought or solved through careful thinking. Challenge children to list solutions or preventive measures for each predicament that they share.

## Performing An Experiment

Children will love chewing bubble-gum and blowing bubbles in preparation for an experiment. Respond to the fun with a comment using the expression from the poem "to [our] own delight." Provide a swatch of fabric or low-pile carpet and a cup of ice cubes for each child. Have them place gum on the swatch, press it down, and then apply ice. Have partners discuss the on-going process and then share their findings with the class.

## Thinking About Cause And Effect

Read aloud as you write a sentence such as this: Bunny's bubble popped and gum stuck to his face. Write *cause* and *effect* and tell children "gum stuck to his face" is the effect, or what happened. Write the words under *effect*. Ask what caused the gum to stick and write "bubble popped" under *cause*. Repeat for other ideas in the poem, such as why there would be ice in the watering trough.

Have children list causes and effects of real happenings at home, brainstorm possible solutions and/or preventions, and write their information in the form of short stories to share with parents.

## Using Words Meaningfully

Unfamiliar words in the poem will become part of children's working vocabulary if you use them in everyday classroom situations. Invite peer cooperation, for example, by suggesting that a "chum" help " 'cause two heads are sometimes better than one;" describe a sticker as sticking "like a parasite;" suggest that a stubborn zipper presents a "predicament" but its owner will "never despair."

Help children see that "thingamujig" is used when there's no word or when the name of an object cannot be recalled. Introduce them to Rich Hall's books on Sniglets for words like "pupkiss," which he defines as the saliva a dog leaves on your cheek or the window. Have children try out their own sniglets on friends and parents.

## Relating The Poem To Other Literature

Children will enjoy recalling the morals of other favorite fables. You will also want to present "Bubble Gum" from this collection (Related Poems).

See Meet the Poet, page 186.

# Bunny Rabbit's Predicament

Come along and meet Bunny! He's a wee little rabbit
Who, once upon a time, had a strange kind of habit.
He adored chewing gum from morning till night
And often blew bubbles to his own delight.

But one day he blew a gum bubble so big
It popped, leaving Bunny with a thingamujig
Stuck to his whiskers, his nose, and his chin-
'Twas an awkward predicament Bunny was in!

Well, he squirmed
And he wiggled
And he snorted
And he sniffed
And he blew his gummy nose in a handkerchief!

And wouldn't you know, that hankie held tight.
It dangled from his nose like a parasite
Which caused Bunny's nose to begin to itch,
And the itching caused the whiskers on Bunny to twitch.

Well, he squirmed
And he wiggled
And he snorted
And he sniffed
But his nose was still fastened to the handkerchief!

Well, along came a chum with a cupful of ice
Which he offered to the rabbit with some gummy advice:
"Your predicament is sticky but the gum will come off.
All we need is more ice from the watering trough."

"My, my, that's peculiar," said Bunny with a sigh,
"But my friend's here to help, so it can't hurt to try."
Then off hopped the rabbit and his chum to the trough,
Got the ice, froze the gum, and the hankie dropped off!

Now, the moral of the tale is "Never despair."
An unsolvable problem is generally rare,
Though you may need some help to get a job done,
'Cause two heads are sometimes better than one!

*Babs Bell Hajdusiewicz*

# RESPONDING TO

# Cat

BY MARY BRITTON MILLER

## Dramatizing The Poem

Ask children to sit on their haunches like a cat. Then, as you read the poem, have them act out the motions of the black cat.

This would be a good time to read "Fog," by Carl Sandburg (Nature: Poster 3). Children can compare the quiet movements of the fog to the movements of a cat.

## Exploring The Power Of Colorful Verbs

Encourage children to notice words the poet uses to describe what the cat does. (yawns, opens her jaws, stretches her legs, shows her claws, stands on four legs, shows her teeth, and so on). Point out the action words, or verbs, (opens, stretches, stands) that help them picture the cat's movements.

You may wish to have children make up a list of additional action words that could be used to describe a cat's movements: *crouch, scamper, pounce, slink, lurk, creep*.

## Sequencing Actions

After repeated readings, have children tell from memory what things the cat does. Elicit children's help in recording each action to form a list. Then have children number the actions in order as they remember them. Suggest that children recite the poem in their minds for help in ordering the actions. Then display the poster so children can read it and check their memory.

## Analyzing Words

Ask children to find words in the poem that have the *aw* sound heard in *saw* or *law*. List the words (*yawns, jaws, claws*) and then have children think of other words with that sound. They may suggest *draw, seesaw, craw, straw, thaw, paw, slaw, raw,* and *gnaw*. Ask children which of the many new words might be used to describe a cat. Challenge them to write sentences using those words.

## Classifying Cats

Point out that cats are part of a large family that includes many wild animals, such as lions, panthers, tigers, and leopards. Children may make a learning web on the bulletin board that looks like this. In each circle, they may tack a report on the animal or a picture of it.

Extend the activity by making a web for famous cats in literature. They could include Puss in Boots, Garfield, Felix, Bill the Cat, and The Cat in the Hat.

# Cat

The black cat yawns,
Opens her jaws,
Stretches her legs,
And shows her claws.

Then she gets up
And stands on four
Long stiff legs
And yawns some more.

She shows her sharp teeth,
She stretches her lip,
Her slice of a tongue
Turns up at the tip.

Lifting herself
On her delicate toes,
She arches her back
As high as it goes.

She lets herself down
With particular care,
And pads away
With her tail in the air.

*Mary Britton Miller*

# RESPONDING TO
# Eletelephony

BY LAURA RICHARDS

## Talking About Talking

Have children tell how the poet has mixed up her words. Help them realize that people sometimes think of two things at the same time, and then words come out all mixed up. Give examples such as these: I mopped the dishwater and emptied the floor, or Let's take the jumpside outrope.

## Using The Poet's Model

Have children clap to show the syllables they hear when saying *telephone* and *elephant*. Ask them to think of and list other animal names that have three syllables. Then have them list objects whose names contain three syllables. To make a mixed-up word, children select one word from each list and follow the poet's model to combine them and make new words. Substitute the new words in the poem: Once there was a dinosaur who tried to use a microsaur — No! No! I mean a dinoscope who tried to use a microscope. . . .

## Using Anthologies

Invite children to use the indexes of various poetry anthologies such as Joanna Cole's *A New Treasury of Children's Poetry*, Childcraft's Volume I *Poems and Rhymes*, or *Poems for Young Children*, compiled by Caroline Royds, to find "Eletelephony." Ask children to look for the poet's name. Then have them read along with you to see if the poem's words are the same. Encourage discussion about why the same poem is found in several different collections.

Challenge children to search for more books containing "Eletelephony." Extend the activity by enjoying "Adventures of Isabel" (Adventure: Poster 1) from this collection and then searching for its inclusion in other anthologies.

## Comparing Illustrations

Have children use this collection and various anthologies containing "Eletelephony" to compare illustrations. Help children identify the artist for each and talk about why one piece of art is different from another.

You may want to discuss the different kinds of telephones artists have drawn and then have children think of how else the elephant's phone might look. Invite children to draw their ideas.

## Using Parentheses

As you read the poem, pause and alter your voice to emphasize the "by the way" aspect of the words in parentheses. Help children recognize that the parenthetical words are not necessary to the sense of the poem. They do, however, add fun and also help the reader know what the poet was thinking as she wrote.

Explain that writers may use parentheses to give additional information, explain other words, or simply let the reader know something that temporarily strays from the topic. You may want to illustrate these points by reading "The Pasture" (Nature: Poster 7), "I've Figured It Out" (Numbers: Poster 5), "I, Myself, and Me" (Me: Poster 3), or "My Favorite Word" (Word Play: Poster 6).

# Eletelephony

Once there was an elephant,
Who tried to use the telephant —
No! no! I mean an elephone
Who tried to use the telephone —
(Dear me! I am not certain quite
That even now I've got it right.)

Howe'er it was, he got his trunk
Entangled in the telephunk;
The more he tried to get it free,
The louder buzzed the telephee —
(I fear I'd better drop the song
Of elephop and telephong!)

*Laura Richards*

# RESPONDING TO
# Fourteen Cats

BY EILEEN ELLEN MURPHY

## Acting Out One-To-One Correspondence

Set out fourteen chairs and have fourteen children pretend to be the cats who sat on them. Let another child play the role of Mrs. Stairs. Have children act out the poem as you read it.

You can then use the chairs to play Musical Chairs. Arrange them in two rows, back to back. Play music while fifteen children march around the chairs. Stop the music and have each child try to find a seat. The one who doesn't is out. Have that person remove a chair, and then let the remaining children repeat the activity until only one chair and two children are left.

## Identifying With The Characters

Ask children what is bothering Mrs. Stairs. Use her experiences to initiate a discussion of sharing. Talk about what it feels like when someone won't share. Ask if children think there should be rules about sharing or if sharing should be voluntary.

## Learning The Meaning Of Words

Read and reread the poem, helping children deduce the meaning of unknown words from their context and from your voice and expression. Draw their attention to words that may be unfamiliar and have children speculate about their meaning. What would a "comfy" chair look and feel like? How did Mrs. Stairs feel when she was filled with "dismay"? What are "hostile glares"?

Suggest that children substitute synonyms for the unfamiliar words and read the lines with new words. They can verify their guesses by looking up the words in the dictionary.

## Making Sound Mobiles

The poem is full of words whose endings sound the same despite their different spellings: *Stairs, chairs, bears, unawares, glares, shares; thought, caught.* Encourage children to think of other examples such as *hair* and *square, chief* and *leaf, pole* and *goal.*

Extend the activity by discussing homonyms — words that sound exactly alike but are spelled differently: *two, to, too; fair, fare; bare, bear.*

Children may wish to make Sound Mobiles. From a hanger, hang oaktag cards that have words with the same ending sounds. Children may also add these rhyming words to their rhyming dictionaries.

## Discovering Internal Rhyme

Ask children to look and listen carefully to the first line in each stanza. Ask what these lines have in common. Help them see that they all begin with *Mrs. Stairs* and end with a word that rhymes with *Stairs.*

Challenge children to find examples of internal rhyme in other poems in this collection. In "Mr. Bear" (Adventure: Poster 6) they will find this and other, similar lines: "Mr. Bear! Mr. Bear! Now don't you dare . . . ." "Old Grumbler" (Me and Others: Poster 8) begins with the line "Old Grumbler swore by the shirt he wore . . ." and has many lines with a similar pattern.

## Playing A Rhyming Game

There are so many rhymes in "Fourteen Cats" that it is possible to play a rhyming game using only sounds from the poem. Let someone be It, pick a rhyming word from the poem, and write it on the chalkboard. Volunteers will call out other words from the poem that rhyme with the word on the board, and It will record them. When no more rhymes can be named, another person becomes It and repeats the activity with another word. See which word gives the most rhymes.

# Fourteen Cats

Mrs. Stairs owned fourteen chairs
And fourteen cats as well,
The chairs were soft as teddy bears
And comfy — you could tell.

Mrs. Stairs, caught unawares
Came home one sunny day
To find the cats in all the chairs
Which filled her with dismay.

Mrs. Stairs gave hostile glares
"I don't like this a bit.
With fourteen cats on fourteen chairs
There's no place I can sit."

Mrs. Stairs was one who shares
But not This Much, she thought,
"Get off!" she snapped, and down they jumped
Annoyed that they'd been caught.

*Eileen Ellen Murphy*

# RESPONDING TO
# If the Spider Could Talk

BY BABS BELL HAJDUSIEWICZ

## Comparing Poems

Children should be familiar with the nursery rhyme, "Little Miss Muffet" to enjoy this poem. Help them use anthologies to locate the rhyme. Read it aloud several times. Ask children why they think the spider frightened Miss Muffet and how they think the spider might have felt. Then read "If the Spider Could Talk," depicting the spider as disappointed but happy to have met its original goal of finding something to eat.

## Listening Purposefully

Encourage children to discuss whether they would act differently than Miss Muffet if they were "in her shoes." Ask them to listen to the poem again and make a list of the reasons the spider thought Miss Muffet should not have run away.

## Making Number Comparisons

Divide the class into groups of five. Designate one child to be Miss Muffet and the others to be the spider. Have children listen to the poem and then use their legs to compare the number of legs a spider has with the number Miss Muffet has. This is a good opportunity to introduce or review counting by twos.

## Sharing Fears

Ask children why Miss Muffet ran away. Write their responses in sentences, such as "Miss Muffet was afraid of the spider because she thought it might hurt her." Then tell children about a fear of yours as you print your words in a sentence, such as "I am frightened of snakes because they hiss." Encourage children to tell about things that scare them and why as you print their responses. You'll want to encourage empathy as children discuss their fears.

## Learning About Spiders

Ask children to think about the poem to recall things that spiders eat. Provide resource books so children can find other kinds of insects spiders might like for a meal.

Stimulate talk about how spiders catch their food by telling children about a cobweb or two you've encountered on cleaning day. Help children search the building for a spider's web.

Show children how to observe spiders under a microscope (or use pictures of spiders) to learn that spiders' eyes vary in number, size, and position on the head according to the species, and that while some spiders have two, four, or six eyes, most spiders have eight.

Ask children to think about why spiders are helpful to humans. Remind them that spiders eat insects that are pesky and/or carry diseases. Spiders also eat insects that destroy crops and gardens.

## Making Spiders

Have children create spiders from cut or torn paper ovals and folded paper strips or pipe cleaners. You may want to reread the poem to help children determine how many legs to put on their spiders. Display the spiders on strings suspended from the ceiling or "hide" spiders around the room for a realistic effect.

## Enjoying Other Literature

Children will enjoy singing and acting out "Eensy Weensy Spider" (Related Poems) and reading or hearing Charlotte's Web, by E.B. White, and other spider stories.

See Meet the Poet, page 186.

# If the Spider Could Talk

If the spider could talk,
Here are words he might say
To the girl who sat eating
Her curds and her whey:

Hey, Little Miss Muffet!
Come back to your seat!
I'm only out searching
For insects to eat.

Have you seen any grasshoppers?
Beetles or flies?
I'm looking and looking
With all of my eyes.

Come see my eight legs —
Four pairs to your one.
While your legs have bones,
My body has none.

Hey, Little Miss Muffet!
Please don't be afraid.
I'm only a spider.
See the web I have made!

A spider won't bite you
Unless it's afraid
Or injured somehow.
Gosh! I wish you had stayed.

Hey, Little Miss Muffet!
Look! Your curds and whey
Has a fly landing in it —
SLURP! It's my lucky day!

*Babs Bell Hajdusiewicz*

# RESPONDING TO

# If You Should Meet a Crocodile

BY ANONYMOUS

## Analyzing The Poem

Ask children to listen to the poem to find three warnings: don't poke a crocodile with a stick; ignore the welcome of his smile; and do not stroke a crocodile. Have them review the text to find the reasons for the warnings: he's sleeping; he's getting thinner and thinner; and he's ready for dinner. Then talk about who will be dinner — YOU — if you don't heed the warnings.

Two other poems in Related Poems contain warnings. "Who to Pet and Who Not To" by X. J. Kennedy warns of petting porcupines, and "The Panther," by Ogden Nash, says "if called by a panther, don't anther." Children can draw tongue-in-cheek warning signs and display them around the room.

## Giving Meaning To Words

Some of the words in this poem, such as *ignore, Nile,* and *stroke,* may be unfamiliar to children. First see if they can figure out the meaning from the context of the verse. Then have them suggest synonyms that could be used in place of the words. Finally have children look up the words in the dictionary. They might also locate the Nile River on a map of Africa.

## Talking About Famous Crocodiles

Ask children to tell about crocodiles they have encountered in their reading. They may mention the one who ticks in James Barrie's *Peter Pan* or Lyle, the crocodile in the books by Bernard Waber. Interested students might want to make an annotated bibliography of books, poems, songs, and other works about crocodiles.

## Find Other Poems By Anonymous Poets

Point out that anonymous poets wrote this and other poems in the collection: "The Dark House" (Adventure: Poster 3), "Hairy Toe" (Adventure: Poster 4), and "Tall and Small" (Related Poems). No one knows or remembers who wrote these poems. Remind children that if they don't put their names on their papers, they, too, will remain anonymous.

At this time, you may want to draw students' attention to the "biography" of Anonymous that is included with the other biographies in this collection. It is found on page 175. Children can imagine what the poet looked like and draw her or his picture. They will also enjoy hearing "Poet Unknown" (Related Poems).

## Doing Research

You may wish to have children see for themselves what a crocodile looks like and how it acts. They can compare the real thing to the one described in the poem. Does a real croc appear to smile? Does it really sleep a lot? Does it really stay in water? Interested students can discover the differences between alligators and crocodiles.

## Writing Verses

Introduce the refrain from the popular song, "See you later, Alligator. In a while, Crocodile." Show children how to make up similar verses about other animals:

Good-by, House Fly;
Gotta go, Mosquito;
Catch you soon, Baboon.

See Meet the Poet, page 192.

# If You Should Meet a Crocodile

If you should meet a Crocodile
　　Don't take a stick and poke him;
Ignore the welcome in his smile,
　　Be careful not to stroke him.
For as he sleeps upon the Nile,
　　He thinner gets and thinner;
And whene'er you meet a Crocodile
　　He's ready for his dinner.

*Anonymous*

# RESPONDING TO
# Mother Doesn't Want a Dog

BY JUDITH VIORST

## Reading Along

After hearing "Mother Doesn't Want a Dog" a few times, children will be eager to join in on the first line of each verse: "Mother doesn't want a dog." They will also be quick to remember the last line, "She will not want this snake."

## Sharing Personal Experiences

Judith Viorst's poem is sure to launch an outpouring of animal anecdotes. Children will want to tell about their pets or the pets they want and how their mothers feel about them. Allow plenty of time for discussion.

Then suggest that children write a response to this poem by listing all the good things about having a dog. Work together to come up with a suitable title that parallels the original.

## Reading Other Works By Judith Viorst

"Mother Doesn't Want a Dog" is from *If I Were in Charge of the World and Other Worries*. It contains many poems that children will enjoy.

Two of Judith Viorst's books, *Alexander and the Terrible, Horrible, No Good, Very Bad Day* and *I'll Fix Anthony*, are also great favorites with children. They will want to hear them read aloud or read them independently.

## Thinking Of Pets Mother *Definitely* Doesn't Want

The child in the poem has a snake that Mother will not be fond of. Children will have fun thinking of other exotic pets that will not please her. They can read these poems from the *Poetry Works!* collection for ideas: "Who to Pet . . ." by X. J. Kennedy (Related Poems), "The Panther," by Ogden Nash (Related Poems), and "If You Should Meet a Crocodile," by Anonymous (Animals: Poster 7).

Have children write the names of the animals they suggest on removable stick-on notes and place the notes over the word *snake* in the last line. Then, as a group, read the last stanza of the poem with the substitutions.

## Thinking Critically To Write

Discuss the idea that the mother in the poem may be against having a dog for reasons other than those stated. Lead children to think about where the family lives and whether there's adequate space for a dog or whether dogs are even allowed.

Ask children to find out if there might be some kinds of dogs better suited for certain kinds of homes. Help children look up different breeds of dogs with that question in mind. Invite children to write a list of breeds recommended for apartment living, those that may need a yard area, and those dogs that require the larger area that a farm or rural home would offer.

## Giving Oral Reports

The poem suggests that pet care might be difficult. Ask children who have pets to describe the care required. You may wish to have special Show and Tell times when children bring in their pets or pictures of their pets and describe how they care for them.

Extend the activity by inviting a veterinarian to visit the class to explain how best to care for common household pets. You might also ask someone from a pet store or zoo to talk about exotic pets such as snakes, monkeys, or ferrets.

See Meet the Poet, page 190.

# Mother Doesn't Want a Dog

Mother doesn't want a dog.
Mother says they smell,
And never sit when you say sit,
Or even when you yell.
And when you come home late at night
And there is ice and snow,
You have to go back out because
The dumb dog has to go.

Mother doesn't want a dog.
Mother says they shed,
And always let the strangers in
And bark at friends instead,
And do disgraceful things on rugs,
And track mud on the floor,
And flop upon your bed at night
And snore their doggy snore.

Mother doesn't want a dog.
She's making a mistake.
Because, more than a dog, I think
She will not want this snake.

*Judith Viorst*

# RESPONDING TO
# Sleepy Tiger

BY BABS BELL HAJDUSIEWICZ

## Dramatizing The Poem

Children enjoy acting out this poem in small groups. Each child can have a turn in the role of the tiger, a visitor to the zoo, and the narrator. Children can make a "bars" prop by attaching several vertical cardboard or posterboard strips to two horizontal strips, one at the top and the other at the bottom.

Children also enjoy using puppets to dramatize the poem. Have them make puppets from brown bags or draw pictures and glue them onto popsicle sticks.

## Viewing Things From Another Perspective

Take children outside in small groups. Have them look in at their classroom through the windows. Discuss how different the classroom and everything in it may look from the outside.

While outside, have children imagine they are birds, squirrels, or other animals that live outside the school. Ask how the classroom and people might look from the animal's viewpoint. Encourage children to share "animal" thoughts such as these: "I'm glad I'm free to run around out here," "How do you people sit like that?" "Why don't you fly?" "Where are your tails?" or "There's no food in there! How can you live with nothing to eat?"

## Enjoying A Related Poem

Have children listen to a tiger's words of warning as you read Mary Ann Hoberman's "Tiger":

>     I'm a tiger
>     Striped with fur
>     Don't come near
>     Or I might Grrr
>     Don't come near
>     Or I might growl
>     Don't come near
>     Or I might
>     BITE!

Ask what words the tiger uses to introduce and describe itself. Ask what warning the tiger gives over and over. Have children recall three things the tiger says it might do if someone comes near.

Children enjoy reciting this poem for an audience. For group presentation, change the opening words to "We are tigers" and substitute *we* for *I* throughout. The use of puppets adds to the fun and may offer encouragement to any who are reluctant to perform.

Discuss the wisdom of the tiger's words. Ask how the tiger's message helps explain why tigers in zoos are kept behind bars and fences.

You may also want to discuss how animals growl or hiss when they're frightened or sense danger. Children may relate stories of times their pets have growled when cornered.

## Noticing Shapes And Patterns

Children will enjoy having a Tiger-Stripe Day when everyone wears striped clothing. Encourage awareness of less obvious stripes such as seams, ribbed socks, cuffs, ridges on shoe soles, and woven patterns in clothing fabrics.

## Relating The Poem To Other Literature

This is a good opportunity to introduce fables and folktales such as "From Tiger to Anansi" from Philip M. Sherlock's *Anansi, the Spider Man: Jamaican Folk Tales* and "The Tiger, The Brâhman and the Jackal" from *Tales of the Punjab* by Flora Annie Steel.

## Analyzing The Form Of The Poem

Place the poem alongside another familiar poem such as "Family of the Sun" (Nature: Poster 2), "Trees" (Nature: Poster 10), or "It's Not Fair!" (Feelings: Poster 2). Help children recognize the common use of couplets, or stanzas with two rhymed lines. Compare the couplet form to that of other poems in this collection.

See Meet the Poet, page 186.

# Sleepy Tiger

The sleepy tiger in the zoo
Opens his eyes and looks at you.

He stares and gawks at you a while,
Then yawns his great big sleepy smile,

And turns his head and stares some more,
Then stands and gives a big loud roar!

To say, "Well, well, it must be true!
We have new animals in this zoo!"

The sleepy tiger in the zoo
Meanders closer to look at you:

"They don't have hair at all like me;
They also have no tails, I see.

"What could these animals be named?
They don't look wild; they're surely tamed."

But, to be sure, he stares some more;
Then stands and gives another roar!

"Aha! You jumped!" he thinks in glee.
"I see you animals are scared of me!

"That's why these bars are everywhere
Keeping me out here, and you in there!"

*Babs Bell Hajdusiewicz*

 # Index to Related Poems

1. Eensy Weensy Spider...........................page 208
2. Poet Unknown..................................233
3. The Panther ..................................230
4. Who To Pet and Who Not To.........................254

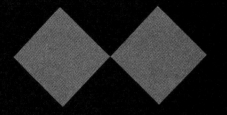

# UNIT 3
# FEELINGS

1. Bed in Summer
2. It's Not Fair!
3. Mumps
4. My Turn to Talk
5. One-Eyed Teddy
6. Solo Sunday
7. Stealing Feelings
8. To Be or Not to Be
9. Wishful Thinking

# RESPONDING TO
# Bed In Summer

BY ROBERT LOUIS STEVENSON

## Sharing Feelings

Ask children to tell what they think the narrator means by "In winter I get up at night . . ." and "I have to go to bed by day." Invite children to share feelings about having to go to bed before dark or getting up before it is light outside.

You may want to read Marjorie Weinman Sharmat's book *Go to Sleep, Nicholas Joe*. Children will enjoy the way Nicholas solves the early bedtime problem by fantasizing that he is putting the whole world to bed. Compare the book to the poem, noting that the poem merely states the problem.

## Using A Clock

Illustrate the 24-hour day by using one clockface for midnight to noon and an identical clock for noon to midnight. Have children move the hands around as classmates talk about the light or darkness outside and the activities they do at each hour. Encourage discussion of why one analog clockface is not sufficient to show all 24 hours. Challenge children to design a single clockface that will show an entire day.

## Responding To An Opinion

Introduce the limerick, "Sad Bedtime" by Babs Bell Hajdusiewicz:

Now that I've learned how to add,
My bedtime at eight is quite sad.
It should be at nine;
One more hour'd be fine —
But now to convince Mom and Dad.

Ask children to compare the narrator's bedtime to their own and tell why they would agree or disagree with the narrator. Encourage discussion of why bedtime limits are set for children and what those limits mean in different homes.

Extend the activity by having children complete this statement: "If I could stay up later at night, I would . . .". Suggest that they illustrate their sentences.

## Exploring Seasonal Changes

Use a globe and a flashlight to demonstrate how the northern hemisphere tilts toward the sun in the summer and away from it in the winter; that is the reason summer has more daylight hours than winter. Note that the reverse is true in the southern hemisphere. Challenge children to say the poem the way a child in Africa, Australia, or South America would: "In summer I get up at night . . ."

Talk about Daylight Savings Time and how moving the clocks ahead or back ("spring ahead, fall back") affects the daylight hours.

This would be a good time to read "Summer" by Frank Asch (Related Poems).

## Placing The Poem In Time

Ask children to find the clue in the poem *(yellow candle-light)* that tells that it was written a long time ago. Challenge them to use an encyclopedia to find out when and where Robert Louis Stevenson lived and when people began lighting their homes with electricity. They will discover that Stevenson lived in England from 1850-1894, and electric lighting came into common use at about the time of his death. In this country, Edison invented the incandescent bulb in 1879.

# Bed In Summer

In winter I get up at night
And dress by yellow candle-light.
In summer, quite the other way,
I have to go to bed by day.

I have to go to bed and see
The birds still hopping on the tree,
Or hear the grown-up people's feet
Still going past me in the street.

And does it not seem hard to you,
When all the sky is clear and blue,
And I should like so much to play,
To have to go to bed by day?

*Robert Louis Stevenson*

# RESPONDING TO
# It's Not Fair!

BY BABS BELL HAJDUSIEWICZ

## Predicting The Subject Of The Poem

Tell children you are going to read a poem entitled "It's Not Fair!" Ask, What might this poem be about? Record children's ideas on the chalkboard or on chart paper. They will probably contribute a number of serious subjects. Then read the poem aloud, surprising them with its silly theme.

After reading the poem, reread their list of serious suggestions. The contrast may provide another laugh.

## Sorting Out An Issue

To encourage children to think about the issue presented in the poem, ask questions such as, How does the person feel about a tail?, Why might it be good to have a tail?, How does the character's opinion change?, or Why is there a change of opinion? Have children quote lines from the poem to support their answers.

## Giving A Choral Reading

Read the first stanza of the poem several times, tracking the words on the poster as you do so. Once children are familiar with some words, encourage them to read them aloud with you each time they occur in the poem.

## Mimicking The Style Of The Poem

Encourage children to think of other silly things that are not fair. Perhaps they wish they had fur like cats, dogs, and polar bears or wings like robins, owls, and turkeys. Work with the group to incorporate the ideas into a new poem modeled on "It's Not Fair!"

## Doing Research About Animals

Children's curiosity about tails may be piqued as they think about the animals in the poem. Have children list the animals named in the poem and research those they have questions about. Challenge children to add to the list of animals with tails and form any generalizations that may seem obvious.

Children will be interested to learn that people bob the tails of some animals, while other animals have naturally short tails. Discussion and research may result in categorizing animals by tail length.

You may want to encourage a study of cats so children can discover that the Manx breed has no tail at all. Some children may want to do research to find out if there are other animals with no tails. At this time, children will enjoy "I Had a Little Pig" (Related Poems).

## Stating And Supporting An Opinion

Invite children to discuss things that they think are unfair. Remind them to support their opinions with reasons. Children may find that their reasoning leads them along the same path as the character's in the poem. They may enjoy writing their opinions on issues that affect them and then sharing their writing with parents at home.

## Using Dialect

Have children list all the words written in dialect and write the standard form of each.

Challenge children to listen to the rhythm of particular lines of the poem to tell why they think the poet used words such as "'stead," "prob'ly," or "tail'd." Have children look for similar examples in other writers' work and tell why each was used. Help children realize that these words not only help poets attain certain rhythmic patterns, but also represent spellings that suggest an informal speech pattern.

See Meet the Poet, page 186.

# It's Not Fair!

It's not fair! It isn't! It's not fair at all!
It's not fair, I tell you! Just not fair at all.

That cats, dogs, and horses, lions, fish, whales,
Tigers and squirrels and monkeys have tails.

It's not fair! It isn't! It's not fair at all!
It's not fair, I tell you! Just not fair at all.

That cows and canaries, camels, sheep, snails,
Wombats and insects and chickens have tails.

It's not fair! It isn't! It's not fair at all!
It's not fair, I tell you! Just not fair at all.

If I had a tail, I could hang from a tree,
And sleep like a 'possum 'stead of sleeping like a me.

If I had a tail, I could wag for a treat,
Or cushion my bottom on hard, old concrete.

If I had a tail, I could chase away flies,
Or swim a lot faster than people my size.

If I had a tail, I know I could fly
Like airplanes and kites and birds in the sky.

If I had a tail . . . well, on second thought . . .
If I had a tail, I might get it caught

In car doors or zippers or bicycle spokes —
Might everyone laugh and think it's a joke?

But, oh, it would hurt! Ouch, it would sting!
And what if it broke? Would I wear a sling?

And . . . now that I'm thinking a little bit clearer,
How would I feel when I looked in a mirror?

If I had a tail, whether bobbed or real long,
I'd prob'ly look goofy since tails don't belong

On humans like me. So maybe it's fair.
'Sides, a tail'd never fit in my underwear.

*Babs Bell Hajdusiewicz*

# RESPONDING TO
# Mumps

BY ELIZABETH MADOX ROBERTS

## Building Background

Ask children to think back to when they had shots before entering kindergarten. Explain that the shots kept them from getting mumps and measles. (Children may have a lot to say about the way the shot hurt their leg.) Describe the symptoms of each disease — the swollen neck glands and sore throat of mumps and the itchy, red spots of measles.

Tell children that the poem you are going to read, "Mumps," by Elizabeth Madox Roberts, is about a family that lived before people had mumps shots. It describes what happened when four children in one family got the mumps.

## Interviewing Others

Since it is likely that none of the children in the class will have had mumps, ask them how they could find out what it was like to have the illness. Elicit the idea of talking to or interviewing adults who may have had mumps. In that way, they can find out how long mumps last, what children ate when they had them, and what remedies were used. You may wish to have children present oral reports about what they learned.

## Conducting A Survey

Talk about the need for vaccinations. To demonstrate their effectiveness, have children conduct a survey. On a form like the one below, ask each to record information about five adults born before the 1960s (when vaccinations for mumps and measles were introduced) and five children.

| Have you had these diseases? | | | | | | | |
|---|---|---|---|---|---|---|---|
| Children | | | | Adults | | | |
| Mumps | | Measles | | Mumps | | Measles | |
| Yes | No | Yes | No | Yes | No | Yes | No |
| | | | | | | | |
| | | | | | | | |
| | | | | | | | |
| | | | | | | | |
| | | | | | | | |
| | | | | | | | |

Help children tabulate the results on a large class chart. Then ask them what conclusions about the effectiveness of vaccination they can draw from the results. You may want to title the chart:

No Measles! No Mumps!
No Spots! No Bumps!

Ask children to suggest appropriate art ideas.

## Using Language Literally And Figuratively

Review the words that Dick used to torment Will and John. Ask why *vinegar, lemon drops,* and *pickles* might make someone with the mumps cry. (Explore the idea of difficulty in swallowing; compare it to a severe sore throat.) Then discuss the word *sour* as used in the second to last line of the poem. Elicit that the poet may have meant both the literal meaning of the word *sour* and the figurative meaning, "not sweet, unpleasant, mean." You may wish to have children see if they can find both meanings in the dictionary.

## Talking And Writing About Feelings

You may wish to have a discussion about why Dick teased John and Will when they had the mumps and he didn't. Elicit the idea of jealousy and feeling left out. Ask how it is possible to be jealous of something bad. Could someone well be jealous of someone sick? Why? Ask how they think Dick felt at the end of the poem, when he too had the mumps. Would he still be jealous? What other emotions might he feel at that point? You may wish to end the activity by having children complete the sentence: "Sometimes I feel jealous when. . . ."

# Mumps

I had a feeling in my neck,
   And on the sides were two big bumps;
I couldn't swallow anything
   At all because I had the mumps.

And Mother tied it with a piece,
   And then she tied up Will and John,
And no one else but Dick was left
   Who didn't have a mump rag on.

He teased at us and laughed at us
   And said whenever he went by
"It's vinegar and lemon drops
   And pickles!" just to make us cry.

But Tuesday Dick was very sad
   Because his neck was sore.
And not a one said sour things
   To anybody anymore.

*Elizabeth Madox Roberts.*

# RESPONDING TO
# My Turn To Talk

BY BABS BELL HAJDUSIEWICZ

## Introducing The Poem

You will find that children readily identify with the poem when you act it out. As you read it a second time, encourage children to act it out with you.

## Personalizing The Poem

Ask children what they think the narrator's story might have been. Invite them to tell of times when they forgot what they wanted to say. Ask children why they think they forgot, how they felt about forgetting, and if they remembered their story later and were able to share it.

## Sorting Out Feelings

This is a good opportunity to discuss how many different kinds of feelings we experience and how our feelings can change from minute to minute. Have children identify each feeling the narrator experiences as you slowly read the poem aloud. Make a list of the words that describe feelings to show the character's mood changes from excitement to calmness, puzzlement, embarrassment, surprise or shock, and disappointment. Encourage talk about how several feelings may be experienced at the same time — shyness and embarrassment or happiness and excitement.

Help children talk about each feeling and name other words that express feelings. Encourage children to draw faces expressing each kind of feeling. A display may be titled A Face Tells It All or Faces with Feeling.

## Thinking To Prevent Forgetting

Write, "Sometimes I forget what I want to say." Read the sentence aloud and explain that this problem or predicament happens to everyone at times, but there are ways to prevent it from happening. Tell children to imagine that they have something to say right now, but that they have to wait for their turn to talk. Ask what they might do in order to remember their thoughts. You may need to pose questions such as, How might writing help? and How could thinking of one word help? to channel children's thinking.

This is a good opportunity to have children think about good listening when others are talking. You may want to introduce the idea that a speaker may feel rushed and anxious if others have their hands up.

## Using Proverbs

Since this poem concerns patient waiting as well as a predicament nobody likes to experience, take the opportunity to discuss the sayings, "Patience is a virtue" and "An ounce of prevention is worth a pound of cure." Explain that a virtue is something good and that being patient nearly always helps us and those around us. Tell children that an ounce is a tiny amount compared to a pound and that it's easier to prevent a problem than to solve it after it happens.

You'll find many opportunities to use proverbs when children show patience, when you observe a child working diligently to free a knotted shoelace, when a child writes a note to remember something, or when someone makes a special effort to replace something when it gets lost.

Provide a proverb as a display heading. Challenge children to use the saying orally and earn the honor of creating an illustration.

See Meet the Poet, page 186.

# My Turn To Talk

My hand goes up when I want to say
Something that happened to me today.
I wait so patiently until
It's time for the others to be still.
I wait and wait to have my say
About what happened to me today.
Then suddenly I look around
And you know what? There isn't a sound!
All my friends are looking at me
And waiting, ever so patiently.
They're waiting to hear what I have to say
About what happened to me today.
But, guess what! Oh, no! It couldn't be!
I've forgotten my story of what happened to me!

*Babs Bell Hajdusiewicz*

# RESPONDING TO
# One-Eyed Teddy

BY ROBERT D. HOEFT

## Completing The Lines

After repeated read-alouds, children will enjoy completing the last line of each stanza by supplying the last word. The meaning of the lines, the rhyming last word of these lines, and the familiarity created by the repetitions should make it easy for children to fill in these words.

## Making Inferences

It is not uncommon for someone to find a button and not know where it came from. Ask children how they think the narrator *knows* it's a teddy bear's eye. What do they think the button looks like? Why is the narrator so sure the teddy can't be found? Do they think sewing the eye on his teddy bear is the best he can do? What would you do? Encourage children to come up with a variety of responses.

## Comparing The Poem To Other Literature

"One-Eyed Teddy" lends itself well to comparison with the children's classic *Corduroy* by Don Freeman. In *Corduroy*, a teddy bear is missing a button, though this button is from its clothing. Compare the forlorn Corduroy, worried about his missing button, with the "poor teddy" imagined by the narrator of the poem.

## Using Fractions

The narrator of the poem says the one-eyed teddy bear can see only half the sky. Show children why that is so by drawing a teddy bear face with two eyes. Point out that if you took away half of the teddy bear's two eyes, it would have only one. With only half its eyes would it see only half as much? Have children close one eye and discuss what they now see.

Explain that while people really function very well with only one eye, it is fun to speculate about what the world might look like to a one-eyed teddy. Encourage discussion of how much of a TV screen it would see, or how much of an apple, a house, or a dog. Ask children to draw pictures of this half-world. You may then want to challenge children to draw pictures of what the

three-eyed teddy would see — one-and-a-half of everything? Extend the study of fractions by reading "Arithmetic Pie" (Numbers: Poster 1).

## Exploring The Principle Of The Whole And Its Parts

Talk about how the narrator has found something which he or she believes to be a teddy bear's eye while the sister thinks it is just a button. Elicit that it is sometimes difficult to recognize a whole object by looking at one of its smaller parts. Point out that if you saw a wheel, you might not be able to tell what the vehicle it was attached to looked like. The end pages of *World Magazine*, a National Geographic publication for children, show photographs that are sometimes hard to recognize as the everyday objects they are. Share these pages with the class as they try to guess what each picture is.

## Demonstrating Word Meanings

Discuss the word *squinting*. Ask different children to demonstrate the meaning of that word. Consider why someone might squint to enable him or her to see better. Discuss the word *vacant*. Ask children to draw a picture of the teddy bear with a vacant space instead of an eye. Help them understand that *vacant* means *empty*.

## Putting On A Teddy Bear Fair

Note that many boys and girls have teddy bears. Teddy bears are a common gift to babies and often remain as fond members of the family. Many adults keep their teddy bears and pass them on to their own children. Some teddy bears are even valuable antiques. Suggest that children bring in teddy bears from their homes, neighbors, and so forth. Have each child introduce his or her teddy bear and describe its name, origin, and any repairs it has had. Some children may wish to bring in other items that have a teddy bear motif such as teddy bear calendars, joke books, cups, or clothing.

56

# One-Eyed Teddy

Sister says it's just a button,
but I know it's a teddy bear's eye.
Somewhere there's a teddy squinting
and seeing only half of the sky.

Somewhere there's a teddy sitting
squinting at far-off Mars,
enjoying the beautiful evening
but seeing only half of the stars.

I'll never find that poor teddy
with the squinting one-eyed face.
I'll never find him and put back
his eye in that vacant space.

But I'll have Mama do some sewing.
It's the best I can do, you see.
Somewhere there's a teddy with one eye
but my teddy will have three.

*Robert D. Hoeft*

# RESPONDING TO
# Solo Sunday

BY BABS BELL HAJDUSIEWICZ

## Identifying The Problem

Tell children that the poet wrote this poem after hearing her own children's complaints. Ask the class to listen to the poem to find out what those complaints were. Then allow some time for students to talk about similar experiences in their own lives.

## Weighing The Problem

You may wish to bring in a thick Sunday paper and compare it to a daily newspaper. Ask children to feel the difference between the two and, if possible, weigh each one. Talk about the advantages and disadvantages of the big Sunday paper.

Examine both papers to find out why the Sunday paper is so big. Notice all the ads, the special magazines, and the comic section.

## Exploring And Creating A Newspaper

Ask children if they have ever wondered what intrigues or interests their parents so much in the Sunday paper. Tell them that, together, you are going to take the paper apart to see what is in it that makes it so interesting and time–consuming. Review each section of the paper: news, magazine, real estate, help wanted, classified, travel, sports, book review, comics (funnies). Offer a brief explanation of what each section is about.

As an extension, you may wish to publish your own Classroom News. Invite children to write one or two articles telling what is newsworthy in your classroom such as a new topic of study, a new student, a new pet, or a funny event. Print or photocopy your newspaper so each child can take one home.

## Making A List/Sharing Solutions

Ask children if they ever feel that their parents or brothers and sisters are too busy to pay attention to them. Suggest that they make a list of things they can do on their own to amuse themselves. Let children compile a list of such activities.

## Finding Non-Rhyming Poems

Note that "Solo Sunday" has no rhyming lines. Hajdusiewicz has simply chosen to state her ideas in poetic form. It is like another poem in this collection, "Whose Face?" by Lonny Alexander (Me: Poster 11), which is also written without rhymes. See if children can recall other poems of this type. They may know "Fog," by Carl Sandburg (Nature: Poster 3), "Dandelion," by Hilda Conkling (Nature: Poster 1), or "Have You Seen Edgar?" by Teresa Lynn Morningstar (Nature: Poster 5).

## Talking To Write

Discuss the title of the poem "Solo Sunday." Ask children if they know the meaning of the word *solo*. Perhaps they have heard of a solo in music or a solo flight. Help them discover that the word means "alone." Have them substitute that word for *solo* in the poem's title and listen for the sound of the words. Children will notice that *solo* and *Sunday* begin with the same sound.

Next, make up other alliterative titles that incorporate days of the week: Super Saturday, Windy Wednesday, Frightful Friday, Messy Monday. Suggest that children write a poem using one of these titles. Have them talk about their ideas before they actually put pencil to paper.

See Meet the Poet, page 186.

# Solo Sunday

You know the paper,
The one that comes on Sundays,
The big fat one
That takes Dad and Mom all day to read
And leaves me all alone
With no one to talk to me?

Why can't the paper be
Skinny on Sunday
And
Fat on Monday
When I'm in school?

*Babs Bell Hajdusiewicz*

# RESPONDING TO
# Stealing Feelings

BY BABS BELL HAJDUSIEWICZ

## Identifying Feelings

Have children read the poem to identify each word that names a feeling. List the words and encourage children to talk about times when they've experienced one or more of the feelings. Elicit other feeling words and discuss each.

## Discussing Related Poems

Read other poems from this collection such as "Mumps," "My Turn to Talk," "Solo Sunday," or "Wishful Thinking" (all from Feelings: Posters 3, 4, 6, 9). Encourage children to talk about how the characters feel and why.

## Appreciating The Poem's Structure

Display this poem poster alongside another familiar poem poster such as "Drinking Fountain" (Me: Poster 1), "Cycles" (Numbers: Poster 4), or "Wishful Thinking" (Feelings: Poster 9). Ask how the arrangement of the words in the poem, "Stealing Feelings," looks different from that of the other poem. Explain that poets sometimes arrange words to set a poem's mood and also to give a clue to how the reader might read the words. Read the comparison poem. Then read "Stealing Feelings," emphasizing each or. Use your voice to illustrate how the feeling grows bigger and bigger until it is all-consuming.

## Thinking About Cause And Effect

Ask children to help write many different feeling words across the chalkboard. Explain that a feeling can be the effect of something. Write *Effects:* before each feeling word. Ask children to think about what might happen to cause someone to have each of the feelings. Write *Cause:* before writing each response under its appropriate feeling word. Children should notice that several different feelings may result from a single cause.

Extend the activity by inviting children to select a feeling word and illustrate a possible cause for that feeling. Have children write a sentence or two to name the feeling and tell about what caused it.

## Thinking About Words With Opposite Meanings

Write a feeling word from the poem. Ask children to name its opposite. Continue for the other feeling words in the poem.

## Rewriting To Say The Opposite

Write the poem as children read it aloud with you. Discuss how a bad feeling seems to grow until it steals all the good feelings. Ask children to think about what a feeling like happiness or excitement might do to bad feelings. Challenge children to rewrite the poem so a good feeling steals from all the bad feelings. Cross out *lonely*, and insert a caret (∧) before it. Ask children to name a good feeling. Write the new word above the crossed-out word. Continue to substitute good-feeling words and model going back to the beginning to reread if meaning becomes lost. Help children realize that the meaning of the new poem requires an additional word substitution near the end.

## Recognizing Spellings Of A Sound

Have children read the poem with you to identify words that have the long *e* sound. List the words. Ask how the long *e* sound is spelled in each. Using chart paper, sort the words into columns headed *ee, ea, e,* and *y.* Challenge children to think of other words with the long *e* sound. Encourage them to decide in which column each new word belongs. Post the list where additions can be made as children encounter other words in their listening and reading.

See Meet the Poet, page 186.

# Stealing Feelings

When I'm feeling lonely
or frightened
or sad
or angry
or hurt
or guilty
or mad,
The feeling
I'm feeling
begins
as
a
feeling
but
soon
begins
stealing
from all
the good feelings
I had.

*Babs Bell Hajdusiewicz*

# RESPONDING TO
# To Be Or Not To Be

BY ANONYMOUS

## Enjoying The Poem

"To Be or Not to Be" can be read and listened to just for the sheer fun of the word sounds. After a few readings, children will be able to join you each time you read, "I dunno."

## Understanding Figures Of Speech

Point out that the poem contains expressions that have meaning beyond their literal definition. These expressions are called *idioms*, or *figures of speech*. Present these examples and see if students are familiar with the figurative meaning of each:

*to crow* to brag or boast
*to be a rooster* to be a strutting proud person
*to roost* to sit on a perch
*to eat crow* to admit to being wrong
*stand more show* put on a fancy appearance, as in "show off"

Reread the poem, comparing the meaning conveyed by the actual words with the implied meanings. Here is an example from the third stanza: "Nobody thinks of eating crow" literally means "no one wants to ingest crow" and figuratively means "no one wants to admit to being wrong."

## Making Decisions

A rooster or a crow — which would children rather be? Note that the poem says the rooster and the crow are alike in that they both roost, but different because a crow can't crow and no one actually eats a crow. Help children sort out the meaning of the words. Then talk about what each bird can do: a rooster, for example, gets to wake up people in the morning, while a crow is able to fly high in the sky. And what about the way the birds look and the way they sound? Children may have a tough time making up their minds and, like the narrator, come up with "I dunno" for an answer.

In that case, present a model for decision making. Show children how to write their ideas in columns like the ones below:

| Crow | | Rooster | |
|------|------|---------|------|
| Pro | Con | Pro | Con |
| | | | |
| | | | |
| | | | |
| | | | |

## Using Other Resources

You may wish to share the book, *In A Pickle*, by Marvin Terban. This book is an exploration of figures of speech, many of which may be more familiar to the children than those in the poem. The book has illustrations that show the literal meaning, as well as short, easily understood written explanations of the figurative meanings of these expressions.

Suggest some other idioms to children: *in a jam; fit to be tied; up a creek; a flash in the pan; fishing for a compliment; egging me on.* Have children select an idiom and then write a sentence and draw a picture explaining it.

## Understanding The Use Of Slang

Ask children if they noticed that there are certain words and expressions in the poem that may be used in conversation but are not written correctly. Explain that these words and expressions are called "slang." You may wish to discuss the fact that slang is usually not acceptable in writing, unless one is trying to paint a picture of the way someone who uses that slang might speak.

You may wish to conduct a joint search for the slang expressions in the poem: *I dunno; mebby; don't seem fair.* Have children suggest the correct forms for each of these expressions.

See Meet the Poet, page 192.

# To Be Or Not To Be

I sometimes think I'd rather crow
And be a rooster than to roost
And be a crow. But I dunno.

A rooster he can roost also,
Which don't seem fair when crows can't crow.
Which may help, some. Still I dunno.

Crows should be glad of one thing, though;
Nobody thinks of eating crow,
While roosters they are good enough
For anyone unless they're tough.

There are lots of tough old roosters though,
And anyway a crow can't crow,
So mebby roosters stand more show.
It looks that way. But I dunno.

*Anonymous*

# RESPONDING TO
# Wishful Thinking

BY PEARL BLOCH SEGALL

## Identifying With Feelings

Most children will be able to identify with the feeling of exclusion that Pearl Bloch Segall writes about in "Wishful Thinking." Encourage them to share their feelings. Ask if they understand what she means when she writes, "Some days I just wish to sail out on the seas." Talk about other fantasies children may have when they just want to get away from it all for a while.

Children will enjoy choosing someone they don't know very well and then trying to get to know "the niceness that's there" in that person. Make sure they tell the other person what they like about them.

## Sharing Common Experiences

Children may be helped to realize that friendship often comes from having common experiences. Encourage sharing in the classroom. Group two, three, or four children to work together on a project where each has an opportunity to contribute.

Activities such as these will help promote sharing, fun, and friendship:
- reading a delightful book together;
- caring for a classroom pet;
- raising the school flag together;
- helping the teacher after school;
- getting milk for the class;
- creating a bulletin board display;
- gathering things like leaves or worms outside.

## Learning About The Poet

Children will be interested to learn that Pearl Bloch Segall is the mother of four children. She wrote this poem about a feeling she remembered from her own childhood in Chicago.

## Relating The Poem To Other Literature

The trials and tribulations of finding and keeping friends are a major topic in children's literature. Children should find such books comforting — they are not alone in wanting friendship.

James Stevenson's book, *No Friends*, combines the real problems of two children who find themselves friendless in a new neighborhood with the tales of their grandfather, who recounts his fanciful version of a time when he was in the same predicament. It is a rollicking, humorous look at a serious problem. Russell Hoban's *Best Friends for Frances* and Helen Craig's *The Night of the Paper Bag Monsters*, and Charlotte Zolotow's *The Hating Book* all deal with the sometimes aggravating disagreements that come between friends.

You may also wish to read some books that deal with small misunderstandings between good friends. Arnold Lobel's series about Frog and Toad and James Marshall's books about George and Martha are both collections of humorous, gentle short stories that warm the heart.

Two poems in this collection by Babs Bell Hajdusiewicz also amplify the ideas expressed in "Wishful Thinking." In "Stealing Feelings" (Feelings: Poster 7), she writes about the way bad feelings can overwhelm good ones, and in "I, Myself, and Me" (Me: Poster 3), she writes about how we talk to ourselves when alone.

## Writing About Friendship

Children can explore "the niceness that's there" in their writing. Suggest that they begin by thinking of the niceness that is inside themselves. Then have them expand their thinking to include friends and family members. They can write their ideas in a book called A Friend Is . . .

# Wishful Thinking

Some days I just wish to sail out on the seas,
When my friends seem to vanish in twos and by threes;
Because I'm not pretty, with blonde, curly hair,
They seem not to notice the niceness that's there.

If only they'd stop just to talk for a while,
Perhaps then they'd notice my spectacular smile!
I'd share all my secrets and stop playing pretend
If only I had my own special friend.

*Pearl Bloch Segall*

#  Index to Related Poems

1. I Had a Little Pig ...................................page 212
2. Summer .................................................239
3. Tall and Small ..........................................241

# UNIT 4
# ME

1. Drinking Fountain
2. Extraordinary Me
3. I, Myself, and Me
4. Me a Mess?
5. Mud Monster
6. My Loose Tooth
7. The Poet Says
8. The Secret Place
9. Silly Sleep Sheep
10. Statue on the Curb
11. Whose Face?

# RESPONDING TO
# Drinking Fountain

BY MARCHETTE CHUTE

## Personalizing The Poem

"Drinking Fountain" expresses the poet's frustration with a water fountain. Children will probably be able to recall similar experiences. Ask if they have had trouble with a tube of toothpaste or a bottle of ketchup. Talk about how they felt in such circumstances.

You may wish to use the poem to inspire a classroom discussion of how people sometimes feel frustrated when events don't go the way we would like even though at other times we might find those same events funny. Judith Viorst's *Alexander & the Terrible, Horrible, No Good, Very Bad Day* expands on the frustration of the main character — and provides a good laugh as well. Contrast the mood of mild frustration of the poem with the extreme annoyance of Alexander in the book.

## Being Inventive

Elicit that, as the poet reminds us, a water fountain may not be a perfect invention: it is not always the right height; the water flow may be too strong or too weak. Ask children to pretend to be inventors, or "invention-fixers." Each should choose a common object (telephone, television, pencil, car, or bicycle) and think about ways to improve it (an electric bicycle, a recumbent bicycle, a bicycle built for ten). Have children draw a picture of their new creation and write a few sentences explaining the new improved product.

## Conducting An Experiment In Perception

Begin by showing children an empty glass. Have them describe what they see. Pour water in the glass until it is *half* full. Again ask children to describe the glass. Note that some people say the glass is half full while others would call the glass half empty. Explain that both answers are correct, depending on one's perspective or point of view. Elicit that sometimes things look different to us, according to our mood. You may wish to introduce the terms *optimist* and *pessimist* to describe people who tend to view the world as usually good or usually bad. Ask children to think about whether they are usually optimistic or pessimistic.

## Recognizing And Using Contractions

Have the children find all the words in the poem that have an apostrophe *(doesn't, you'd, don't)*. You may wish to have the children underline or circle these words. Explain that the apostrophe takes the place of missing letters (doesn't = does not; you'd = you would; don't = do not). Re-read the poem, substituting the expanded forms in place of the contractions. Ask the children if this change has any effect on the way the poem sounds or feels. You may wish to make a list of other common contractions with the children.

## Recognizing Initial Consonant Blends

Draw attention to the blend at the beginning of the title. At the beginning of *Drinking*, you can hear the sound of two letters blended together. Challenge children to find the blends at the beginning of *climb, drink,* and *small*.

Write these words at the top of three columns. Then ask children to think of other words that begin with the same blends. The resulting list might look like this:

| climb | drink | small |
|-------|-------|-------|
| club  | draw  | smile |
| clang | drop  | smell |
| click | dress | smart |
| class | drip  | smoke |

Leave the list where children can add to it as they encounter new words.

# Drinking Fountain

When I climb up
To get a drink,
It doesn't work
The way you'd think.

I turn it up.
The water goes
And hits me right
Upon the nose.

I turn it down
To make it small
And don't get any
Drink at all.

*Marchette Chute*

# RESPONDING TO
# Extraordinary Me

BY BABS BELL HAJDUSIEWICZ

## Stating And Supporting An Opinion

Have children list all the reasons the character presents for being extraordinary or first-rate. Encourage children to express their opinions of the creature's self-evaluation. Do they agree that the creature is lovely? Ask children to identify words or sentences from the poem that explain their opinions.

## Using Meaningful Words And Phrases

Help children make the poem's words and phrases their own by modeling the use of each. For example, you may say "That truly is preposterous!" when silliness occurs; "It's so obvious" when everyone knows or sees something; or "You must behold . . ." to direct children's attention.

You may want to initiate discussion of the saying "Beauty is in the eyes of the beholder" with a story about a less-than-pretty stray dog who begins to look pretty when its new owners discover its personality.

## Using Numbers

Have children point to and identify each number word on the poster and tell what it describes. Ask which number from one through six is not used in the creature's self-description. Help children discover how that number could describe the sides and corners of the creature's face. Have children explore how many ways the five nostrils could be arranged in two rows.

## Studying Shapes

Ask children to draw and identify the shape of the creature's face and then its eyes. Encourage comparisons of those shapes with human faces and eyes. Draw a triangle that points down and have children identify its shape, count its corners and sides, and talk about why the creature never frowns.

## Using Directions

Show how the compass rose on a map denotes north as the opposite of south, east to the right of north, and west to the left. Have children draw a plus sign or cross and mark the endpoints with the four directions. Show them how to connect E to S and S to W to form a triangle with one corner pointing south.

## Rereading To Create In Detail

Read aloud and discuss a postscript the creature might have written:
P.S.  I am unique, one of a kind,
    Though I confess I wouldn't mind
    If you should choose to draw another,
    'Cause I'd love a friend or brother.
  Provide cardboard boxes and other materials for children to work with in small groups. Display the poem poster where children can refer to it as they construct their creatures. Invite discussion of different interpretations as each group introduces its "friend or brother."

## Identifying Rhyming Words

The poem lends itself to a study of rhyming words. Have children list each pair of rhyming words and add them to a rhyming dictionary. Children will be interested to note rhyming sounds that are spelled differently. Point out that there are no other true rhymes for *mouth* and *south*.

## Giving A Dramatic Reading

Budding actors in the class will enjoy reading this poem aloud with suitably dramatic expression. Suggest that they take turns making tape recordings of their readings.

See Meet the Poet, page 186.

# Extraordinary Me

I think you'll never ever see
　　A creature lovelier than me.
Please do forgive if I seem bold,
　　But, really now, you must behold
My beauty! It's so obvious
　　It truly is preposterous
That compliments don't come my way
　　From everybody every day.
For instance, without more delays,
　　See how my round eyes look all ways.
One here and here, two there and there;
　　Six eyes in all! My face is square.
Blue eyes up front, two red in back,
　　And on the sides? One purple, one black.
And then, of course, there is my nose
　　With its five nostrils in two rows.
And though I prob'ly needn't tell
　　How keen this makes my sense of smell,
I'd hope that you'd appreciate
　　Each part that makes me quite first-rate.
Look here! See my triangular mouth
　　It has three corners; one points south.
With two points up and one point down;
　　I guess you see why I don't frown.
Which only proves that I am rare,
　　A unique being; I declare
I'm extraordinary! Yes?
　　But you agree by now, I'd guess,
That you will truly never see
　　A creature lovelier than me.

*Babs Bell Hajdusiewicz*

# RESPONDING TO
# I, Myself, And Me

BY BABS BELL HAJDUSIEWICZ

## Introducing The Poem

Allow children to hear you think out loud as you make various decisions. For example, you may reach for a chair or other object, pause to say, "No, I think that (object) would be (more comfortable/better)" and then perhaps stop again to say, "I need to ask **myself** which (object) is best for **me**."

Invite children to share stories of times they have stopped to think of different choices before deciding to do something. Encourage children to talk about the reasoning process they use to make decisions.

## Using Props To Act Out The Poem

Children will enjoy designating themselves and their likenesses as *I, me,* and *myself* by using two mirrors or photos of themselves as they read or recite the poem.

## Sharing Feelings

Help children talk about how they feel when alone. Ask them what plan the character in the poem made. What plan would they make in a similar situation? Ask how long they think it might take them to make a plan.

Extend the activity by having children list what they enjoy doing alone. Invite children to title and illustrate their lists. You may also want to have children talk about and list things they like to do with others and then look for classmates who share their interests.

For added fun, share the poems "Just Like Me," "I and My Echo," and "The Me Key," (all in Related Poems).

## Recognizing Different Interpretations

Help children appreciate how a poem may be interpreted differently according to the reader's situation. Ask children to imagine the poem's narrator is feeling lonely. Talk about how the character might feel when the family comes in. Then present other scenarios such as the following for children to respond to:

- the character is in the middle of a good book;
- he or she has just made a yummy snack — for one;
- he or she decides to take a nap.

Have children predict how adults might interpret the poem. Invite them to share the poem with parents and other adults and report how their predictions compared to actual responses.

## Using Pronouns

Have children identify the pronouns that name themselves in the poem. Note that people often have difficulty knowing whether to say *I* or *me* when talking or writing. Tell children that mnemonic devices help us remember things and are often written as poems. Read "No Pronoun Problems" (Related Poems) and then take every opportunity to recite it when you and children are talking or writing.

See Meet the Poet, page 186.

# I, Myself, And Me

If I come in and no one's home,
   I tell myself that I
Am really not so all alone;
   There's Me, Myself, and I.

"Me," I say, "what shall we do?"
   "Let's ask Myself," says Me.
Myself and I, we then sit down
   To make a plan with Me.

Then just about the time that we,
   (That's I, myself, and Me)
Get all our talking sorted out,
   In comes my family.

*Babs Bell Hajdusiewicz*

# RESPONDING TO
# Me a Mess?

BY BABS BELL HAJDUSIEWICZ

## Reciting With The Teacher

After hearing the poem once, children will enjoy reciting the prefix *un* in many of the words in "Me a Mess?" You may want to cover each prefix with a removable stick-on note, which you remove as children say *un*.

## Expanding Vocabulary

Ask children to notice what sound is repeated in the poem. After participating in the oral reading exercise, they should easily be able to identify the prefix *un* as the most frequently occurring sound in the poem. Explain that the prefix *un* can mean "not." Review words with the prefix *un* and explain that they mean the opposite of the root word. For example, *unclean* means "not clean;" *unbuckled* means "not buckled." Pay particular attention to the more difficult words such as *undignified, unbecoming, unfortunately, unaware*, being sure to clarify the meaning of the root words.

Challenge the class to expand the list of words with the prefix *un*. You may wish to note that all words that begin with *un* are not necessarily words with the prefix *un*. Examples of such words are *uncle, under* and *underwear*.

## Giving Other Prefixes

Explore other prefixes and their meanings: dis- (*disappear, discover*); out- (*outside, outnumber, outgrow*); re- (*review, return, rewrite, retread*); bi- (*bicycle, bifocals*); in- (*inside, into, income*); pre- (*preview, prefix, premature, predict*).

You may wish to make mobiles of prefixes. Using a hanger as a base for each prefix, hang words that begin with that prefix from the hanger.

Extend the activity further by asking each child to name a word with a prefix, for example, a word with the prefix *un*. When no one can think of another word, begin again with a new prefix.

## Exploring Antonyms

Point out that there are a number of ways to say the opposite of a word. For instance, instead of *unclean* the poet might have used the word *dirty*. Substitute the word *dirty* in "Me a Mess?" and see how it changes the flow of the poem.

Next elicit antonyms of common words: cold/hot, tall/short, empty/full, in/out, slow/fast, love/hate, big/little. Try playing a word game called What Am I? One person is It. It says "I am the opposite of *cold*, what am I?" The first person to give a correct answer becomes the new It. The game can also be played as charades.

## Relating to Other Literature

Marjorie Weinman Sharmat's *Mooch the Messy* explores the problems of a messy animal. It is a good book to read aloud, and will encourage a discussion about the disadvantages of being messy.

## Using Imagery To Create

Note that the poet does not tell us if the messy character is young, old, male, female. Our only idea comes from the picture drawn by the illustrator of the poster. Have children pretend they were asked to illustrate the poem. Ask them to imagine what the messy person. Some readers may want to suggest that the I of the poem is not a person, but an object of clothing such as a dirty pair of jeans.

## Writing To Describe

Discuss with children what the house of a messy person might look like. Have children write a few sentences describing an extremely messy room.

## Learning From The Poem

Ask what a messy person might look like. Talk about the basics of good grooming. Construct a Good Grooming chart and illustrate it with pictures cut from magazines that show people practicing good grooming habits.

See Meet the Poet, page 186.

# Me a Mess?

Unclean and unbuckled,
Unfastened, untied,
Unfit to be seen,
I'm undignified.
Unfolded, unbuttoned,
Unbecoming, no less.
Unfortunately I'm
Unaware I'm a mess.

*Babs Bell Hajdusiewicz*

# RESPONDING TO
# Mud Monster

BY BONNIE KINNE

## Relating To The Poem

Invite children to tell about times they have stepped in mud. Ask why "Mud Monster" is a good name for a poem about mud. You may also want to tell about a time you stepped in mud, how you felt, and how that experience has led you to avoid mud puddles. Have children consider why an older child or adult might step around a mud puddle, while a small child might purposefully step in mud. Ask children how old they think the owner of the boots, shoes, socks, and toes in the poem might be.

Encourage children to talk about and compare the nature and behavior of monsters they have read about or seen on television or in movies.

## Writing A Sequence Of Events

Give each child a long, narrow sheet of paper. On it, have them draw a series of pictures that depict the events of the poem. Under each picture, they can write the words from the poem that describe what is happening.

## Comparing Characters

This is a good opportunity to read *Mud Puddle* by Robert N. Munch. Discuss how mud is a problem to the characters in the story and the poem. Ask how the characters attempt to solve the problem and how successful they are. Invite discussion of whether children think "Mud Monster" would be a good name for the mud puddle in Robert N. Munch's story and, if so, why.

Read "Arithmetic Pie" (Numbers: Poster 1) to discuss another character's experience with mud.

## Reading For Details

Discuss why the reader would think the monster is a male. Ask how the poet's spelling of *help* gives a clue for reading with expression.

## Experimenting With Suction

Provide small paper cups and a tray of mud or a similar substance such as chocolate pudding. Nest cups to simulate boots, shoes, and socks. Press upright cups into the mud and then lift, allowing the mud to "gobble" the bottom cup. Children enjoy repeating the experiment to learn how the amount of suction varies depending on how deeply the cups are submerged.

## Writing A Poem . . . And A Song

Write a few words like *muddy, yucky, dirty, slimy, squirty, grimy, cruddy, ooey,* or *gooey.* Help children note how each word ends in a *y* that has the sound of long *e.* Ask children to think of more words to describe mud. List at least eight words in a column. Have children read the words with you to check for the long *e* sound at the end of each. Then lead children to chant the words several times.

Remind children that by putting music to a poem they can create a song. Ask children to sing the words in the column with you to the tune of "Twinkle, Twinkle, Little Star."

You may want to take this opportunity to model the process of revising. Write two lines: "Twinkle, twinkle little star. How I wonder what you are." Read or sing the words, emphasizing how *star* and *are* rhyme. Chant or sing the list of words about mud. Ask which words would need to rhyme in order to follow the pattern of the song. Brainstorm words that rhyme with the words about mud. Create a longer list of "mud" words, if desired. Then have children suggest ways to rearrange their "mud" words so the rhyming words fall at the ends of the lines. Model crossing out a word or circling it and drawing an arrow to show where to reinsert it. Model rereading for help in placing each word where it sounds best.

# Mud Monster

The mud monster
Gobbled up my boots.
Then he gobbled up my shoes,
And he started on my socks,
But before he reached my toes,
I yelled Hellllllllp!

*Bonnie Kinne*

# RESPONDING TO
# My Loose Tooth

BY RUTH KANAREK

## Reading And Reciting

As you read the poem, children will enjoy saying the repetitive phrase "wiggly, jiggly loose tooth" each time it appears. They might also be divided into three groups, with each group reading one stanza. Have a "director" lead the groups by pointing to the words on the poster as group members say them.

## Writing About Losing Teeth

Children will have many stories to tell about losing their teeth. Explain that there are many ways they can use these experiences in their writing. Suggest the following:

- a letter to the tooth fairy;
- a first-person account of How I Lost My First Tooth;
- a story called What the Tooth Fairy Does with Teeth.

Children will enjoy writing these stories on tooth-shaped paper.

## Relating To Other Literature

Encourage children to compare their lost-tooth experiences with those described in these books: The Mango Tooth, by Charlotte Pomerantz, Arthur's Loose Tooth, by Lillian Hoban, and Air Mail to the Moon, by Tom Birdseye. Together, these books explore the anxieties produced by waiting for the tooth to fall out and the custom of putting the lost tooth under a pillow and getting money from a tooth fairy. The Tooth Witch, by Nurit Karlin explores the same problems from the tooth fairy's perspective and suggests that the tooth fairy makes the teeth she collects into stars in the sky.

Two poems in this collection also deal with losing teeth and money. The first, "This Tooth" by Lee Bennett Hopkins (Related Poems), is a humorous look at waiting for a tooth to fall out. The second, "What Coin Do I Have?" by Babs Bell Hajdusiewicz (Related Poems) is about different coins. It can be sung to the tune of "He's Got the Whole World in His Hands."

## Discovering The Truth About Losing Teeth

Help the students gather information about why teeth fall out. Discuss good dental habits: brushing regularly; drinking milk for calcium; avoiding sweets; regular dental check-ups. You may wish to invite the school nurse or a dental hygienist to visit the classroom to discuss good dental hygiene. The class may follow up by making a poster about healthy teeth.

## Using Literal And Figurative Expressions

There are two expressions in the poem which have both literal and figurative meanings: "hanging by a thread" and "a hole in my head." Explain to children that these expressions are part of a group of expressions that have two kinds of meanings: what they seem to mean and what they really mean. Explore each expression for its literal and figurative meaning:

1. tooth hangs loosely as if by a thread/tooth is barely hanging on
2. a real empty space in my head/some good sense missing from my head

You can model using these sentences in daily speech and review other expressions with literal and figurative meanings, such as "cut across the lawn"; she "skipped breakfast"; they were "pulling my leg."

## Gathering Oral History

Tell children that long ago, money was worth more. Salaries were lower and so were prices. A subway ride cost a nickel, as did a candy bar and an ice cream cone. Explain that as years go by, items become more expensive and even the going rate from the tooth fairy changes! Have children ask older brothers and sisters, parents and grandparents if they received any rewards for losing their teeth. Have children record their answers and share them with the class. In addition to discovering what a lost tooth was worth a long time ago, children may discover other customs that were used to celebrate losing a baby tooth.

# My Loose Tooth

I had a loose tooth, a wiggly, jiggly loose tooth.
I had a loose tooth, hanging by a thread.

So I pulled my loose tooth, this wiggly, jiggly loose tooth.
And put it 'neath the pillow when I went up to bed.

The fairies took my loose tooth, my wiggly, jiggly loose tooth.
So now I have a nickel and a hole in my head.

*Ruth Kanarek*

# RESPONDING TO
# The Poet Says

BY BABS BELL HAJDUSIEWICZ

## Thinking Critically

Stimulate discussion by asking questions such as, Why might someone write a poem? How is a poem a part of a person? or Why might a writer be thought of as a sharing person?

You may want to introduce the idea of reading someone's mind. Encourage children to think about advantages and disadvantages of being able to tell what others are thinking. Talk about clues such as facial expressions, actions, personality, and body language that help us learn what someone is thinking.

## Thinking About Paper

Read "Paper I" by Carl Sandburg:
Paper is two kinds; to write on,
to wrap with.
If you like to write, you write.
If you like to wrap, you wrap.
Some papers like writers,
some like wrappers.
Are you a writer or a wrapper?

Have children list some kinds of paper they would use as writers and those they would use as wrappers. Writing paper may include stationery, computer paper, newspaper, and construction paper. Wrappers might use napkins, waxed paper, freezing paper, brown paper, and gift wrap. Have children compare the lists to look for kinds of paper that might be used by writers as well as wrappers.

Children will enjoy an anonymous poet's fantasy about paper, "If All the World Were Paper" (Related Poems).

## Extending The Poem

Write "The Author Says" and ask children how the words of the poem might change if an author of books or stories were speaking. Write the poem making the suggested substitutions.

Extend children's thinking by changing the noun in the poem's title to words like *Illustrator, Sculptor, Songwriter,* or *Playwright.* Encourage children to think of the kind of tools each creator would use. You may want to extend the activity further by substituting the names of other creators such as an engineer building a skyscraper or bridge, a chef cooking a meal, or a carpenter building a table.

## Having A Reason To Write

Display a few unfamiliar pictures that evoke thought and imagination. Ask each child to study any one or all of the pictures. Tell children you wonder what is in their minds as they examine the picture, but you cannot see their thoughts. Invite children to "take some paper, a pencil or pen" to write what's in their mind. If necessary, scribe for children so their words can be read by others. Have children share their writing with one or two friends. Then bind several copies so children can read their classmates' thoughts. These books can also be checked out of the class library so children can share a part of themselves and their friends with parents.

## Enjoying More Poets' Thoughts

For another "part" of Carl Sandburg, read and sing his thoughts about "Fog" (Nature: Poster 3). The tools of poets in "Poets and Pigs" (Word Play: Poster 7) make for an interesting comparison. "Poet Unknown" (Related Poems) introduces children to writers who share their thoughts anonymously.

## Holding A Poetry Reading

Urge children to stage a reading of their favorite poems. Suggest that they introduce the program with "The Poet Says." Then have children take turns reciting poems. Some may want to pretend to be the poet and tell about him- or herself before sharing the work.

See Meet the Poet, page 186.

# The Poet Says

A poem is a part of me —
A part of me you do not see.
You see my head.
You see my hind.
But you can't see what's in my mind.

So I must write that part of me
The part of me you cannot see.
I take some paper,
A pencil or pen,
To write what's in my mind, and then . . .

You have a poem
To read and . . . see!
I've given you
A part of me.

*Babs Bell Hajdusiewicz*

# RESPONDING TO
# The Secret Place

BY TOMIE DEPAOLA

## Discussing The Details

Since most children have had a secret place at some time or other, they will readily identify with the narrator of Tomie dePaola's poem. Discuss what book the child might have brought to his secret place, why he would need a flashlight, and what kind of pencil his grandfather might have given him. Have children read the text to find the answer to this question: Why was it his "secret place for about a week"? Have children suggest things the narrator's mother might have said when she found out what he had been doing to the sheets. Suggest to children that this poem might be autobiographical. Since Tomie dePaola became an artist when he grew up, perhaps his mother did not get too angry — maybe she enjoyed his talent.

## Personalizing The Poem

Ask children to describe a secret place of their own, real or imaginary. Ask where such a place might be — under a table or chair covered with a blanket, a tree house, a clubhouse, or a tent. Discuss how children would create such a place, what tools they would use, and what they would do in it when it was finished. What would they take to their secret place? Who would be allowed in?

## Observing The Structure Of The Poem

Have children talk about the way this poem is built, with no rhyme and short stanzas with an alternating number of lines. Encourage children to observe the poet's use of dashes. Ask them what these dashes do. (They allow the poet space to explain further, create the effect of someone explaining as they speak.

You may also wish to ask children to notice the one stanza that is made up of a single line: "It was very white." Have children volunteer their thoughts on how and why this line stands alone. (It is used for emphasis; to show how tempting the whiteness of the sheet was for the poet/artist.)

At this time you may want to present some other poems that have one- or two-word lines or one-line stanzas. Try "Stealing Feelings," by Babs Bell Hajdusiewicz (Feelings: Poster 7) "Hey, Bug!" by Lilian Moore (Me and Others: Poster 4) and "Moochie," by Eloise Greenfield (Me and Others: Poster 6).

## Relating The Poem To Art

Explore with children why the white sheet was such a tempting drawing surface for the child in the poem. To demonstrate this, you may wish to bring in or have a volunteer bring in a white or light-colored sheet. Allow children to experiment with crayons, paint, and markers in decorating the sheet.

## Enjoying Related Books

Crockett Johnson has written a series of books about an inventive young man named Harold, who can create a whole world with just one purple crayon. He doesn't just color his sheets — he covers his entire bedroom wall! Two of the most popular titles are *Harold and the Purple Crayon* and *A Picture for Harold's Room*.

See Meet the Poet, page 184.

# The Secret Place

It was my secret place —
   down at the foot
   of my bed—
   under the covers.

It was very white.

I went there
   with a book, a flashlight,
   and the special pencil
   that my grandfather gave me.

To read —
   and to draw pictures
   on all that white.

It was my secret place
   for about a week —

Until my mother came
   to change the sheets.

*Tomie dePaola*

# RESPONDING TO
# Silly Sleep Sheep

BY HELEN C. SMITH

## Introducing The Poem

Before reading this poem, you may want to explain to children that to help them get to sleep, some people count imaginary sheep jumping over a fence. That was what Helen C. Smith was doing when the idea for this poem came to her.

## Identifying Humor

Note that "Silly Sleep Sheep" begins with a serious topic: trying to get to sleep. Have children quote the serious lines. Then point out that the poem takes a humorous turn. Ask children to identify the lines of the poem that are funny. Children may notice that the poet does not keep her funny intentions a secret — the title lets the reader know that this is a funny poem.

## Sharing Feelings

Ask children if they have ever had trouble going to sleep and why. They may give reasons such as not being tired, being in strange surroundings, worrying about something, or being afraid of ghosts or monsters. Talk about how noises and shapes that seem very ordinary during the daytime can seem frightening at night. This theme is explored by Paulette Bourgeois in her book *Franklin in the Dark*. It is the story of a turtle who overcomes his fear of climbing into his small, dark shell.

You may also want to discuss ways, other than counting sheep, of falling asleep. Make a list of children's suggestions.

## Dramatizing The Poem

Have children draw and cut out pictures of sheep. After they glue cotton on their sheep, children may attach them to popsicle sticks to make stick puppets. (You may want to note that even though children have made a lot of sheep, they have made far fewer than the million mentioned in the poem.)

Show children how to use their puppets to act out the poem. Set up a scene with a doll in a bed and a fence. Then, as you or a child read the poem, children can make the sheep puppets jump the fence.

## Using Alliteration

Point out the letter *S* at the beginning of each word in the title of "Silly Sleep Sheep." Then cover the first word with a removable stick-on note. Have children think of other words that begin with *s* to write instead of "Silly." They may suggest *six, seven,* or *stupid*. Do the same thing with the other words in the title.

Extend the activity by reading other poems that use alliteration in the title. Try "Poets and Pigs" by John Schaum (Word Play: Poster 7) and "Solo Sunday" by Babs Bell Hajdusiewicz (Feelings: Poster 6).

## Comparing The Poem To Other Literature

"Silly Sleep Sheep" closely parallels the story told by Holly Keller in *Ten Sleepy Sheep*. In this book, a reluctant sleeper tries to prolong his bedtime ritual until he takes his grandfather's advice and counts sheep. The sheep arrive, decked out for a party. They make quite a racket until the little boy must finally put *them* to sleep. You may wish to discuss the strong similarities between the poem and the book. This may lead to a talk about how more than one person can have the same idea. Point out that this is a coincidence and not a case of copying.

# Silly Sleep Sheep

One sheep, two sheep, three sheep, four . . .
There must have been a million more!
As I lay there wanting sleep,
I counted all those silly sheep.
They didn't jump the fence for me
but gathered all around to see
if I would jump the fence instead
so all of them could go to bed!

*Helen C. Smith*

# RESPONDING TO
# Statue On The Curb

BY BABS BELL HAJDUSIEWICZ

## Dramatization

"Statue on the Curb" lends itself well to dramatization. Ask one child to be the pedestrian and have others be cars, trucks, and buses. You may wish to have children who are pretending to be vehicles wear or carry signs or pictures showing what they are supposed to be. Once children have practiced in the classroom, take them to an actual street corner where they can demonstrate what they have learned about crossing safely.

## Meeting A Traffic-Safety Expert

Review what the poet suggests one should do before crossing the street — look left and right; watch out for cars, trucks, and buses; stay on the curb if anything is coming. Ask children what other rules help them travel safely around their neighborhood.

Invite a police officer or traffic control guard to visit the classroom and discuss safety on the streets, both on bicycles and on foot. Help students make a chart that lists safety rules. Have the class write a joint thank-you letter or individual letters to the person who visited your class. Remind students to mention something new that they learned from the expert's visit.

## Tape Recording The Poem

A group of children may enjoy recording a dramatic reading of the poem, complete with sound effects. One child can be the narrator, while others can produce the sounds.

Before they begin, have children practice making car, truck, and bus noises. Then talk about the places in the poem where those sounds would be most effective. Help them make a practice recording to listen to and to decide what parts they like and where they want to make changes. Then have them incorporate the changes into a final recording.

## Learning About Statues

Challenge children to name some statues — the *Statue of Liberty*, a Civil War general in a local park, or even a mannequin in a store. Show them a picture of a famous sculpture such as *The Thinker* by Rodin. Children may enjoy posing like the statues.

Work with children to write a group story about a child who goes for a walk and becomes a different statue at every corner — sometimes *The Thinker*, sometimes the *Statue of Liberty*. Have volunteers illustrate the story.

## Looking For Safety Signs

Discuss some of the signs that help us walk and drive safely through towns and neighborhoods. You may wish to read the class a book about traffic signs, such as *Signs* by Ron and Nancy Goor. Then have children construct signs from oak tag. Display these signs on a special bulletin board display.

## Expanding Vocabulary: A Game

Ask children why the poet pretends to be a statue. (A statue doesn't move; a statue stands perfectly still.) Tell children you are going to play a game in which they are all to turn into statues — that is, freeze in place. Allow children to walk about or move freely as you name things that might be seen, heard, or felt while out on a walk — *wind, sidewalk, grass, bush, tree, flower, sunshine, bird, friend, kitten*. Tell them that if you say a word that indicates danger, however, they are to freeze like statues. These words might include *car, truck, bus, honking horn, screeching brakes, traffic, red light, stop sign, danger*.

## Comparing The Poem To Other Literature

The book, *Try it Again, Sam*, by Judith Viorst, tells the story of a boy named Sam who longs to be able to walk to his friend's house by himself. The back of the book includes a list of rules for safety. You may wish to compare this book to the poem. Children might also compare the poem as it appears on the poster with the way it appears in the August/September 1988 issue of *Humpty Dumpty* magazine.

See Meet the Poet, page 186.

# Statue On The Curb

When crossing the street,
I watch out and beware
Of cars, trucks and buses
All going somewhere!

I stop at the corner,
Look left and look right;
Then step off the curb
If nothing's in sight.

But if there's a car
Or truck down the way,
I pretend I'm a statue
And on the curb stay!

*Babs Bell Hajdusiewicz*

# RESPONDING TO
# Whose Face?

BY LONNY ALEXANDER

## Exploring Self-Image

Be sure to have some shiny metal spoons on hand before reading this poem. You may also want to assemble some shiny pot lids, a mirror or two, some aluminum foil, and other objects in which children can see their reflection. After reading the poem, allow some time for children to see how they look in each one. Encourage them to find other places in the room where they can see themselves: in a window, a faucet, a brass doorknob, or a shiny tabletop. Talk about how their image is distorted.

Two poems that relate to the way people feel about themselves are found in this collection. "The Me Key," by Biji Surber Malaker (Related Poems), is a little confidence booster. "Just Like Me" (Related Poems) is the old trick that everyone falls for — once.

## Using Metaphors

Have children list the comparisons made by the narrator of the poem. They will note that the face is described as looking like a stringbean, a skinny hippopotamus, and a hay-filled scarecrow.

Suggest that children look at themselves in a spoon and think of their own comparisons. What do they look like? They may enjoy drawing a picture of the way they look in the spoon and then under it write questions that improvise on the text of the poem:
Whose is that funny banana face?
Does it belong to a skinny goldfish?

## Examining Compound Words

Challenge children to find words in the poem that are really two words joined together: *stringbean, scarecrow, whenever, myself*. Then have them think about compound words that refer to their own heads: *eyeball, eyebrow, eyelash, earlobe, hairline, cheekbone, forehead*.

## Writing With Adjectives

Ask children to try to imagine the poem without descriptive words or adjectives. Cover all these words with removable stick-on notes: *funny, stringbean, big, bulgy, long, pointed, huge, wide, skinny, hay-filled, silvery*. Read what is left of the poem. Ask, What kind of eyes, nose, mouth, hippopotamus, or spoon is being described? We have no idea! Maybe the spoon is made of wood; maybe the hippo is fat. Help children understand that descriptive words help paint the picture we see in our minds.

Suggest that children write a description of a face, using plenty of adjectives to describe each part of it. They can then give their description to a friend and have that person draw a picture of the face they wrote about.

## Expanding On The Theme

Some children might be interested in writing a story about a character who sees its reflection in a spoon and thinks it has learned how it really looks. The character might despair because it is so ugly or rejoice because it is so beautiful. It might then go off searching for someone who looks the way it does, only to have the truth revealed in some way. These stories can be read aloud to the class. Children will enjoy "Extraordinary Me" (Me: Poster 2).

# Whose Face?

Whose is that funny, stringbean face
with the big, bulgy eyes,
the long, pointed nose,
the huge, wide mouth?

Does it belong to a skinny
hippopotamus?
Does it belong to a hay-filled
scarecrow?

No! It belongs to ME!
It's my face whenever I look at myself
in the back of a silvery spoon!

*Lonny Alexander*

 **Index to Related Poems**

1. I and My Echo.........................................page 211
2. If All the World Were Paper.............................214
3. Just Like Me...........................................219
4. No Pronoun Problems....................................226
5. Poet Unknown..........................................233
6. The Me Key ............................................221
7. This Tooth ............................................244
8. What Coin Do I Have? ..................................250

# UNIT 5
# ME AND OTHERS

1. Alas!
2. From Mars to Safety
3. Goops (Table Manners)
4. Hey, Bug!
5. Jonathan Bing
6. Moochie
7. Nancy Hanks
8. Old Grumbler
9. Rudes

# RESPONDING TO
# Alas!

BY BABS BELL HAJDUSIEWICZ

## Enjoying A Poem With A New Twist

Recite or read aloud the traditional nursery rhyme several times until children are familiar with its words and its rhythm and rhyme:

Jack and Jill
Went up the hill
To fetch a pail of water.
Jack fell down,
And broke his crown,
And Jill came tumbling after.

Tell children to listen to another story about Jack and Jill going up a hill. As you begin to read or recite the seat-belt version, children may appear puzzled at what seems like the same rhyme they heard before. They will, therefore, be very attentive and delighted when you say "But, alas!" with a knowing look.

## Identifying Humor

After several readings, explain that "Alas!" is called a parody because it is a funny imitation of the original poem. Ask children to recall the idea that makes "Alas!" funny or humorous. Have children identify the specific words that make "Alas!" a parody. Then encourage children to think about how the rhyme could be taken seriously and why.

## Becoming Safety Conscious

Invite children to talk about why Jack fell and why Jill didn't fall. Ask children to tell about their own use of seat belts in cars. Ask them why they think there are laws that require people to wear seat belts. Discuss ways that are used to remind people to "buckle up": signs on highways, buzzers or chimes in cars, TV messages. Children will enjoy looking for such reminders for several days and then reporting their findings.

## Thinking To Write

Help children think of other ways Jack and Jill might go up a hill and how the illustration might change accordingly. For instance, on a motorcycle they would need helmets. Children will enjoy rewriting the last line and illustrating their new rhyme.

You may want to introduce another poem "If the Spider Could Talk" (Animals: Poster 6).

## Experimenting With Motion

Invite children to bring in toy people or animals and model cars, trucks, or other small vehicles. Challenge children to suggest ways to use these objects along with tape or string to show what happened when Jack and Jill were riding in a car.

You may want to have children perform motion experiments a given number of times and tally their results. Help children compile their findings and draw conclusions from them.

## Using The Dictionary

Model the use of a dictionary or have children use various dictionaries to define "vehicle." Encourage discussion of the qualities of a vehicle: it carries people or things; travels over land, water, or in space; has an engine or is pulled by an animal. Invite children to debate whether such things as skateboards, surfboards, or roller skates would be considered vehicles.

Children may enjoy creating a "Dictionary of Vehicles" by drawing and labeling vehicles on separate sheets of paper, arranging the sheets in alphabetical order, and then binding the pages to make a book.

## Enjoying More Poetry

Children will enjoy "One For Me," "Bill and Jim and Joe and Zack," "Where's My Seatbelt," "My Organs," and "I'll Always Wear You" (Related Poems).

See Meet the Poet, page 186.

# Alas!

Jack and Jill
Went up the hill
To fetch a pail of water.
Jack fell down
And broke his crown,
But, alas!
Jill was wearing her seat belt!

*Babs Bell Hajdusiewicz*

# RESPONDING TO
# From Mars to Safety

BY BABS BELL HAJDUSIEWICZ

## Talking About Dreams

Ask children to share their good and bad dreams, and encourage talk about how they feel when they awaken from each kind of dream, who might come to comfort them during a nightmare, and how they are comforted.

Help children think about how parents often express their wish that their children have good dreams with words such as "sweet dreams," "sleep tight," and "pleasant dreams." Children will enjoy discussing any specific "tucking in" words their parents use.

To help children realize that sometimes we incorporate real events into our dreams, share a pertinent dream of yours or ask children if they've ever dreamed about something and then awakened to find that the dream situation had really happened while they were sleeping. Ask children to share such dreams of theirs and tell how any real event was woven into the dream.

## Thinking Critically

Help children think of the events in the poem as real happenings woven into the child's dream. The crash, for instance, might be the dreamer's mom stumbling when coming into a dark room to comfort the child, or the flight in the sky and the "hiss" might be the mother holding and rocking the child while saying "shhh." Encourage children to tell the poem's story from this perspective.

## Dramatizing The Poem

A pair of children may enjoy pantomiming this poem while a third person reads it aloud. A costume designer can make a suitably scary mask from a paper bag for the creature from Mars, while a sound-effects person can collect objects that will make ". . . crash! . . . boom! . . . kerbang!" noises at appropriate times.

## Learning About A Planet

Ask children why they think the author chose to include a creature from Mars. Have children list questions they might like to ask about Mars, use resource materials to find answers, and then check to see if their research in any way changes their thoughts on the author's use of a creature from Mars.

This would be a good time to read "Family of the Sun" (Nature: Poster 2).

## Identifying Words For Sounds

Ask children to say the sound a dog or cat makes as you write words like *wolf, arf, meow,* and *mew.* Have children read the words and then name more animal sounds for you to write. Ask children to listen for more words for sounds as you reread the poem. Add the words to the list. Have children write each word in a sentence.

You may want to introduce the word *onomatopoeia* as the name for words that imitate sounds. You'll want to share "Glug! Gurgle! Glug!" (Word Play: Poster 2) "Hairy Toe" (Adventure: Poster 4), and various other poems which make use of onomatopoeia.

## Creating New Words

Invite children to think of sounds for which there may not be a word, consult their dictionaries to check their predictions, and then list any new words along with a definition for each. Children may enjoy illustrating their words for a display titled Hear It and Say It.

See Meet the Poet, page 186.

# From Mars to Safety

I was playing outside
Having lots of fun,
When all of a sudden
There was no sun.

I heard a crash!
A boom! Kerbang!
I saw a flash!
I heard a clang!

I spun around
And what did I see?
A creature was standing there
Staring at me!

It asked me if
I'd like to go
With it to Mars —
Well, I couldn't say "no"!

I didn't have a choice, you see.
It had its arms curled all around me!
So I said "yes," that I would do
What it was obviously forcing me to.

The creature held me;
I started to cry.
I cried very softly
Up there in the sky.

The creature looked mean;
I heard him hiss!
I started to scre-e-e-eam!
When I woke to Mom's kiss!

*Babs Bell Hajdusiewicz*

# RESPONDING TO
# Goops (Table Manners)

BY GELETT BURGESS

## Introducing The Poem

As you read the poem, children will love watching you act it out. Pretend to lick your fingers, use your index finger as a knife, motion to show spilling, wrinkle your nose and put hands on hips to accent "disgusting," chew with an open mouth and smack your lips, and point to yourself before scanning the group with a pointing finger.

## Listening To Recall Information

Ask children to listen for reasons the poet is "glad that I am not a Goop" as you read aloud. List the behaviors in the poem. Then ask children to think of other things a Goop might do and add these suggestions to the list.

## Naming Opposites

Create a second column beside the behaviors of the Goops listed above. Encourage children to use complete sentences to tell what the Goops should do instead. Write each opposite sentence beside its corresponding behavior.

Extend this activity by having children picture one of the Goops' disgusting behaviors beside a picture of what the Goops should do. Displays of the drawings might be titled Listen Up, Goops! or How Not to Be a Goop.

## Categorizing Behaviors

Tell children that two very different little mice have come to live in a family's house. One mouse has good manners and is named Good Manners Mouse while the other little mouse is named Poor Manners Mouse. Read "Who Is This Mouse?" by Babs Bell Hajdusiewicz and ask children to name the mouse:

Who is this tiny, little mouse
Who lives with me inside my house?
He always shares
His cheesy squares.
His name's _____ Manners Mouse.

Continue, using the same two beginning lines and substituting the following for lines 3, 4, and 5:

1) He asks for cheese
   He never says "please"!
   His name's _____ Manners Mouse.
2) He never burps;
   And doesn't slurp.
   His name's _____ Manners Mouse.
3) He picks his nose
   So I suppose
   His name's _____ Manners Mouse.
4) He pulls my hair —
   I must beware!
   His name's _____ Manners Mouse.
5) He'll boast and brag
   And hit in "tag."
   His name's _____ Manners Mouse.
7) He doesn't peek
   In "hide-and-seek."
   His name's _____ Manners Mouse.

Challenge children to change a "Poor Manners Mouse" stanza to a "Good Manners Mouse" stanza and vice versa. Encourage children to think of other examples of good and poor manners to create more stanzas.

## Enjoying Related Poems

Read "Bad and Good" (Word Play: Poster 1) and "Rudes" (Me and Others: Poster 9). Ask children to compare and contrast the ideas of each poet to see that the main idea of each poem is manners, each poem stresses poor manners, and there is repetition of the same or a similar behavior.

Gelett Burgess has written many more poems about the Goops in the books, *Goops and How to Be Them* and *More Goops*.

## Creating A Book

Work with children to create a Goops Book of Etiquette. Questions such as these will help them get started:

What would the Goops do when they were introduced to someone?

How would a Goop behave at the theater?

How would a Goop act in the hallway?

First, help children phrase their responses as rules for good Goops: Good Goops always stick out their tongues at someone they meet, or A good Goop always jumps on theater seats.

# Goops (Table Manners)

The Goops they lick their fingers,
    And the Goops they lick their knives;
They spill their broth on the tablecloth-
    Oh, they lead disgusting lives!
The Goops they talk while eating,
    And loud and fast they chew;
And that is why I'm glad that I
    Am not a Goop — are you?

*Gelett Burgess*

# RESPONDING TO
# Hey, Bug!

## Reading Dramatically

Children will enjoy seeing you pretend you're talking to the bug as you read this poem. At the end, appear to follow the imaginary bug's path up the wall to the ceiling, out the door or window, or under the chair seat.

## Examining Motivation

Children delight in pretending the bug doesn't stay because it doesn't like *oatmeal* cookies. What kind does it like? Maybe sugar cookies, or peanut butter, chocolate chip, or snickerdoodles — let children decide.

Then talk about the real reasons why a bug might not stay. Ask children to put themselves in the bug's place. How would they feel if they were little insects on the hand of a very large person? Help them see that the bug wants to find a meal, not be one.

## Making A Walking Book

Working together, children can make a book that illustrates each aspect of the poem. They can then join the pages as shown. As they read the book, they should "walk" their fingers along the finished book from left to right.

## Considering Point Of View

This would be a good time to read "If the Spider Could Talk" by Babs Bell Hajdusiewicz. (Animals: Poster 6) Draw children's attention to the fact that each poem is told from a different point of view: one is told by a person; the other by the bug.

Extend the activity by having interested children write their own poem from the point of view of a bug. They might call it "Hey, Melinda!" or "Hey, José!"

## Enjoying Other Poetry

Two other poems in this collection would be fun to read at this time. After acting out the fingerplay "Eensy Weensy Spider" (Related Poems) children will have fun trying to make up hand motions to go with "Hey, Bug!"

It would be interesting to compare the outcome of the limerick, "Antsy Pants" (Related Poems) to the outcome of "Hey, Bug!" Children may conclude that it is sometimes a good thing if a bug — a mosquito, bee, blackfly, or hornet — doesn't stay. Lead children to discuss their feelings about bugs. Do they like some better than others?

# Hey, Bug!

Hey, bug, stay!
Don't run away.
I know a game that we can play.

I'll hold my fingers very still
And you can climb a finger-hill.

No, no.
Don't go.

Here's a wall — a tower, too,
a tiny bug town, just for you.
I've a cookie. You have some.
Take this oatmeal cookie crumb.

Hey, bug, stay!
Hey, bug!
Hey!

*Lilian Moore*

# RESPONDING TO
# Jonathan Bing

BY BEATRICE CURTIS BROWN

## Enjoying The Poem

Children will enjoy joining in to chant "Poor old Jonathan Bing" during repeated read-alouds. Pause after the word *poor* to allow the children to complete the phrase. You may also pause for the children to chorus "He'd forgotten his hat!" at the end of the first stanza and "He'd forgotten his tie!" at the end of the second stanza.

## Dramatizing The Poem

"Jonathan Bing" lends itself easily to dramatization. Roles include Jonathan, a soldier, the Archbishop, several children to "be" the carriage, and the remainder to be "everyone" who points in the first stanza. Someone may also be the narrator, reading the lines as the characters perform, or you may present the action as a play.

## Comparing The Poem To Other Literature

You may wish to read other works that deal with confusion and embarrassment caused by choice of clothing. *The Emperor's New Clothes* by Anne Rockwell and *The 500 Hats of Bartholomew Cubbins* by Dr. Seuss are stories in which clothing — or lack of it — leads to problems. Help children compare the problems and feelings of Jonathan Bing to those of the Emperor and Bartholomew Cubbins.

## Expanding Vocabulary

Discuss words in the poem that reveal that Jonathan Bing is going to visit royalty: *King, palace, soldier.* Elicit additional words that might be useful in describing a visit to a king. *(queen, prince, princess, throne, crown, castle)*

## Linking Uniforms To Occupations

Review some of the characters mentioned in the poem: soldier, King, Archbishop. Each of their jobs may involve wearing a uniform. Discuss other workers who wear recognizable uniforms: nurse, doctor, sailor, baseball player, etc.

You may construct a chart or mural with the children, titled Who Wears This? One side will display a drawing or magazine cutout of a uniform; the other side will display the name of the matching profession.

You may play a game, Who Am I? The child chosen to be It will describe what he or she is wearing, and the class must guess what kind of work that person does.

## Using Adjectives

Ask children what kind of hat Jonathan Bing chose to wear.("a new hat") And what kind of a tie? ("a beautiful tie") Suggest changing these descriptive adjectives to others: a feathered hat; a baseball hat; a top hat; a felt hat; a polka-dotted tie; a striped tie. Explore the images created by substituting these new adjectives.

## Placing The Poem In Time

Ask children when they think this poem took place — recently or a long time ago. Suggest that the mode of travel — carriage — suggests it was a long time ago. Elicit other modes of travel that might make the poem sound more contemporary and change the tone: train, plane, car, bike, skateboard. You may substitute each of these words and see if it creates a different effect.

## Writing A New Ending

Elicit other ways to change the ending of the poem. What would the King do after he receives Jonathan's note? (go and visit Jonathan) Or instead of giving up, what might Jonathan have done? (gone on in his pajamas; dressed up and tried again)

## Making A List

Discuss what caused Jonathan's predicament — forgetting, excitement causing forgetfulness. Ask children what Jonathan could have done to be sure he was ready to visit the king. Elicit that he could have made a list. Work with children to compose a list of things Jonathan should have remembered.

# Jonathan Bing

Poor old Jonathan Bing
Went out in his carriage to visit the King,
But everyone pointed and said, "Look at that!
Jonathan Bing has forgotten his hat!"
(He'd forgotten his hat!)

Poor old Jonathan Bing
Went home and put on a new hat for the King,
But up by the palace a soldier said, "Hi!
You can't see the King; you've forgotten your tie!"
(He'd forgotten his tie!)

Poor old Jonathan Bing,
He put on a *beautiful* tie for the King,
But when he arrived an Archbishop said, "Ho!
You can't come to court in pajamas, you know!"

Poor old Jonathan Bing
Went home and addressed a short note to the King:

If you please will excuse me
I won't come to tea;
For home's the best place for
All people like me!

*Beatrice Curtis Brown*

# RESPONDING TO
# Moochie

BY ELOISE GREENFIELD

## Dramatizing The Poem

After repeated read-alouds, children will enjoy reciting the third and fourth lines: "Peeka Boo! Peeka Boo!" Pause after the word *game* and signal children that it is their cue to speak. You may wish to have them add hand motions (covering their face) as they speak.

Volunteers can come up in pairs to reenact the poem. One will portray the older child playing peekaboo; the other will be the baby who laughs and gets hiccups.

## Making Inferences

Ask children who they think is telling this little story. They may suggest a big sister or brother, a babysitter, or even a parent or grandparent. Then explore the meaning of the poem further by having children quote lines to answer these questions:

What does the narrator think of peekaboo?
What does the game make Moochie do?
Why does the narrator keep playing?

Ask them to summarize their answers by telling how they think the narrator feels about Moochie.

If children had to describe the mood of the poem in one word, what would they use? They will probably think of words like *funny, silly,* and *affectionate.*

## Personalizing The Poem

Use the poem as a springboard for sharing experiences children have had with babies. Ask, What babies have you known? Have you ever had to entertain a baby? What games did the baby like? Do they remember what they liked to play when they were little?

## Using Art To Expand The Poem

Discuss what might be fun for a baby in the game of peekaboo. (surprise and recognition) Tell children that they can construct their own peekaboo pictures. Let them draw or cut out a picture of a familiar object and then let them cut out two flaps, one for each side of the paper. With a stapler, attach a flap to each side of the paper so only part of the child's picture is visible. Children can display their pictures at Show and Tell and see if their classmates can guess what is beneath the peekaboo flap. You may wish to provide examples of such pictures by showing children two books that use this idea. One is Anno's *Peekaboo,* a wordless exploration of the game; the other is Tana Hoban's *Look Again.*

## Surveying Hiccup Cures

Ask children if they have ever had the hiccups. Ask what they did to stop the hiccups. You will certainly get a variety of answers. Make a list of all the possible hiccup remedies the class suggests: having someone surprise or scare them; eating raw sugar; taking a drink of water; holding their breath, and so on. Then have children conduct a survey to see how many people favor one remedy over the other. (You can give each child a sheet of paper listing the remedies and have them interview five people and check off their responses.) Combine the results of each child's survey and display the results in chart form.

## Relating To Other Literature

Several excellent books explore mixed feelings about having a baby around. Jan Omerod's *101 Things to Do with a Baby* is both humorous and realistic. Another in a similar vein is *I Love My Baby Sister (Most of the Time)* by Elaine Edelman.

Other books expand on the fatigue alluded to in the poem. *Nobody Asked Me if I Wanted a Baby Sister*, by Martha Alexander, and Russell Hoban's classic, *A Baby Sister for Frances*, deal with older sisters' reactions to younger siblings.

# Moochie

Moochie likes to keep on playing
That same old silly game
Peeka Boo!
Peeka Boo!

I get tired of it
But it makes her laugh
And every time she laughs
She gets the hiccups
And every time she gets the hiccups
I laugh

*Eloise Greenfield*

# RESPONDING TO
# Nancy Hanks

BY ROSEMARY CARR AND STEPHEN VINCENT BENÉT

## Relating The Poem To History

Before reading the poem, tell children that Nancy Hanks was the mother of Abraham Lincoln. She died in Pigeon Creek, Indiana, of something called the "milk sickness" when Abe was nine years old.

A number of Lincoln biographies have been written for youngsters. Susan Dye Lee, Katie Billinstean Smith, and Rae Bains have all written books called *Abraham Lincoln* that describe his early life. Included in each book is the story of Sarah, the woman Tom Lincoln married after Nancy Hanks died, and how she encouraged Abe, taught him to read, and showed him how to laugh again. All three books will help children answer the questions in the poem.

## Writing A Letter

Ask children how they think Nancy Hanks would feel if she knew what really happened to "poor little Abe." Suggest that they write a letter to Nancy Hanks telling her what did happen to Abe. This may be a class project or an individual project. Remind them to answer as many questions from the poem as they can: "Did he grow tall? Did he have fun? Did he learn to read?" and so on.

## Writing With A Partner

This is the only poem in the collection that was written by two people, in this case Rosemary Carr and Stephen Vincent Benét. Ask why two people might work together to write one poem. Discuss possible methods of collaboration.

You may wish to have children experiment with team writing to see which method of collaboration works best for them. Ask which they prefer, writing with a partner or writing alone. Talk about when it would be good to write with a partner, noting those times when a writer needs to discuss ideas with someone.

## Using Asking Sentences

Ask children to notice how many lines of the poem end in a question mark. You may wish to have them point to these sentences. Elicit that these are "asking sentences," or questions. Talk about the words that begin many of these sentences: *where, what, did, do.* Practice making questions. You may write "telling" or declarative sentences and have the children convert them into "asking" sentences.

## Comparing The Poem To Other Literature

The Newbery Award–winning book, *Sarah, Plain and Tall*, is a good book to compare with the story of Abraham Lincoln. Abe Lincoln lost his mother and was raised by a cheerful stepmother (also named Sarah), much like Anna and Caleb, the children in the book.

## Using Figurative Language

The poem contains several examples of figurative language that you may want to explore and explain to the class: "Tom, who's a rolling stone," "pinching times," and "Did he get on?" Ask the children if they know what each of these expressions means.

Explain that Tom was Abe Lincoln's father. Ask them what they think is meant by a "rolling stone." Confirm that Tom Lincoln moved his family often. You may wish to refer to the expression "a rolling stone gathers no moss."

"Pinching times" can be explained by referring to another expression — "penny pinching." Have the children hold a penny and see what it might mean to "pinch a penny" — to hold on tight to their money. Suggest that "pinching times" might be times when the family had little money and had to be careful with whatever they did have.

"Did he get on?" can be explained as relating to the expression "to get on in the world." Have the children guess what that might mean. Explain that it means "to go far" in the figurative sense, to do well.

# Nancy Hanks

If Nancy Hanks
Came back as a ghost,
Seeking news
Of what she loved most,
She'd ask first
"Where's my son?
What's happened to Abe?
What's he done?

"Poor little Abe,
Left all alone
Except for Tom,
Who's a rolling stone;
He was only nine
The year I died,
I remember still
How hard he cried.

"Scraping along
In a little shack,
With hardly a shirt
To cover his back,
And a prairie wind
To blow him down,
Or pinching times
If he went to town.

"You wouldn't know
About my son?
Did he grow tall?
Did he have fun?

Did he learn to read?
Did he get to town?
Do you know his name?
Did he get on?"

*Rosemary Carr and Stephen Vincent Benét*

# RESPONDING TO
# Old Grumbler

BY OSCAR BRAND

## Singing It Out; Acting It Out

After hearing "Old Grumbler" a couple of times, children will want to join in on the echo part of the last line in each stanza. If time permits, they can also act out the story. Interested students can make props and oaktag name tags for the actors.

## Telling The Story In Sequence

Have children tell where Old Grumbler went and what he did. List their responses in the order in which they are given. Then, as you reread the poem, have children number the actions in the order in which they happened.

## Identifying Cause And Effect

Write this sentence starter on the chalkboard:
   What happened when Old Grumbler . . .
Complete the question with an action from the poem:
   . . . forgot the fat in the pot? Say that when Old Grumbler forgot the fat, he caused something to happen. Ask children to supply the effect:
   It all went up in flame.
Continue with other examples from the poem. Help children understand that each of Old Grumbler's actions was the cause of an effect.

## Making Inferences

Encourage children to use the text along with what they already know to answer and discuss questions such as these:
- Why do the man and his wife trade jobs?
- How long does each do the other's job?
- Why does the man need to rock the cradle?
- How many children does the couple apparently have?
- Why did the fat go up in flame?
- Why might the hen go astray?
- Why would yarn get lost in the hay?
- Why might the cow go dry?
- Why would the cow hurt the man?
- Where was the sun setting?
- Why does the man agree with his wife at the end of the poem?

## Comparing The Poem To Other Literature

Explain that "Old Grumbler" is a Scottish ballad, or narrative poem, that Oscar Brand has adapted for singing. The Norse version, "The Husband Who Was to Mind the House," from *Popular Tales from the Norse*, by George W. Dasent is fun to read and compare.

Suggest that children write their own prose version of this story. It could be about a husband and wife or about a teacher and student, a farmer and a factory worker, even about two animals, one wild and one domestic.

## Exploring Word Meanings

Discuss some of the words Oscar Brand has chosen. You may begin with the title, "Old Grumbler." Ask children to speculate about the meaning of *grumble* — "to complain or whine."

Another point to note is the poet's use of several words for the cow's actions: *reared, flicked, flenched, kicked, rapped him in the eye.* Each word has a somewhat different meaning, but all the words together express the cow's extreme displeasure. Children may want to experiment with strings of verbs in their own writing. What, for example, would a dog do if a stranger walked onto the property? Or how would a person react when bitten by a mosquito?

See Adding Music, page 179.

# Old Grumbler

Old Grumbler swore by the shirt he wore
And the green leaves up in the tree,
That he could do more work in a day
Than his wife could do in three . . . three, than his wife could do in three.

Mother Grumbler, she just looked at him,
Saying why not try it now?
Let you do all the work in the house
And I'll go follow the plow . . . plow, and I'll go follow the plow.

Well, she turned on her heels and went to the fields
And left him the ladle-o.
He was stirring the pot when he soon forgot
He should rock the cradle-o . . . oh, he should rock the cradle-o.

Then he went to churn the jar of cream
That stood within the frame.
And he soon forgot the fat in the pot
And it all went up in flame . . . flame, and it all went up in flame.

Then he went to watch the speckled hen
For fear she'd go astray.
And he dropped the yarn in the middle of the barn
And lost it in the hay . . . hay, and lost it in the hay.

Then he went to milk the old grey cow
For fear she would go dry.
She reared and flicked and flenched and kicked
And rapped him in the eye . . . eye, and rapped him in the eye.

Then he looked to the east and he looked to the west
And he saw the setting sun.
And he saw his wife on her way back home
And his work not nearly done . . . done, and his work not nearly done.

So he took her hand and he made her stand
And he said, "Now, I agree!
A woman does more work in a day
Than a man can do in three" . . . three, than a man can do in three.

*Oscar Brand*

# RESPONDING TO
# Rudes

BY BABS BELL HAJDUSIEWICZ

## Analyzing Rude Behavior

Have children list the behaviors of the Rudes and tell why each is a rude thing to do. Elicit and discuss other rude behaviors. Ask children to choose a behavior they think is particularly rude. Have them write a few sentences to describe the behavior, tell why they feel it is rude, and why they would not want to be around someone who does it.

## Discussing Peer Pressure

Ask how and why Rudes might "try to get you somehow to join their club and be a Rude," "try their best to get your attention," and "teach you all the tricks of the trade." Encourage children to think of times in their own life when others have tried to get them to do something wrong. Talk about how difficult it can be to resist peer pressure. Ask children to think of good ways to say "no."

## Personalizing The Poem

After a few readings, you will probably notice use of the poem's language in children's conversations. You will also find opportunities to use ideas or actual lines from the poem to remind children of rules and expectations or to recognize politeness. For example, you may say, "I noticed there were no Rudes at lunch today" when you witness good manners in the lunchroom. You may also offer gentle support with words like "Rudes try their best to get your attention" when you see a child who's trying hard to resist temptation.

## Making Cartoons

Each child can choose one example of rude behavior from the poem. Suggest that they use that behavior as the basis for a two-frame cartoon. First they should draw a cartoon of a Rude exhibiting the crude behavior. In a speech balloon over the Rude's head, children can write what the Rude is saying. In a second box, children can draw another cartoon showing how they would resist the Rude's pressure.

## Locating Rhyming Words

Help children notice that rhyming words in the poem are found at the ends of the lines. Say a word and show children how to scan the ends of lines to quickly locate a word that rhymes with the word you said. Suggest that children add the rhyming words to their rhyming dictionaries.

## Learning How To Identify A Rhyming Pattern

Teach children how to use letters to represent the rhyming pattern in "Rudes:" *AABBCCC*. Challenge them to notice that the fourth stanza strays from that pattern.

Children will enjoy finding different patterns in these poems in the collection:

"Bed in Summer" (Feelings: Poster 1) *AABB*
"Cat" (Animals: Poster 3) *ABCB*
"Fourteen Cats" (Animals: Poster 5) *ABAB*
"Adventures of Isabel" (Adventure: Poster 1) *AABBCCDDEE*

## Enjoying Related Literature

Ask your librarian for *No Fighting! No Biting!* by Else Holmelund Minarik, which children can read independently. You may also want to have children identify and discuss the Rudes in Miss Nelson's class as you read aloud *Miss Nelson Is Missing!* by Harry Allard.

Children will enjoy these poems, found in this collection, about manners and related behavior: "Bad and Good" (Word Play: Poster 1), "Shut Up!" (Related Poems), "Goops" (Me and Others: Poster 3), and "Who Is This Mouse?" (Related Poems).

See Meet the Poet, page 186.

# Rudes

The Rudes don't know or even care
When they are getting in your hair.
They interrupt when you are talking;
Their behavior is absolutely shocking!
They pinch, they hit;
They scratch, they spit.
They don't play fair when they are "it."

The Rudes, they are so terribly rude!
They open their mouths when their food's half-chewed.
They pick their noses in public places;
They stick out their tongues and make ugly faces.
They bite, they fight;
They seem to delight
In showing you how to be impolite.

Rudes love to eat soup, but how they slurp!
There's never "excuse me" whenever Rudes burp!
They don't remember a "thank you" to say
When you give them a gift on their special day.
Rudes stare, they swear;
They seldom share.
They make fun of you and pull your hair.

They'll call you names like stupid and dumb.
You know, Rudes are really quite troublesome!
And that's not all! Listen carefully now:
Rudes try real hard to get you somehow
To join their club
And be a Rude;
If you say "no," you'll be pursued.

They'll try their best to get your attention.
To them, rude behavior is a nifty invention.
They'll teach you all the tricks of the trade
So you can march in their Rude parade.
They're crude, they're shrewd;
They want you as a Rude.
Will you join their club? Will you be a Rude?

*Babs Bell Hajdusiewicz*

# Index to Related Poems

1. Antsy Pants.....................................page 197
2. Bill and Jim and Joe and Zack........................199
3. Eensy Weensy Spider....................................208
4. I'll Always Wear You....................................213
5. My Organs ...........................................224
6. One For Me..........................................228
7. Shut Up!.............................................236
8. Where's My Seatbelt? ................................252
9. Who Is This Mouse? .................................253

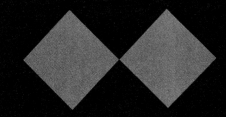

# UNIT 6 NATURE

1. Dandelion
2. The Family of the Sun
3. Fog
4. The Frost Pane
5. Have You Seen Edgar?
6. Last Word of a Bluebird
7. The Pasture
8. Silly Trees
9. Tommy
10. Trees
11. When Icicles Hang by the Wall

# RESPONDING TO
# Dandelion

## Relating Poetic Images To The Actual Object

Before reading, ask children if they know what a dandelion looks like. Ask them to point one out on the poster. If possible, have them pick some dandelions.

After reading, ask children if they can see the dandelion's resemblance to a soldier. Ask, What is the golden helmet? (the petals) What is its green gun? (leaves) Where is the golden beard? (the part of the flower that curves downward under the main petals) Ask children if they have ever seen a lawn where the dandelions were winning the fight with the grass.

## Learning Scientific Names

You may wish to label a flower with the scientific names of its parts: the sepals, the petals, the stamen. Help children find a real dandelion or a picture of one. Suggest that they draw a picture and label its parts.

## Using Metaphors

Ask children in what ways the poet thinks a dandelion is like a little soldier. They will note the poet's words such as *golden helmet, guarding, green gun, yellow beard, stand so stiff,* and *grass to fight.* Explore the differences between comparisons with and without the word *like.* Which do children prefer — "O Little Soldier" or "Dandelion, you look like a little soldier?"

Refer to other poems that use metaphors. In "Fog" (Nature: Poster 3) by Carl Sandburg, fog is seen as a cat. "Have You Seen Edgar?" by Teresa Lynn Morningstar (Nature: Poster 5), personifies a snowflake. You may also want to note that these poems are all unrhymed.

## Creating A New Metaphor

Challenge children to think of other metaphors for a dandelion. Does it look like a lion? A pillow? The sun? Allow children time to brainstorm. Once the class has agreed on a comparison, work to extend the metaphor into a poem. If, for example, they choose to compare a dandelion to a lion, ask them to suggest words such as *growl, stalk, yellow,* and *mane* that relate to lions. Then decide which of those words they would like to use in the poem. Write what they dictate.

## Talking About Writing By Children

Note that this poem was written when the poet was eight years old. Read another example of writing by a youngster — "Hamster," by Alison Hajdusiewicz. (Related Poems)

Publications by and for children may interest your students. *Stone Soup* is a magazine that is written by children and includes poetry, short stories, illustrations, and book reviews. Children interested in writing book reviews may write the magazine and offer their services. The magazine will send them a book to review. The magazine *Highlights for Children* also publishes children's poetry and illustrations.

## Painting In The Impressionist Style

Many Impressionist artists such as Claude Monet and Auguste Renoir have painted pictures of gardens and fields filled with flowers. Their landscapes were bathed in light, the flowers appearing as lively blotches of color that seem to reflect warmth. Show children prints of some of these pictures and have them note the artists' technique. Then challenge them to create their own flower gardens using dabs of color.

112

# Dandelion

O Little Soldier with the golden helmet,
What are you guarding on my lawn?
You with your green gun
And your yellow beard,
Why do you stand so stiff?
There is only the grass to fight!

*Hilda Conkling*

# RESPONDING TO
# The Family of the Sun

BY ANONYMOUS

## Singing The Poem

Children can sing the words of the poem to the familiar tune of "Farmer in the Dell." You may want to repeat the first stanza after each verse or create a new chorus such as this:
The family of the sun, the family of the sun, What's another planet in the family of the sun?

Children will enjoy related poems such as "From Mars to Safety" (Me and Others: Poster 2), "Old Man Moon" (Related Poems), and "The Purple People Eater" (Adventure: Poster 7).

## Remembering The Planets In Order

Have children create a mnemonic device to remember the order of the planets from the sun. First list planet names in order, circling each initial letter. Then create a sentence in which those letters begin each word. One group of children used to chant, "My very educated mother just showed us nine planets."

## Making Diagrams And Charts

Give children long sheets of shelf paper. On it they can draw and label the planets as you name them in order from the sun. Help interested students record each planet's actual distance from the sun.

A group of students might work together to make a chart that lists important facts about each planet. On it they might list the planets, the distance of each from the sun, the size of each, and two or three other interesting facts about each one.

## Creating A Model Of The Solar System

After some research into the relative size and appearance of the planets, encourage students to make a model of the solar system. To make the planets they will need ½-inch wide construction-paper strips, paste or a stapler, and string.

First have students curl a strip so the ends meet, and paste or staple ends together. Then have them take another strip and wrap it around the first circle crosswise. They will paste it, and then continue to wrap two or three more strips until they make a ball. When it is finished, they can attach a string to the top and hang it from the ceiling. By varying the length of the strips and the color of the construction paper, children can make planets of different sizes and colors. Then challenge children to make a sun. Arrange the planets in order from the sun.

## Appreciating Our Earth

Encourage discussion of Earth's resources and how pollution harms them. Focus the discussion on preserving the oceans, trees, natural food sources, and clean air. Children can then draw pictures and write stories for a Save the Family of the Earth bulletin board. Interested students can also write to their representatives in Congress, expressing their concern for the environment.

## Making An Outline

Use the poem's title as a main topic, and list the planets as subtopics. Under each subtopic, have children list two or more interesting facts. They may use their outlines to make oral or written reports.

## Staging A Musical

To present the poem as a musical, have children play the parts of the sun and planets as classmates sing the song. Younger children may hold name cards or pictures they've drawn to identify their "characters," while other groups may want to create simple paper-bag costumes.

See Meet the Poet, page 192.

# The Family of the Sun

The family of the sun, the family of the sun.
Can we name the planets in the family of the sun?

Mercury is hot and Mercury is small;
Mercury has no atmosphere. It's just a rocky ball.

Venus has thick clouds that hide what is below.
The air is foul, the ground is hot, it rotates very slow.

We love the earth, our home, its oceans and its trees.
We eat its food, we breathe its air, so no pollution, please!

Mars is very red. It's also dry and cold.
We'll maybe someday visit Mars. Now wouldn't that be bold!

Great Jupiter is big; we've studied it a lot.
We've found that it has fourteen moons along with its red spot.

Saturn has great rings; we wondered what they were.
But now we know they're icy rocks, though once they seemed a blur.

Uranus and Neptune — we don't know much about.
In time and with more studying, will we know more? No doubt!

Pluto's last in line. It's farthest from the sun.
It's small and cold and icy, too. To land there shan't be fun!

The family of the sun, the family of the sun,
Did you count nine planets? Yes, and now our journey's done.

*Anonymous*

# RESPONDING TO
# Fog

BY CARL SANDBURG

## Using A Metaphor

Ask children to think of a cat entering a room quietly. Compare that to the noisy way a dog comes in. Ask children to listen to "Fog" to find out what animal Carl Sandburg compares fog to.

Talk about the first two lines: "The fog comes/on little cat feet." Children will enjoy moving like the fog to demonstrate their understanding of the poet's image.

## Rewriting

Say that the poet used the image of the cat as a metaphor, a way to explain how the fog acted. Challenge children to employ an alternative method of expression, using straight descriptive passages to describe the fog. Have children read their passages aloud and notice whether the words they use to describe the fog could also be used to describe a cat.

## Appreciating Brevity

Have children count the number of lines in this poem. Now suggest that they count the number of words. Ask, Is this a long or short poem? Do you think it is too short to give you the poet's message? Do you think the poet may have wanted it to be short on purpose? Could the fact that it is so short have anything to do with the nature of the topic? Discuss children's opinions of short poems.

## Singing The Poem

If possible, play the accompanying music (Adding Music, page 177) on the piano and encourage children to join in the singing. Talk about how the minor key creates an eerie feeling.

## Using Comparison When Writing

Ask children to find the word in the poem that tells us about the sound of fog. Are there other forms of weather that are silent? (snow, sunshine, misty rain) What weather forms make noise? (rain, wind, hail) Let children take turns describing the noises of all these weather forms. Encourage them to write a sentence about one of these weather phenomena and the sound it makes. Perhaps they could compare the weather to an animal.

## Performing An Experiment: Creating Fog

Pour approximately one inch of extremely hot water into a wide-mouth glass jar. Put the jar in a dark closet or in a dark box. Place a metal tray of ice cubes on top of the jar. Aim a flashlight beam at the middle of the jar and you will see a small cloud or patch of fog. Help children draw a conclusion from this experiment about how clouds and fog form. (Warm air rises to meet cold air. Mist forms.)

## Comparing Illustrations

Since this is a very well-known poem, suggest to children that they might be able to find the poem in several anthologies. Have them locate the poem in a few volumes and compare the accompanying illustrations. Read "The Index" (Related Poems) before children try to find the poem.

## Relating The Poem To Social Studies

Ask children to tell what they know about a harbor. Have they visited one? What have they seen there? Repeat the procedure to elicit descriptions of a city. Now help them paint a mural showing a harbor with a city skyline in the background. Encourage them to cut out and glue to the scene buildings, signs, and modes of transportation that they have drawn.

See Adding Music, page 177.
See Meet the Poet, page 187.

# Fog

The fog comes
on little cat feet.

It sits looking
over harbor and city
on silent haunches
and then moves on.

*Carl Sandburg*

# RESPONDING TO
# The Frost Pane

BY DAVID MCCORD

## Writing Without Paper

Is there a cold window in the classroom? Children will love to use it to create their own "Write-me-out-a-picture-frost/Across the pane . . ." Remind them that they will have to clean the window afterward.

A mirror placed in the refrigerator will also work well. Have children breathe on it and write.

## Conducting And Recording An Experiment

For this experiment, children will need a large can without a label, ice cubes, water, and salt. Have them fill the can with ice and pour salt and water over it. Volunteers can take turns stirring the icy water for four or five minutes. A thin layer of frost should become visible on the outside of the can. It was created from the moisture in the air around the can which condensed and froze when it met the ice cold metal. Compare the cold can to the cold glass in a windowpane in winter.

Children can draw a picture of the experiment, record the steps they took as they conducted it, and report any conclusions that can be drawn from it.

## Enjoying Related Literature

Read "Eletelephony" (Animals: Poster 4). Point out the words that are made up of a combination of two words: *elephant* and *telephone*. Compare them to the made-up words in "The Frost Pane." Ask what two words were combined to make *nalphabet* and *nelephant*.

## Naming Summer And Winter Activities

David McCord has written about something he can do in winter but can't do in summer. Ask children if they can think of other activities that can only be done in winter — things such as skiing, making snow forts, licking icicles, and making steam clouds with their breath. Then talk about the opposite, things that can only be done in summer — swimming, building sandcastles, smelling newly mown grass, picking flowers. This would be a good time to read "Summer" by Frank Asch (Related Poems).

## Talking About And Writing Opinions

Ask, What two seasons does the poet talk about? Which does he seem to prefer? Then have children identify the four seasons. Ask them which is their favorite. Suggest that they express their opinion by completing this sentence: My favorite season is _____ because _____ .

## Making A Bar Graph

Take a vote to see who prefers summer and who prefers winter. Ask a child to record the results of the vote on the chalkboard.

Suggest that students can picture the results of the voting. Make a graph grid with numbers along the vertical axis and *summer* and *winter* along the horizontal axis. Show children how to draw bars that reflect the results of the voting.

## Discussing And Using Hyphenated Words

Draw children's attention to this phrase: "write-me-out-a-picture-frost." Elicit that it is not one word but a string of words joined together to express a single idea that David McCord wishes to communicate to the reader. Suggest some other hyphen-linked words:

An I-can't-find-my-boots look;

A blowing-down-the-leaves wind.

Brainstorm with the group to extend the list and then have children create their own. They will enjoy illustrating their hyphenated words.

# The Frost Pane

What's the good of breathing
On the window
Pane
In summer?
You can't make a frost
On the window pane
In summer.

You can't write a
Nalphabet;
You can't draw a
Nelephant;
You can't make a smudge
With your nose
In summer.

Lots of good breathing
On the window
pane
In winter.
You can make a frost
On the window pane
In winter.
A white frost, a light frost,
A thick frost, a quick frost,
A write-me-out-a-picture-frost
Across the pane
In winter.

*David McCord*

# RESPONDING TO
# Have You Seen Edgar?

BY TERESA LYNN MORNINGSTAR

## Introducing The Poem

Read this poem on a day when big, fat flakes of snow are falling. Give children squares of black paper on which to catch the flakes and study them. Maybe they'll catch Edgar! (If you live in an area where no snow falls, read stories such as Ezra Jack Keats' *The Snowy Day* or Virginia Lee Burton's *Katy and the Big Snow.*)

## Dramatizing To Talk About Feelings

Invite one child to be Edgar as the other children join hands in small groups. Designate a cloud area and have children pretend to "jump off the cloud" and slowly shrink to simulate falling to Earth. Repeat this activity several times with different children playing the part of Edgar. Then talk about feelings associated with being singled out as special, being alone, being light and tiny as a snowflake, and trying something for the first time.

This is a good opportunity to introduce other poems in this collection that focus on self, being alone, and self-confidence: "The Me Key" (Related Poems), "I, Myself, and Me" (Me: Poster 3), and "Solo Sunday" (Feelings: Poster 6).

## Learning About Snow

Talk about what might have happened to Edgar in these and other situations:

- he was made into a snowman;
- he landed on your tongue;
- he fell onto some salt.

Provide a large pot labeled Snow Soup and have volunteers bring in handfuls of snow to put in it. (In warm climates, use crushed ice.) Stir the "soup," and then let it sit for a few hours. Have students observe that when the snow melts, it thaws and becomes liquid. Mark the level of the water in the pot and then observe changes over several days, noting that the water evaporates. Explain that the water returns to the air in the form of gas, or water vapor. Some of this water vapor may form clouds, and if it freezes, it will again fall to Earth as snow.

## Making Snowflakes

*Snow Crystals* by Wilson Bentley presents vivid illustrations of snowflakes. To have children make their own snowflakes, show them how to fold paper circles or squares in quarters and cut shapes from all edges. Fold in eighths and cut shapes into the folded side. Open and display.

Hang the snowflakes in the windows or against a dark-colored background. Note that each of the paper snowflakes is unique, just like each snowflake in nature.

## Using Personification

Explain to children that giving inanimate objects names and human qualities makes those objects seem like people. Have children identify the poet's words and phrases that suggest snowflakes are human. Elicit other examples of personification that children may be familiar with: people pretending their animals talk or toddlers claiming their blankets or stuffed animals are hungry or angry.

Read other poems in this collection in which children can identify words and phrases that personify objects: "Dandelion" (Nature: Poster 1), "Last Word of a Bluebird" (Nature: Poster 6), or "Silly Trees" (Nature: Poster 8). Challenge children to look for personification in their favorite stories.

# Have You Seen Edgar?

Did you see
Edgar the snowflake
Parachuting through the sky?
I wonder
If he was afraid
To jump off the cloud.
It was his first time, you know
Or at least, I think so.
Did you see
The other snowflakes
Hold out their hands to each other
And come down
Like fluffy little feathers?
But Edgar wasn't afraid.
Edgar came down all by himself.
Did you see
Edgar when he landed?
I wonder
If he wished
He could go back up and do it again
Or if he was glad
To stop falling
And just sit down for awhile.
Did you see Edgar vanish?
I wonder
Where he went:
Have you seen Edgar?

*Teresa Lynn Morningstar*

# RESPONDING TO
# The Last Word of a Bluebird

BY ROBERT FROST

## Imagining The Action

Ask children to tell the story of the poem in their own words. Ask, Who is speaking? Who is listening? Help children see that this poem is a kind of relay message: Someone (Crow) told me to tell someone else (Lesley) that someone else (bluebird) had a message for her!

## Acting Out The Poem

Children will enjoy demonstrating how the bluebird acted as winter approached. They can cough and shiver and perhaps try to get a drink from the frozen watering trough.

## Talking About Seasonal Changes And Animals Responses

Ask children to talk about the bird's reasons for flying away. Talk about some of the wintery changes mentioned by the bluebird — north wind blowing hard, ice. Ask children what people do to keep warm when winter comes. Talk about animals' responses to the same conditions — flying south, hoarding food, hibernating. You may wish to have children draw a picture of an animal in summer and in winter.

## Finding Out More About Birds

This would be a good time to introduce children to *A Field Guide to Birds* by Roger Tory Peterson. It is available in most libraries. In it, students can find out about the habits of bluebirds. They can also compare them to other blue birds such as blue jays and indigo buntings. Challenge students to find out which blue bird does not fly south in winter.

Many people enjoy making bird lists to keep track of all the birds they have seen. Suggest that the class keep such a list, noting the names of birds and when and where they were seen. Look up unfamiliar birds in Peterson.

## Discussing Talking Birds

Ask children if they have ever heard a real bird talk. Say that some birds mimic or copy human speech. Ask children if they have ever seen or heard a parrot or a mynah bird that can talk and sound like a person. Discuss whether talking birds are actually expressing *their* thoughts or just imitating sounds. It would be interesting to note the meaning of the expression "to parrot"; to repeat without understanding.

You may wish to have children do some research into talking birds. They can write reports and present their findings to the class.

## Expanding The Idea Of Communication

Ask children if they have ever felt that an animal was telling them something. How did this animal speak? By wagging its tail? Jumping up? Licking? Talk about conveying a message without words — using body language. Let the children take turns coming to the front of the room and trying to convey a message without speaking. (nodding yes and no, shrugging shoulders, getting angry.)

## Enjoying Rhyme

Divide the class into small groups. Give each group one of the rhyming words from the poem: *oh, do, bird, night, cough, fly, good, ax, sing*. See how many other words each group can think of that rhyme with the lead word.

## Learning About The Poet

Robert Frost often wrote about seasonal changes as he observed them near his home in New England. Children who want to learn more about Frost will enjoy reading *Robert Frost: America's Poet* by Doris Faber. They will also want to read another of his poems, "The Pasture," (Nature: Poster 7) as well as the biography found in this collection. Suggest that interested students write a paragraph in which they explain why they think Robert Frost's work is loved by so many people.

See Meet the Poet, page 185.

# The Last Word of a Bluebird (As Told to a Child)

As I went out a Crow
In a low voice said, "Oh,
I was looking for you.
How do you do?
I just came to tell you
To tell Lesley (will you?)
That her little Bluebird
Wanted me to bring word
That the north wind last night
That made the stars bright
And made ice on the trough
Almost made him cough
His tail feathers off.
He just had to fly!
But he sent her Good-by,
And said to be good,
And wear her red hood,
And look for skunk tracks
In the snow with an ax —
And do everything!
And perhaps in the spring
He would come back and sing."

*Robert Frost*

# RESPONDING TO
# The Pasture

BY ROBERT FROST

## Talking About Feelings

Ask, whom do children think the narrator is inviting to join in the trip to the pasture? Why do they think the narrator is asking someone to come along? Elicit that the narrator may not want to be alone, may enjoy having company, or may wish to share the experience. Broaden this into a discussion about the times that we might wish to be in the company of a friend. Also draw forth the notion that sometimes it is fun to be alone. The class may wish to make lists of times when they would prefer to be alone and to be in the company of others.

This would be a good time to read two other poems in the collection that explore the question of being alone or with others. They are "Solo Sunday" (Feelings: Poster 6) and "I, Myself, and Me (Me: Poster 3) both by Babs Bell Hajdusiewicz.

## Adding Details

Ask children to picture the scenes described by Robert Frost in "The Pasture." Where would they find a pasture? What else might they see if they decided to go along with the narrator? Butterflies in the grass? Wild flowers? Other farm animals? Talk about the sounds and smells of the spring season, the time when calves are born. Ask children to think of something they might like to do — drink the cold spring water, pat the calf — if they went to the pasture.

Read Robert Frost's "The Last Word of a Bluebird" (Nature: Poster 6). Ask children if they think the poet might have been writing about the same place in both poems. Have them explain their answers.

## Using New Words

Unfamiliar words in this poem can be approached in a number of ways. Suggest that children listen for the word *fetch* as they read or recite the nursery rhyme, "Jack and Jill". Then have them read the line in "The Pasture" that contains that word. Help them figure out that *fetch* means "to get something and bring it back."

A word that may cause confusion is *spring*. Talk about its meaning in the poem (a place where water flows up from under the ground) and then have children think of its other meanings, including "leap," "recoil," and "a season of the year."

Another way to learn the meaning of words is to act them out. Ask children to spring like a spring. Then have them "totter," to move the way the calf in the poem moves.

## Writing Examples Of Alliteration

Give children some examples of alliteration: gorgeous girl; silly song. Ask them to see if they can find any examples of hidden or subtle alliteration in the poem. Tell them that the words must begin with the same letter and sound but need not be right next to each other — "*totters* when she licks it with her *tongue*"; "and *wait* to *watch* the *water* clear, I may."

Have children make up their own examples of alliteration. You may wish to let them practice alliteration using their names: Raucous Randy; Sweet Sara; Daring Dave. As an extension, children can do a self-portrait under an alliterative caption containing their name.

## Linking The Poem To Science

Ask children what animal is mentioned in the poem. Elicit that a calf is a baby cow or bull. See how many other kinds of farm animals children can think of that have different names for mother, father, and child: mare, stallion, colt; ewe, ram, lamb; sow, boar, piglet. You may wish to have children make a poster of animal names showing the names of adult animals and their offspring.

See Meet the Poet. page 185.

# The Pasture

I'm going out to clean the pasture spring;
I'll only stop to rake the leaves away
(And wait to watch the water clear, I may):
I shan't be gone long. — You come too.

I'm going out to fetch the little calf
That's standing by the mother. It's so young,
It totters when she licks it with her tongue.
I shan't be gone long. — You come too.

*Robert Frost*

# RESPONDING TO
# Silly Trees

BY BABS BELL HAJDUSIEWICZ

## Acting Out The Rhyme

Children will enjoy mimicking the motions you model as you read and reread the poem. You can point to your self and shake your head for "And me? Oh, no!"; spread your arms for "upon our limbs and in our hair," and so forth. Discuss how people's arms and legs are often referred to as "limbs."

At this time you may also want to introduce "Trees" (Nature: Poster 10).

## Identifying Silly And Serious Ideas

Write a silly sentence such as "The tree said it was cold" along with a sentence such as "The tree has no leaves." Track the words as you read the sentences aloud. Ask children to tell why one is silly and the other is not.

Discuss how ideas that are silly are also called "foolish," "pretend," or "nonsense," while those that are not silly may be called "serious," "true," or "real." Children will enjoy talking about times when they or others have acted silly or when they have been serious about something. Brainstorm lists of silly and serious sentences.

## Categorizing Trees

Discuss how some trees change their appearance throughout the year. Provide books in which children can locate information about common deciduous and evergreen trees. Then have children create lists of "Silly Trees" (trees that lose their leaves) and "Serious Trees" (trees that are evergreen).

## Using Knowledge To Write And Illustrate

Have children use information from lists of silly and serious trees to complete and illustrate rhymes such as the following and then create their own:

I am truly a serious tree.
A (an) _____ is what they call me.
We are very silly trees,
_____ , _____ , and hickories.

## Recording Observations

Children will enjoy adopting a deciduous and an evergreen tree near the school or their home to observe for changes throughout the year. Have children record their observations weekly or monthly by drawing and writing about what they see.

## Making Words And Ideas Meaningful

Encourage children to share the poem with their parents and then search their neighborhoods for trees and shrubs that are "silly" or "serious." Invite children to share their observations.

## Using Contractions

Write the poem without contractions so children can compare the look and rhythm of the two versions. You may also want to have children circle each contraction, name the words used for each, and then write those words above the contraction.

Provide books, stories, and other poems in which children can find contractions and their expanded forms. A class chart titled "Two Ways to Say It" or "The Long and Short of It" might result.

## Being "Glad I'm Me"

To stimulate thinking about reasons one might be "glad I'm me," suggest first lines such as "I'm glad I'm Randy and not some candy," "I'm glad I'm me and not a bee," or "I'm glad I'm Bill and not a hill." Children will enjoy building second lines or creating their own poems to illustrate and display under a heading such as "I'm Glad I'm Me."

See Meet the Poet, page 186.

# Silly Trees

I'm glad I'm me, and not a tree!
Some trees and I, we don't agree
On how to dress and what to wear
Upon our limbs and in our hair.

In summertime when it is hot,
Those trees wear all the clothes they've got.
And then in winter when there's ice and snow,
They stand there nude from head to toe!

You'd think they'd learn from year to year
to wear their clothes in weather severe.
And me? Oh, no! You'll not find me
Standing nude in winter like a silly old tree!

*Babs Bell Hajdusiewicz*

# RESPONDING TO
# Tommy

BY GWENDOLYN BROOKS

## Remembering Lines

After reading the poem several times, you may wish to divide the class into two groups and let each half recite one stanza. Students in each half of the class may stand when it is their turn to recite. After several recitations, you may wish to have the groups switch and read the alternate stanza.

## Dramatizing The Poem

"Tommy" can be dramatized by pairs of children — one is the child who plants the seed and the other the seed who will spring into a plant. You may ask the "plant" what kind it is. You may also want to ask children who Tommy is. Is it the plant? the child who did the planting? Why did Gwendolyn Brooks title the poem "Tommy"?

## Comparing The Poem To Other Literature

Two excellent books express the wondrous feeling of planting. In *The Carrot Seed*, by Ruth Krauss, a child continues to care for his seed despite the pessimism of those around him until he is eventually rewarded with a carrot!

The story called "The Garden" in Arnold Lobel's *Frog and Toad Together* tells a tale that parallels the one Gwendolyn Brooks describes in "Tommy." Children will enjoy finding similarities between the two.

## Planting Seeds

Read these lines from "Tommy": "I watered it and cared for it/As well as I could know." Talk about what we need to know to grow plants. How do we provide soil, water, and sunlight? Compare how plants get what they need when they are planted outdoors with how they get those things when planted indoors. Reread the poem to find out if the seed was planted indoors or out.

Bring in two or three seed packets and read the planting directions. Then plant the seeds and help children keep a record of their plants: What I Planted, When I Planted It, and How Long It Took to Grow. Have them compare their records with the descriptions on the seed packets.

## Creating A Mural

Elicit from the children the names of as many different kinds of growing things as you can — flowers, fruit, vegetables, trees. Then have them name specific kinds of flowers, fruits, vegetables, and trees. On brown mural paper, have the children paint, color, and paste a mural of Things That Grow. Encourage them to be as colorful and creative as possible. Scrunched-up colored tissues or wrapping paper will make lively, colorful flowers; assorted colorful buttons can be budding blooms on a plant; twigs can be glued on as trees; old seed catalogs can provide colorful pictures of fruits and vegetables.

## Playing What Am I?

You can play the game What Am I? using plant names as answers. The child who is It comes to the front of the class and describes herself or himself as anything that grows in the ground — a flower, a tree, a vegetable, or a fruit. The rest of the class must guess what plant the person is. The person who guesses correctly takes the next turn as It. Here is a sample description: "I grow in the ground from a seed. My top is green and my bottom is long and orange. You eat me. What am I?" (a carrot)

## Expanding Vocabulary

Read "Tommy," in a monotone, trying not to accentuate any words. Ask children which word is the most powerful and dramatic in the poem — which suggests the most action. Children should choose the word *popped*. Discuss how this word sounds like the action it suggests. Ask what other word the poet might have used to convey the same meaning. (*pushed, grown, forced, climbed*) Substitute any of these alternate words and see if it alters the effectiveness of the poem. (If children choose the word *consulting* you may do this exercise with that word as well, using *asking* in place of consulting.)

See Meet the Poet, page 183.

# Tommy

I put a seed into the ground
And said, "I'll watch it grow."
I watered it and cared for it
As well as I could know.

One day I walked in my back yard,
And oh, what did I see!
My seed had popped itself right out,
Without consulting me.

*Gwendolyn Brooks*

# RESPONDING TO
# Trees

BY HARRY BEHN

## Introducing The Poem

"Trees" is written in a pattern of rhyming couplets. After a few read-alouds, children will find it easy to supply the last word of each stanza. Point to each rhyming word as children say it.

## Painting Word Pictures

Tell children that often a poet paints a picture with words. Ask if this poem paints pictures. Help children isolate those phrases that create strong pictorial images: "spread a shade for sleepy cows"; "gather birds among their boughs"; "fruit in leaves above"; "leaves to burn on Hallowe'en"; "in the Spring new buds of green"; "touch the beams of morning sun"; "moon floats on the sky." Children may wish to illustrate one or more of these phrases with the picture it creates in their minds.

## Understanding Personification

Explain to children that although a tree is alive it is not human. You may wish to elicit from children some of the attributes that differentiate humans from trees. Explain to children that sometimes a poet likes to make something that is not human sound as if it is. See if they can find examples of ways the poet suggests that a tree is like a person: making the actions of the tree seem voluntary as in "spread a shade for sleepy cows;" "gather birds;" "give us fruit;" "[give us] wood." Ask children if the tree intends to do these things or if they are just examples of ways that people and animals take advantage of a tree's existence. Ask children if a tree can talk or hum. Discuss why the poet may have chosen to depict the tree as so human-like. (to make us more sympathetic to the tree, to make us understand the tree better)

## Relating The Poem To Other Literature

Over the years, many poets have written about trees. Perhaps you remember Joyce Kilmer's "I think that I shall never see/A poem lovely as a tree . . ." Point out to children that each writer approaches the subject from his or her own experiences and thoughts.

Children will enjoy comparing Harry Behn's "Trees" to *The Giving Tree*, by Shel Silverstein. They will find that both writers see trees as generous friends.

Trees and the changing seasons receive a more humorous treatment in Babs Bell Hajdusiewicz's poem "Silly Trees" (Nature: Poster 8).

## Writing About Trees

Children will want to create their own word pictures of trees. Some may choose to write about real trees while others will have fun making up something more fanciful.

## Examining Real Trees

Explore with children the different types of trees: deciduous trees that shed their leaves, evergreens, redwoods, palm trees. Collect pictures from old magazines and use them to make a poster about the many kinds of trees.

You may also wish to broaden children's understanding of fruit trees. Ask children to name different kinds of fruit that grow on trees. Then have children name fruits that do not grow on trees. You may wish to incorporate this information into a chart called How Our Fruit Grows.

## Listing Products That Come From Trees

The poem lists many things that trees give us. A glance around the classroom will reveal many more, including paper, pencils, and books. Encourage children to recall their own experiences with trees and to think of how trees were "kind" to them. Children will have fun listing all the gifts from trees.

# Trees

Trees are the kindest things I know,
They do no harm, they simply grow

And spread a shade for sleepy cows,
And gather birds among their boughs.

They give us fruit in leaves above,
And wood to make our houses of,

And leaves to burn on Hallowe'en,
And in the Spring new buds of green.

They are the first when day's begun
To touch the beams of morning sun,

They are the last to hold the light
When evening changes into night,

And when a moon floats on the sky
They hum a drowsy lullaby

Of sleepy children long ago . . .
Trees are the kindest things I know.

*Harry Behn*

# RESPONDING TO
# When Icicles Hang by the Wall  BY WILLIAM SHAKESPEARE

## Listening For Enjoyment

The first time you read "When Icicles Hang by the Wall," children should simply listen to enjoy the richness of Shakespeare's language. On the second reading, they may be asked to think of wintery pictures for each line of the poem. Encourage them to think about how the images evoke sensations: the sound of the wind, the smell of roasted crabs, the sight of Marian's red nose.

Some lines may need explanation — but only if children ask. They will first enjoy trying to figure out the meaning of these lines from context. If you pantomime the actions, it will help.

"blows his nail"
(blows on his fingernails or hands to keep them warm)
"keel the pot"
(stir a hot liquid to keep it from boiling over)
"the parson's saw"
(the minister's sermon)

## Learning About The Author

Tell children that William Shakespeare lived in England nearly 400 years ago. People spoke somewhat differently then, which explains why many of the expressions Shakespeare uses are unfamiliar to us today. (You may want to note that Shakespeare would likewise find a lot of our expressions hard to understand.)

A picture and biography of Shakespeare can be found in this collection. Ask children to notice things about his appearance that give clues to the fact that he lived long ago.

## Relating To Other Poems

Another poem in this collection, "Summer," by Frank Asch (Related Poems), provides contrasting subject matter. Note that the Asch poem presents a single image, whereas the Shakespeare poem uses multiple examples and offers a more complex picture of a wintery day.

The line about greasy Joan keeling the pot brings to mind "The Song of the Witches," from Macbeth, by Shakespeare:

Double, double toil and trouble;
Fire burn and caldron bubble.
Fillet of a fenny snake,
In the caldron boil and bake.

Children may be familiar with the lines and will certainly delight in chanting them along with you.

## Enjoying Other Artistic Expression

While artists and composers seem to derive more inspiration from spring and summer, it is possible to find paintings and musical compositions about winter.

One of the most charming is the February picture from the Very Rich Book of Hours of the Duke of Berry. This picture from Medieval England looks as if it could have been an illustration of Shakespeare's poem. It is reproduced in The Story of Painting, by H.W. Janson and Dora Jane Janson, and in numerous other art history books.

Two Impressionist painters have also given us pictures of winter. Camille Pissarro's Snow in Louveciennes shows a simple backyard scene enlivened by light and shadow, while Claude Monet's The cart; road under the snow at Honfleur is an example of the nearly monochromatic pallette of a grey winter day. Both paintings are pictured in The Great Book of French Impressionism, by Horst Keller.

Two very different pieces of music evoke the different feelings of winter. Children will like the bouncy rhythms and lively sound effects of The Sleighing Ride, by Leroy Anderson. They can compare this to the more somber "Winter" section of Antonio Vivaldi's Four Seasons. Both pieces have been recorded by many artists.

See Meet the Poet, page 188.

# When Icicles Hang by the Wall

When icicles hang by the wall,
   And Dick the shepherd blows his nail,
And Tom bears logs into the hall,
   And milk comes frozen home in pail.
When blood is nipped and ways be foul,
Then nightly sings the staring owl,
   "Tu-whit, tu-whoo!" A merry note,
While greasy Joan doth keel the pot.

When all aloud the wind doth blow,
   And coughing drowns the parson's saw,
And birds sit brooding in the snow,
   And Marian's nose looks red and raw;
When roasted crabs hiss in the bowl,
Then nightly sings the staring owl,
   "Tu-whit, tu-whoo!" A merry note,
While greasy Joan doth keel the pot.

*William Shakespeare*

#  Index to Related Poems

1. Hamster ...............................................page 210
2. Old Man Moon ................................................227
3. Summer ......................................................239
4. The Index.....................................................216
5. The Me Key ..................................................221

# UNIT 7
# NUMBERS

1. **Arithmetic Pie**
2. **Calendar Rhyme**
3. **Countdown to Recess**
4. **Cycles**
5. **I've Figured It Out**
6. **If All the Seas Were One Sea**
7. **Lining Up**
8. **Old Noah's Ark**

# RESPONDING TO
# ARITHMETIC PIE

BY BABS BELL HAJDUSIEWICZ

## Staging A Skit

Children may enjoy presenting the poem as a play for parents or other classes. For whole class participation, have children help change singular pronouns to plural as in *"We'll* take the whole pie," "*our* tummies," or "one-fourth for *us*." Children can smudge their faces and hands and dress in play clothes as they present large cardboard "mud pies" divided into fractional parts.

## Identifying And Comparing Fractional Parts

Duplicate a number of "mud pie" circles for children. Some should be whole and others divided into halves, thirds, or quarters. Allow time for children to cut out the circles and cut them into fractional parts. Have children compare the sizes of the fractional parts. They will enjoy reassembling wholes and matching identical-size parts.

Demonstrate how to write the fractions and help children label each fractional part. Help them see that two ¼'s are equal to ½.

## Making Arithmetic Pizza

Collect the cardboard circles that come with pizza. Have available a variety of dried beans, popcorn kernels, cereals, or other small objects. Tell children to divide their cardboard into two, three, or four equal wedge-shaped sections. Working one section at a time, have them use the dry materials to decorate each section in a different way. Suggest that children make up clever names for the different toppings.

## Cooking With Fractions

Bring in measuring spoons, cups and pie plates. Provide water and sand or other dry material so children can experiment with measuring fractional parts.

Ask children to bring in favorite recipes that use fractions. Ask parent volunteers to provide ingredients so children can make one or two recipes.

## Making Inferences

Ask children to listen for fractions as you read aloud the limerick, "Choices" by Babs Bell Hajdusiewicz:

If the choice is one-half or one-third,
My answer depends on one word:
For COOKIE, one-half;
One-third if it's MATH;
And neither if SPINACH is heard.

Encourage children to talk about why each choice might make sense and then tell what fraction they would choose for each word. Have children substitute other words in the poem.

## Using Fractions

Read aloud "Fractions Take the Cake" by Heidi LaFiamma:

I never cared for math that much,
But fractions I can take
'Cause without fractions, Mom would have
No recipes to bake.
I couldn't live without those pies
And cookies my mom makes.
So maybe some of math's okay,
Since fractions take the cake.

Ask children what they think the poet learned from looking at recipes. Challenge children to use magazines and newspapers to find recipes that use fractions.

See Meet the Poet, page 186.

# Arithmetic Pie

Arithmetic pie is tasty and sweet.
As soon as it's hard, we'll each have a treat.
I'll take the whole pie and cut it into
Two equal parts, one for me, one for you.

Each part is one half; what a big piece of pie!
Maybe one half for you but not me! I might die!
My tummy would hurt! One half is absurd!
Perhaps we'd be smarter to each eat one third.

With three equal parts there'd be one for Mother.
We'd each eat one third and she'd eat the other.
But what about Dad? He drools over pies!
I'll cut it in fourths; each piece the same size.

Here's one fourth for me and one fourth for you
And equal size pieces for Mom and Dad, too.
Hey! Where are you going? Come back here and eat!
I'm serving my mud pie arithmetic treat.

Arithmetic pie, arithmetic pie,
You're made out of mud so no one will try
A half, third or fourth, not even a lick;
What a waste of all this arithmetic.

*Babs Bell Hajdusiewicz*

# RESPONDING TO
# Calendar Rhyme

BY BABS BELL HAJDUSIEWICZ

## Introducing The Poem

Separate the pages of a current calendar and post the months in order horizontally. Read the poem slowly as you point to the number at the end of each month with thirty days.

## Identifying "All The Rest"

Display separated calendar pages in order horizontally. Provide twelve index cards for each child. Ask children to name and count the months mentioned in the poem. Tell children to count out that number of cards and on each one write one of the months that was named. Ask how many blank cards are left. Refer back to the poem to learn that they represent months that have 31 days. Have children place their cards next to their corresponding calendar pages. They can then write the names of the remaining months on each card. Have them also write the number of days for each month on the cards.

To challenge children, you may want to suggest that they make a complete calendar on each month's card. Have children put the cards in order. Then help them punch holes in the cards and tie them together with yarn to make a calendar.

## Using A Mnemonic Device

Ask children how they help themselves remember things like what to bring to school each day, what chores to do, or how to get to a friend's house on their bike. Explain that remembering certain things is sometimes difficult, so people think of ways to help them remember. Share the old saying about tying a string around a finger before reading "A String to Remember" by Babs Bell Hajdusiewicz:

I'm trying to remember
To remember
To remember
To always remember
To never forget.
And that's why
You see this string
Tied around my finger.
It's to remind me that
I'm trying to remember
To remember
To remember
To always remember
To never forget.

Tell children that a mnemonic device, often written as a poem, is something that helps us remember specific information. Discuss why the poem "Calendar Rhyme" is a mnemonic device. At this time you may also want to share the mnemonic-device poem, "No Pronoun Problems" (Related Poems).

## Discussing Leap Years

Write the current year's date on the chalkboard. Ask what year it will be next year and write the number under the current year. Remind children that you've added one to the current year to know what next year will be. Continue to add one until your list includes several years. Then subtract one from the current year and continue the process in order to list past years.

Have children check the number of days in the month of February to tell if the current year is a leap year. Tell children that 1992 can be divided by 4, so it is a leap year. Have children count forward 4 and backward 4 or add 4 and subtract 4 to find and circle each leap year in the list.

See Meet the Poet, page 186.

# Calendar Rhyme

Thirty days are in September,
April, June, and November.
All the rest have thirty-one,
But February, it is done
At twenty-eight, though leap one more
Whenever the year divides by four.

*Traditional Rhyme*
*adapted by Babs Bell Hajdusiewicz*

# RESPONDING TO
# Countdown to Recess

BY BABS BELL HAJDUSIEWICZ

## Introducing The Poem

Considering the ending of this poem, you may want to read it just before recess or another free period. In this case, children will not only enjoy the meaningful words, but also find meaning in the poem's title.

Develop number or number-word recognition by placing number or word cards in order on the chalktray as each number is introduced in the poem. To reinforce the meaning of each number, refer to available objects as they are mentioned. For example, point to a tree outside for "1," touch the legs of a table or chair for "4," fold thumbs for "8 fingers are mine," and so on.

## Counting Objects

Write the numbers in order across the chalkboard. Have children reread the poem to find things that some of the numbers can be used to count. Challenge children to think of other things to count with each number. List ideas under their appropriate numbers.

## Counting To Twelve

Have children count aloud with you from one through twelve. Invite children to use the familiar tune of "Twinkle, Twinkle Little Star" to sing "Counting to 12" by Babs Bell Hajdusiewicz:

Zero, one, two, three, four, five,
Six, seven, eight, nine, sakes alive!
Look! I've learned my numbers well —
Next come ten, eleven, twelve.
I can sing a number song!
Won't you come and sing along?

You may want to have individual children or a small group sing the song. On the last line, have children motion to others to join them to sing the song again.

## Recognizing Counting As Adding 1

Place a number card for zero on the chalktray. Then lay out addition-fact cards in order beginning with $0+1$, $1+1$, $2+1$, $3+1$, and so on through $11+1$. Tell children to notice how the poem's words help them add one to each number as they count. Write each number

above its fact card as you read the poem.

You may want to reinforce the relationship between adding 1 and counting by reading "Adding 1" (Related Poems).

## Enjoying Other Related Poems

Read aloud as you write the words of Babs Bell Hajdusiewicz's poem "Adding" on chart paper:

Guess what adding is —
It's making two groups one.
Lay out two groups of sticks and I
Will show you how it's done.

Two plus two is four;
Five plus one is six.
The trouble is, when you are done,
You still will have just sticks!

Sticks, sticks, and then more sticks,
These sticks become a bore!
I want to learn to add my coins
To buy things at the store.

A nickel and a penny add
Together to make six.
Six cents has much more value than
A silly pile of sticks!

Invite children to use sticks and real or play coins as they sing the poem's words with you to the tune of "Row, Row, Row Your Boat."

You may also want to introduce some of the following poems from this collection: "Adding 2," "Things in Two's," "Beehive" "Sad Bedtime" "Measurement Logic," "None," and "Zero" (all in Related Poems).

See Meet the Poet, page 186.

# Countdown To Recess

Zero's the number I say when there's none;
   Zero is first; it comes before 1.
1 counts the number of trunks on a tree.
   2 is for counting my legs and my knees.
Then 3 comes along for tricycle wheels;
   Breakfast, lunch, dinner — 3 daily meals.
Next comes a 4 for legs on a bear,
   A table, a stool, or most any ol' chair.
But what do you think I can count with a 5?
   My toes? My fingers? 5 bees in a hive?
Now add 1 to 5 and 6 will come next.
   6 is to count the legs of insects.
Can 7 be next? Yes, 6 and 1 more
   Is 7, my goodness! I'm 3 more past 4!
To think of the number that comes before 9,
   I fold in my thumbs and 8 fingers are mine.
Then 9, "Go to bed," says mama who then
   Hopes I'm asleep long before clocks strike 10.
And 10 is the number that's made when a 1
   Is followed by zero. But counting's not done.
When I count to 10, I've only begun;
   11 comes next — 1 ten and 1 one.
Then I say 12, a dozen, no less.
   But — though counting is fun
I need a recess!

*Babs Bell Hajdusiewicz*

# RESPONDING TO
# Cycles

BY JOHN SCHAUM

## Singing The Poem

As you read, recite, or sing, you may want to stress the words *no wheels* and *no one* to emphasize the silly nature of the last line of each verse.

Some children may be familiar with the words and the melody through their study of piano. (See page 176). At this time, children will also enjoy "Poets and Pigs," another work by John Schaum (Word Play: Poster 7).

## Listing For Numbers

As you read, recite, or sing, have children hold up one, two, or three fingers or a closed fist when they hear each word that suggests a number. Read the poem again and have children hold up objects, number cards, or number-word cards. Another variation would have children showing the number in some way instead of saying it:

(Hold up one card) wheel makes a unicycle.
(Hold up two cards) wheels make a bicycle.

## Decoding Words

Children will be interested in the formation, pronunciation, and spelling of the words *unicycle, bicycle, tricycle,* and *icicle.* Have children identify the prefix in each word and then list other words such as unicorn, biceps, and triangle, that have those prefixes. Encourage the use of dictionaries to expand the lists.

Have children think about all the words they listed that begin with *uni, bi,* and *tri* to confirm the meaning of each prefix before defining the word. Help children compare the spellings and pronunciations of the root words in unicycle, bicycle, tricycle, and icicle.

You may also want to have children notice the plural endings of words in the poem.

## Thinking About Wheels

Ask children to think about the shape of the wheels of each vehicle named in the poem. Then share the poem "Wheels Wheels Everywhere" by Babs Bell Hajdusiewicz:

Wheels, wheels, wheels, they're everywhere!
Under cars, trucks, bikes, trains, chairs.
Are wheels circles? Are they square?
Can triangles roll somewhere?
Oh, no, no, no, wheels have to be
Circles to roll easily.

Encourage children to sing the poem with you to the tune of "Twinkle, Twinkle Little Star" as they look for wheels in the classroom, the building, or outside.

Ask questions such as "What shapes cannot be wheels and why?" and "What other vehicles have wheels?" Children will name wheelbarrows, wheelchairs, and golfcarts, and then expand to non-vehicular items that make use of wheels: pizza cutter, pulley, lawn tools.

Children may also enjoy reading and singing "Circles," (Related Poems). Have children draw or cut out pictures of vehicles with wheels, write something about their pictures, and then compile the pages for a *Wheels* book. Some children may want to make books that are more specific, such as "Things With Three Wheels."

## Using Another Meaning Of Cycles

Challenge children to think of another use of the word *cycle* by showing pictures or diagrams of the life cycles of animals or the cycle of the seasons. Ask children to think of wheels and their shape to tell why the word is appropriate. You may also introduce *wheel* as an action word rather than a noun, as in "He will wheel the cart to the lunchroom."

See Adding Music, page 176.

# Cycles

One wheel makes a unicycle.
Two wheels make a bicycle.
Three wheels make a tricycle,
But no wheels make an icicle.

Circus clowns ride unicycles.
Boys and girls ride bicycles.
Younger folks ride tricycles,
But no one rides an icicle.

*John Schaum*

# RESPONDING TO
# I've Figured it Out

BY BABS BELL HAJDUSIEWICZ

## Figuring It Out

"I've Figured It Out" has a surprise ending. After reading, talk about what children expected to hear at the end and why they were surprised by the boy's reasoning.

Point out that the title of this poem does not appear anywhere in the poem. Challenge children to find some words in the poem that might also make a good title. Remind them that a title usually expresses a main idea. Children may enjoy another poem with silly reasoning, "Crunchin' Luncheon" (Related Poems).

## Identifying With The Character

Tell children about something you once wondered about or figured out, only to find later that the truth was not what you thought. Did you ever wonder, for example, why hotels and motels exist when people have their own houses and beds or think that characters live inside the TV set? Invite children to share similar misconceptions they once had or ideas they are currently trying to figure out.

## Learning About Dinosaurs

"Dinosaur Bones" by Jean H. Marvin offers another explanation for the lack of dinosaurs in stores.

Dinosaurs don't rumble through the park
Or down my sidewalk after dark.
In museums, still as stones,
They stand in nothing but their bones.

Invite children to research types and sizes of dinosaurs to learn names and descriptions of smaller dinosaurs such as the Deinonychus or Archaeopteryx.

## Exploring Animal Ownership

Plan a trip to a local pet shelter as another kind of "store" the poem's character may have visited. Ask its director to share the center's procedures and explain the responsibilities of pet ownership.

If the question of dinosaur ownership comes up, refer children to *Danny and the Dinosaur*, by Syd Hoff, the story of a boy who plays with a dinosaur for a day. Children will also enjoy reading about a more manageable pet in "Hamster" (Related Poems).

## Measuring For Size Relationships

Children will enjoy discovering how absurd it would be if a huge animal entered their classroom. Provide rulers or measuring tapes so children can measure the width and height of the classroom door. Challenge children to research animal sizes to find the largest one that might fit through the door.

Children may share stories of problems their families have had fitting furniture through doors at home. Have children measure and compare the sizes of doors in the building, interior and exterior doors at home, and any community store doors. Help children form generalizations about standard commercial and residential door sizes.

Introduce the poem "Measurement Logic" (Related Poems) from this collection. After reading it, children may try measuring with various objects and then construct individual measuring tapes using strips of paper, cloth, ribbon, or other available material.

See Meet the Poet, page 186.

# I've Figured it Out

I used to ask where I might go
To get a dinosaur.
I went to every place in town,
To every single store.
But all they did was say to me
(Those people in the stores)
"Why, Honey, we sell cats and dogs.
We don't have dinosaurs!"

I never ask that question now
'Cause I'm a wiser lad.
I have the answer, though it has
Me feeling awf'ly sad.
It makes no sense, no sense at all,
That owners build their stores
With doors that are so narrow and
Too short for dinosaurs.

*Babs Bell Hajdusiewicz*

# RESPONDING TO
# If All the Seas Were One Sea

BY ANONYMOUS

## Using Synonyms To Describe

Ask children to think of synonyms such as *great, colossal, enormous, gargantuan, king-sized,* or *monumental* that may be used in place of *big* in the poem. Have children read the poem using each suggested word and then tell why they prefer one adjective over another.

## Studying The Poem's Structure

To help children appreciate another poem in which one element builds on the next, you may wish to share the classic story *The House that Jack Built*, where each new bit of information builds on the previous one. You may also choose to introduce the cumulative songs "Poor Old Lady" and "There's a Hole in My Bucket" (Related Poems). In addition, children will enjoy reading Paul Bunyan stories and comparing their exaggeration to that found in "If All the Seas Were One Sea."

## Illustrating To Show Sequence

Have children isolate the elements of the cycle — *sea, tree, ax, human,* and *splash* and note how each line of the poem shows a part of the continued sequence. Children may then work in groups to draw a series of twelve pictures depicting many seas, a big sea, many trees, one big tree, many axes, one big ax, and so forth. Ask children to write the appropriate text on each page. Help children attach their pictures in order to make wall friezes.

## Thinking About Cooperative Efforts

Tell children about the Hands Across America event that took place in recent years. Describe how people all over the United States coordinated a time and place to join hands and form one long human chain. Provide a map to help children appreciate the vastness of the distance people covered. Children may want to organize a "hands across the school" to experience the power of many working together. Similarly, cooperative efforts may be realized through working together to make paper chains or other decorations for the classroom or school building.

## Considering Pros And Cons

Encourage discussion of what life might be like for a giant. Elicit advantages such as never needing a ladder or the respect you would command, and disadvantages such as the difficulty of finding a large enough house or trying to hide. Have children draw a giant and write a few sentences telling why it would or would not be fun to "walk in a giant's shoes."

## Using Suffixes To Make Comparisons

Ask children to think of something big, then something bigger, and then something still bigger. Draw each item suggested and then help children talk about the objects as you use the *-er* ending to compare two things or the *-est* ending to compare three or more.

Children will enjoy using the *Guinness Book of World Records* or the *World Almanac* to find the biggest example in various categories such as sea animals (the whale), flowers (the sunflower), or buildings (New York's World Trade Center).

## Using The Globe

Challenge children to locate the oceans on the globe. Ask them if a whale could travel from ocean to ocean, all around the world. Do they think all the oceans are really one ocean? Have them explain their answers.

See Meet the Poet, page 192.

# If All the Seas Were One Sea

If all the seas were one sea,
What a BIG sea that would be!
And if all the trees were one tree,
What a BIG tree that would be!
And if all the axes were one axe,
What a BIG axe that would be!
And if all the humans were one human,
What a BIG human that would be!
And if that BIG human took that BIG axe
And chopped down the BIG tree,
And let it fall into that BIG sea
Hmmm! What a BIG splash THAT would be!

*Anonymous*

# RESPONDING TO
# Lining Up

BY BABS BELL HAJDUSIEWICZ

## Introducing And Dramatizing The Poem

Ask four volunteers to help as you read the poem aloud. Stand with your profile to the class. Point to yourself and say, "If I am first. . . ." Motion for one child to stand in front of you as you say, "Then you can't be unless you stand in front of me." Continue to read as you point to yourself or motion to each child to show where to stand in the line. Once all five of you have formed the line, you'll want to build drama by saying the words "unless we all turn around . . ." slowly and then quickly say "real fast" as you turn an about-face and motion, if necessary, for children to turn also. Have all children respond to the ending question, "What is your word?" by naming the new ordinal number for their position.

As children learn the poem, they'll enjoy dividing into groups of five to recite the poem in unison and act it out.

## Recognizing Ordinal Number Words

Place word cards for *first* through *fifth* in order on the chalktray. Have children answer the question at the end of the poem by selecting the word that describes their position. Vary the activity by displaying the word cards out of order.

## Writing About Feelings

Suggest to the class that sometimes we want to be first and sometimes we'd rather be last. Compile a list of times we'd want to be first (to get dessert) or last (at the doctor's for a shot). Children may prioritize the items on each list using ordinal numbers. Alternately you may want to have children write a composition describing when they would want to be first or last.

## Exploring Relativity And Perspective

The poem "Lining Up" illustrates that whether you are first or last depends upon the direction from which you view the line. Explore other relationships that depend upon relative position:

left/right
near/far
in front/in back
heavy/light
above/below

You may perform a series of simple experiments to illustrate how each of the above is relative. Take two children. Label each one's left hand and right hand with the words *left* and *right*. Then have each child face the other. Ask, Why does one's right appear opposite the other's left? Then have children face the same way and see where right and left are.

Position children, books, or objects around the room and have children describe their relative position: Mary is near; Joe is far. Change the position of the speaker and have the speaker again say who is near and who is far. Repeat for *above, below; in front, in back.* For *heavy* and *light* give children various objects to lift. What at first appears to be heavy (a book), will appear to be light when compared to something heavier (a desk, a person).

## Fun With Order In Words: Palindromes

Explain to children that some words are spelled the same both forward and backward: *Eve, Bob, pop, nun, mom, dad, tot, gag.* Elicit from children as many examples as they can think of. You may wish to make a chart or mobile of such words. These words are called palindromes. As an extension, you may explore phrases and sentences that are palindromes: *Too hot to hoot. Pull up if I pull up.* These two examples and others appear in a book called *Too Hot to Hoot*, by Raymond Stuart. The book shows mixed-up palindromes and the last page reveals the solutions when held against a mirror, a perfect way to illustrate a sense of order and reverse order.

See Meet the Poet, page 186.

# Lining Up

If I am first, then you can't be
Unless you stand in front of me.
Then I am second. I'm behind
The one who is the first in line.
If someone else now joins our line,
They will be third and stand behind.
Then fourth is next and fifth is last,
Unless we all turn around real fast.
Now who is first and who is third?
Your number changed! What is your word?

*Babs Bell Hajdusiewicz*

# RESPONDING TO
# Old Noah's Ark

## Dramatizing The Poem

You may wish to have children act out the poem. They can make oak-tag signs to show what animal they represent. (You may wish to rotate the signs so different children have a chance to be different animals.) The animals include: elephant, crocodile, kangaroo, giraffe, flea, hippopotamus, bees, bear, monkey.

Encourage the participants to act out the motions suggested by the poem and by the nature of the animal. The elephant, for example, might swing its trunk; the crocodile crawl on its belly; the kangaroo jump; the giraffe stand tall; and the flea make itself tiny. Children will also enjoy creating masks or props to identify their animal characters.

## Relating To Math

To encourage children to experience the poem and numbers simultaneously, it may be fun to line them up in groups as suggested by the poem — one by one, two by two, three by three, up to and including ten by ten. Encourage them to observe the drastic changes in the number of groups or rows. Have children march in these formations as you say lines like "The children went in one by one, the new school day had just begun," ". . . two by two, to see the animals in the zoo," ". . . three by three, they did not stop to disagree," ". . . four by four, 'twas rather tight through a skinny door," ". . . five by five, they're on foot — too young to drive." Challenge children to create other rhymes for each of the numbers and continue through "ten by ten."

## Arranging And Rearranging By Numbers

Provide twenty blocks, counters, or other small objects for each child. Have children arrange the objects in vertical rows two by two, three by three, through ten by ten. Ask what happens when the rows each have two, four, five, or ten objects as compared to three, six, seven, and nine objects.

## Classifying Animals

Have children notice that the poem describes big animals (hippopotamus, elephant) and small animals (flea, ant). Have children name as many kinds of animals as they can for each category. They may wish to make a poster or a chart showing large and small animals in pictures and in words. As an extension of this activity you can narrow the categories involved to include such things as animals that hop (kangaroos, frogs, rabbits); animals that fly (birds, bees, butterflies, bats); animals that crawl (snakes, worms); animals that walk (horses, dogs, cows); animals that swim (fish, dolphins, whales).

## Stretching The Imagination By Writing

Ask the children, If you were an animal on Noah's ark, what animal would you be and why? Have them write a few sentences about their choices. They may wish to illustrate their selections. Be sure to tell them that they need not limit themselves to animals mentioned in the poem.

## Relating The Poem to Other Literature

You may want to have children look at Peter Spier's award-winning illustrations in the book *Noah's Ark* and compare the text of the book to that of the poem. Children will also enjoy learning "Over in the Meadow" (Related Poems). They will have fun acting it out.

## Extending The Poem

Ask children's opinions of the poem's surprise ending. Encourage them to create a line to substitute for the last line. You may want to challenge older children to continue the poem for eleven by eleven and so on. Have them decide whether it is easier to rhyme one-syllable words or two-syllable words.

See Meet the Poet, page 192.

# Old Noah's Ark

Old Noah once he built an ark,
And patched it up with hickory bark.
He anchored it to a great big rock,
And then he began to load his stock.
The animals went in one by one,
The elephant chewing a carroway bun.
The animals went in two by two,
The crocodile and the kangaroo.
The animals went in three by three,
The tall giraffe and the tiny flea.
The animals went in four by four,
The hippopotamus stuck in the door.
The animals went in five by five,
The bees mistook the bear for a hive.
The animals went in six by six,
The monkey was up to his usual tricks.
The animals went in seven by seven,
Said the ant to the elephant, "Who're ye shov'n?"
The animals went in eight by eight,
Some were early and some were late.
The animals went in nine by nine,
They all formed fours and marched in a line.
The animals went in ten by ten,
If you want any more, you can read it again.

*Anonymous*

 # Index to Related Poems

1. Adding 1 ................................................ page 195
2. Adding 2 ..................................................... 196
3. Beehive ...................................................... 198
4. Circles ....................................................... 204
5. Crunchin' Luncheon ....................................... 206
6. Hamster....................................................... 210
7. Measurement Logic........................................ 222
8. No Pronoun Problems.................................... 226
9. None ......................................................... 225
10. Over in the Meadow ...................................... 229
11. Poor Old Lady ............................................. 234
12. Sad Bedtime................................................. 235
13. There's a Hole in My Bucket ........................... 242
14. Things In Two's............................................. 243
15. Zero.......................................................... 255

# UNIT 8
# WORD PLAY

1. Bad and Good
2. Glug! Gurgle! Glug!
3. Have You Ever Seen?
4. In and Out
5. Keep a Poem in Your Pocket
6. My Favorite Word
7. Poets and Pigs
8. Railroad Reverie
9. Yellow Butter
10. Yummy Humpty Dumpty

# RESPONDING TO
# Bad and Good

BY ALEXANDER RESNIKOFF

## Enjoying Dramatic Nonsense

Children love the ridiculous aspects of this poem and the images suggested by the particular combination of words. Suggest that they add a dramatic "Now *that* . . . that's *ba-a-a-a-d*!" after the first verse and "Now *that* . . . that's go-o-o-o-d!" after the second verse.

## Thinking Seriously

Ask why the behaviors mentioned in the poem are respectively bad and good. Encourage discussion of what age a person might be who pours catchup on his dad or puts a foot in her food. Ask why babies or toddlers might do these things and how it happens that they eventually learn more self–control.

## Enjoying Related Poems

Children will enjoy "Rudes" (Me and Others: Poster 9), "Goops" (Me and Others: Poster 3), and "Who Is This Mouse?" (Related Poems). You may also want to read "I'll Always Wear You" and "Bill and Jim and Joe and Zack" (both in Related Poems), poems about good things to do when riding in a car.

## Thinking About Behavior

Have children list good and bad things to do and tell why each behavior is acceptable or not. Suggest a behavior like talking in a loud voice to encourage thinking about when and where a behavior may be appropriate or inappropriate.

## Categorizing Behaviors

Make a list of good and bad things to do in the classroom, at home, in a car, while waiting for a medical appointment, on the playground, or at other times. Invite children to illustrate the behaviors and write about each.

You may want to bind the pages to create a book about opposite behaviors. Title the front cover "Good Things to Do . . . and" and arrange pictures of all good behaviors so that they will appear as right-hand pages. Turn the book upside–down and title the back cover "Bad Things to Do." Arrange illustrations of bad things to do so they will appear on the right side when the book is read upside–down.

## Identifying Words For Opposites

Write *bad* and *good* to begin two columns on a sheet of chart paper. Ask children to think of other words that are opposite in meaning. Post the list in the classroom. Encourage children to add words they encounter in their reading and listening.

## Noticing A Word's Spelling

Show children that *catchup* is sometimes spelled *catsup* or *ketchup*. Have children survey spellings on containers in the school cafeteria, at home, and in restaurants they may visit. Suggest that they note the spelling on each container along with the product's brand name. Have children compare their findings to discover such things as the most common spelling, a spelling consistently found with a brand name, or a spelling rarely found.

## Rewriting And Revising

Have children read the poem to you as you write it. Tell them you want to change the poem to say different things. Cross out *catchup* and ask for words that would make sense in its place. List and try each word and let children decide on one. Write a caret(∧) before the crossed-out word and write the new word above it. Then do the same thing to find a replacement for *foot* in the second verse.

# Bad and Good

Do you know what is bad?
I'll tell you what is bad:
To sprinkle catchup on your dad,
'Specially when he's mad.

Do you know what is good?
I'll tell you what is good:
To keep your foot out of your food
When mommy says you should.

*Alexander Resnikoff*

# RESPONDING TO
# Glug! Gurgle! Glug!

BY BABS BELL HAJDUSIEWICZ

## Dramatizing The Poem

Children will enjoy pretending to drive as you read this poem aloud. Those who haven't been in a car that runs out of gas can use an explanation of the sputtering sound and jerky movements that occur.

## Thinking About Sounds

Invite children to imitate the sounds described in the poem and the many other sounds made by a car or other vehicle: the engine's sound as a car is started or turned off, the vehicle coming to a sudden halt, the windshield wipers at full speed, and so on.

Challenge children to think of other categories such as *animals* or *sporting events* that suggest many sounds. Encourage them to imitate the sounds.

## Identifying Words For Sounds

Help children think about words for sounds by talking about the sounds animals make. Then invite children to listen for sound words as you reread the poem. List the identified words and then add to the list as children think of words for sounds they might hear in the kitchen, during a storm, or on the playground.

Have children work with partners. One child can make a sound while the other identifies it. Encourage children to start a class list of sound words.

You may want to introduce the word *onomatopoeia* as the name for words that imitate sounds. You'll want to share other poems in this collection that make use of onomatopoeia: "Bubbles Popping" (Adventure: Poster 2), "From Mars to Safety" (Me and Others: Poster 2), and "Railroad Reverie" (Word Play: Poster 8).

## Drawing Events In Sequence

Discuss the cyclical sequence of filling the car with gas, traveling a long distance, running out of gas, and filling the car with gas again. Invite children to draw a picture for each portion of the story and then use the pictures to retell the story.

Extend the activity by having children draw other series of events such as washing clothes, ironing them, wearing the clothes, and washing them again.

## Using Position Words And Compound Words

Have children use a toy car or other object to demonstrate the meaning of words such as *uphill* or *around*. They can ask classmates to name the word and identify it in the poem.

Ask children to identify the position words that are compound. Encourage children to list other compound-word pairs that use *up* and *down* such as *upstairs* or *upstream*. Have children follow the pattern to list words that begin with *in* and *out*.

## Using Analogies To Innovate On Text

Point out to children that gasoline is fed to a car much as food is fed to people. Ask children how the poem might read if the words "bites of food" were substituted for "gasoline." You may want to help children follow the rhythm as they write by clapping to the words as follows:

The bites of food go in — to my mouth
(clap)      (clap)      (clap)      (clap)

Encourage children to think of sound words that would be appropriate in place of "glug, gurgle, glug." Write the poem as children make the substitutions.

Children may also want to rewrite the poem using other analogies, specific foods they eat, their animal's favorite brand of food and the animal's name, and so forth.

See Meet the Poet, page 169.

# Glug! Gurgle! Glug!

The gasoline goes into my car.
Glug!
Gurgle!
Glug!
It makes my car go very far.
Glug!
Gurgle!
Glug!
Uphill,
Downhill,
Up and down.
Uphill,
Downhill,
Up and down.
But suddenly my car won't go.
Sputter!
Sputter!
Sput!
What is wrong?
I do not know!
Sputter!
Sputter!
Sput!
The other cars around me pass.
Sputter!
Sputter!
Sput!
Ah! I think my car is out of gas!
Sputter!
Sputter!
Sput!
The gasoline goes into my car.
Glug!
Gurgle!
Glug!
It makes my car go very far.
Glug!
Gurgle!
Glug!
Uphill,
Downhill,
Up and down.
Uphill,
Downhill,
Up and down.

*Babs Bell Hajdusiewicz*

# RESPONDING TO
# Have You Ever Seen?

BY ANONYMOUS

## Exploring Meaning

Children enjoy this poem once they catch on to the humorous pattern. To help them understand it, model picking out the key words in the first question. Write *sheet, river,* and *bed*. Ask children to tell something about each word — "it goes on a bed" for sheet or "you sleep on it" for bed. Encourage children to think of the relationships among the words as you write their definitions under the words. Continue to list ideas until children see that *sheet* and *bed* are related. You may have to tell children that a riverbed is the area between river banks that is usually covered by water.

Examine other lines in the same way until children are familiar with the pattern of the poem.

## Illustrating The Poem

After clarifying the precise vocabulary and studying examples of things in the poem, you can invite children to illustrate the funny meaning of each line — a sheet on a river or a mountain with toes, for example. Help them write the appropriate line under each picture.

## Writing With Homographs

Have children list all the homographs from the poem: *bed, head, foot, hose, eye, wing, ribs, trunk, teeth, hands, plot, bark*. Then have them think of other homographs and make up funny ways to use them, following the question format of the poem:

Can you scratch the back of a chair?
Did you ever hear what the tongue of a shoe said?
What did the eye of the potato see?
Would you put a sheet of ice on your bed?
Can a hot dog bark?

## Comparing The Poem To Other Literature

For a further explanation of homographs, read two funny books by Cynthia Basil that explore the concept of homographs. One is *Nailheads and Potato Eyes* and the other is *How Ships*

*Play Cards.*

"Poets and Pigs" (Word Play: Poster 7) plays with a pun. Children will enjoy reading it at this time.

## Telling A Circle Story

For this activity, have children use the original poem and any new questions they have made up. The first person turns to his or her right and asks a question: "Have you ever seen a sheet on a river bed?" The child who is asked says "no" and then turns to the next person on the right and asks another question: "Or a single hair from a hammer's head?" Children continue until they have completed the circle.

## Expanding A Line Into A Story

You and the children can have fun writing a story based on the idea of a single line of the poem. It might be about a fish that always wanted a sheet on its riverbed, or a bald hammerhead that always wanted hair.

Another approach would be to use the last line of the poem. Challenge children to think of a way to tie together the sound of a dog's bark and tree bark. They might come up with a sentence such as this: "Joe heard the bark and put his ear to the tree trunk." Another character might come up to Joe and ask him what he is doing, and the story that results can consist entirely of pun-filled dialogue between the characters.

## Introducing Anonymous

Who is Anonymous? Children will want to speculate about why we do not know who wrote this poem. Perhaps the name was lost. Maybe the poem has been passed by word of mouth from person to person for so long that no one knows who originated it. Maybe the poem has been changed a little bit each time it was recited, and today the author would not recognize it.

See Meet the Poet, page 192.

# Have You Ever Seen?

Have you ever seen a sheet on a river bed?
Or a single hair from a hammer's head?
Has the foot of a mountain any toes?
And is there a pair of garden hose?

Does the needle ever wink its eye?
Why doesn't the wing of a building fly?
Can you tickle the ribs of a parasol?
Or open the trunk of a tree at all?

Are the teeth of a rake ever going to bite?
Have the hands of a clock any left or right?
Can the garden plot be deep and dark?
And what is the sound of the birch's bark?

*Anonymous*

# RESPONDING TO
# In and Out

BY BABS BELL HAJDUSIEWICZ

## Dramatizing The Story

This and other narrative poems in this collection lend themselves to production as plays or skits to present to other classes and/or parents. Children will enjoy pantomiming or speaking the roles as you or a child provides the narration. Each of the characters could wear a sign with his or her name on it.

## Playing With Words

Write *in stinks* and *instincts* so children can see and tell how the words are alike and different in spelling and pronunciation. Help them realize that the poet has made a play on words. Then share these other examples of word play: *able — a bull; Philip — fill up; hourglass — our glass;* and *people — peephole.*

This would be a good time to introduce "Pete and Repeat" and "I and My Echo" (both in Related Poems). Older children will enjoy hearing the story from Greek mythology of Odysseus and the Cyclops, in which mistaking the name *Noman* for *no man* brings the Cyclops to his doom. Of course, this is also the time for the classic example of word play, Bud Abbott and Lou Costello's "Who's on First?"

## Holding A Fast-Reading Contest

This is not an easy poem to read aloud. Challenge good readers to a contest to see who can read the most lines with the fewest mistakes in the shortest time. Most children will collapse with laughter before they get very far. Compare this poem to another tongue twister such as "How much wood would a woodchuck chuck if a woodchuck could chuck wood?"

## Learning About Instincts

Ask children to describe the "in-stincts" of skunks. Say that although we joke about the odor, spraying is serious business to a skunk. It is its innate, unlearned means of protection. This would be a good time to introduce "Trunk Skunk Stunk" (Related Poems).

Have children name other animals and their instinctive means of protection. Note that a porcupine throws its quills, a dog barks, and a bee stings, while an octopus spouts ink.

## Using Context To Gain Meaning

Ask how a person listening to the poem is able to tell if the words *in* and *out* refer to positions in space or to the characters' names. Help children see that their meaning is derived from the way the words are used — from the context in which they appear. Then ask how readers can tell the difference. Children will notice that names are capitalized whereas position words are not.

## Paraphrasing The Poem

Point out that this would be a good story even if it did not rhyme. Suggest that children tell or write it in prose form. They might want to start it with the time-honored fairy tale introduction "Once upon a time. . . ."

See Meet the Poet, page 186.

# In and Out

Momma Skunk had baby skunks.
She named them In and Out.
One day she shooed them out to play,
"Go out now, In and Out!"

"And, Out, stay out and don't come in
Without your brother, In.
If you get tired of playing out,
Come in, but bring In in."

But In, who liked to play small tricks,
Hid out while Out went out.
And Momma Skunk was unaware
That only Out was out.

When moments later, Out appeared
Inside to search for In,
Momma Skunk admonished Out,
"You were to bring In in!"

"But, Momma, In did not go out,"
Said Out to Momma Skunk.
"My, my!" said Momma, "Can In be
Asleep in his top bunk?"

When In was not upon his bed,
Out ran outside to see
If In had sneaked out . . . sure enough!
Out found him easily.

"Oh, Out, how did you find our In?
You're quicker than two winks!"
" 'Twas easy, Momma, surely you
Remember our In-stincts!"

*Babs Bell Hajdusiewicz*

# RESPONDING TO
# Keep a Poem in Your Pocket

BY BEATRICE SCHENK DE REGNIERS

## Introducing The Poem

Present this poem after children have had an opportunity to learn and enjoy many poems. Then it will be most meaningful.

As you read, children will enjoy pretending to pull a poem out of their pocket and saying it aloud. Perhaps they could even write a favorite poem on paper, put it in their pocket, and then pull it out and read it.

This is a good poem to recite just before children go home for the day. Then ask them what little poem will sing to them tonight when they're in bed.

## Comparing Poems

Read "The Poet Says," by Babs Bell Hajdusiewicz (Me: Poster 7). It reminds us that a poem evokes a response, first from the poet and then from the listener or reader. Talk about how a poet might feel when she finishes a poem — satisfied, pleased, relieved? Suggest that the poem may have come from a picture the poet has kept in her pocket for a long time before she brings it out and puts it on paper.

## Capturing The Mood

Beatrice Schenk de Regniers has written a poem that makes you smile. Ask children what words she has used to conjure up this happy mood. Talk about how a poem can "sing to you" or ways in which a picture can "bring . . . a dozen dreams to dance to you." Note that *sing* and *dance* are both words that evoke a happy feeling.

## Picturing Poems

Before they work independently, have children think of some of their favorite poems. It may help if you display a number of **Poetry Works**! Posters in the room. Have children think of the pictures each poem creates for them.

Then suggest that children draw a picture of themselves in bed. In dream balloons above their heads, they can draw the pictures they see when their favorite poem sings to them.

## Looking At Fine Art

As the poem says, pictures can bring "a dozen dreams to dance to you," so this would be a good time to show slides of paintings and sculptures. These can usually be obtained from a library or art museum.

The slide presentation could be organized in a number of ways. If there is an art museum nearby, you may want to show examples of the art in its collection and then follow up with a visit. It is also interesting to compare the way a number of artists treat a single subject such as the ocean, babies, or cats.

The presentation can be made more interesting if accompanied by music, perhaps a Mozart string quartet or Antonio Vivaldi's *Four Seasons*. Some teachers like to provide a place where children can use a viewer and look at slides again on their own.

## Exploring Alliteration

Ask children what the words *poem, picture,* and *pocket* have in common. Young children can listen for the initial sound of *p*. Older children will enjoy learning the big word *alliteration* to describe a series of words that begin with the same sound. Suggest that children list all the things beginning with the same sound as *poem* that they could put in their pocket. You may want to have them use those words in an alliterative sentence like this:

In my pocket I put a pencil, paper, a pen, a peach, a potato, a poodle, a pig, and a parrot.

Children will also enjoy this classic alliterative tongue twister:

Peter Piper picked a peck of pickled peppers.

# Keep a Poem in Your Pocket

Keep a poem in your pocket
and a picture in your head
and you'll never feel lonely
at night when you're in bed.

The little poem will sing to you
the little picture bring to you
a dozen dreams to dance to you
at night when you're in bed.

So —

Keep a picture in your pocket
and a poem in your head
and you'll never feel lonely
at night when you're in bed.

*Beatrice Schenk de Regniers*

# RESPONDING TO
# My Favorite Word

BY LUCIA AND JAMES L. HYMES

## Identifying With The Character

Encourage children to think of questions for which they would like "yes" responses. Questions may be real, "May I have a dog?" or fantastic, "Will you let me go up in a rocket to the moon?"

Talk about questions that usually get "yes" answers from parents or teachers and those that are usually answered "no." Discuss the reasons why adults may answer the way they do.

## Talking About Questions

Have children look at the third stanza. Ask, How do we know that the child is asking for something, since he or she doesn't say "May I have some candy?" Encourage children to comment on the question mark as the sign that tells us how to read those words. You may wish to have children listen to the questioning sound in your voice as you read this poem. Suggest that children experiment with reading "Some candy?" with alternate forms of punctuation — an exclamation mark or a period.

## Turning Statements Into Questions

Show children how to turn declarative sentences into questions and vice versa. Then have one child come to the front of the room and make a statement or ask a question. Ask volunteers from the class to give the alternate form.

## Using Quotation Marks

Ask children to look for the quotation marks in the poem. Ask them when and why these marks are used. Help them see that quotation marks are used to show that someone is speaking. You may wish to explore the difference between quoting someone directly and indirectly. Use sentences such as these as examples: You said, "I don't want to go." You said that you didn't want to go.

Children can practice writing with quotation marks, using the poem as a model. Have them write an imaginary dialogue between themselves and a teacher or parent. The child will ask for things ("Can I have an ice cream cone?" said [name]) and the grownup will respond, "Yes, yes, yes," said [name]).

## Finding Synonyms

Encourage the class to explore alternate ways of saying yes, no, and maybe. (Yes, O.K., all right, sure, of course, definitely) You may also wish to have them research ways of saying the three words in other languages.

## Conducting A Yes/No Survey

Have children think up a topic to survey by asking a question for which the answer is yes or no. They might ask "Do you like rock and roll? Ice cream? Potato chips? Watching television? Divide the class into small groups and have each group survey a different topic. Later the groups may share their results.

## Writing Creatively

Draw children into a discussion of the word favorite. Ask, "How many favorite things can we have?" Elicit a variety of possible favorites — favorite food, favorite flavor, sport, color, and so on. Have each child make a book entitled My Favorite Things or What I Like Best. On each page, the child may record his or her favorite in one area. Encourage children to illustrate their work.

# My Favorite Word

There is one word —
My favorite —
The very, very best.
It isn't No or Maybe,
It's Yes, Yes, Yes, Yes, YES!

"Yes, yes, you may" and
"Yes, of course" and
"Yes, please help yourself."
And when I want a piece of cake,
"Why, yes. It's on the shelf."

Some candy? "Yes."
A cookie? "Yes."
A movie? "Yes, we'll go."

I love it when they say my word:
Yes, Yes, YES! (Not No.)

*Lucia and James L. Hymes, Jr.*

# RESPONDING TO
# Poets and Pigs

BY JOHN SCHAUM

## Introducing The Poem

You can help young children understand the joke in this poem by talking about the various meanings of *pen* before reading. As you read, add to the suspense by covering the last line until it is time to read it. Read the poem a second time and encourage children to act out the last two lines.

## Singing The Words

You'll find music to accompany this poem in Adding Music. Children will enjoy comparing the way the poem sounds with and without the melody. Have one group present a dramatic reading of the verse; then have another group sing it. Spend a few minutes talking about which version children prefer and why. Extend the activity by having children perform other poems with and without music in the same manner. Do they feel the same way about every poem, or do some poems sound better with a melody than others? Discuss their reactions.

## Tracking The Words

Sometimes it is fun to have a child act as teacher and point to the words on the poster as classmates read them. Short poems like this are well–suited to this activity.

## Using Words With Multiple Meanings

Remind children that the meaning of some words depends on the words around them. Write two sentences on the chalkboard and have children identify the word in both whose meaning is changed by the surrounding words. Use these or other examples:

Zeb heard the dog *bark*.
Molly saw the tree *bark*.

Challenge children to compare a multiple-meaning word to a chameleon. Invite small groups to list as many "chameleon words" as they can and briefly define each meaning in words or simple illustrations.

For fun while studying multiple meanings, set up a riddle board where children can post riddles that depend on surprising word

meanings for their humor. The classic example of this kind of humor is, of course, What's black and white and red all over?

## Listening For Rhyming Words

Ask children to name and point to the rhyming words — *think* and *ink* — in the verse. Note that *oink* ends with the same three letters as the rhyming words but does not have the same sound.

Encourage children to list other words that rhyme with *think* and *ink* and add them to their rhyming dictionaries. For an added challenge, they can try to find words that rhyme with *pigs*, and *pen*.

## Identifying Letters And Their Sounds

Have children identify the sound of *i* in *pig* and then find other words in the poem and elsewhere that have the short *i* sound. The words in the poem also lend themselves to a study of the sounds of short *e*, the initial consonant *p*, and the final blend *nk*.

## Enjoying Related Poems

You may want to introduce other, more serious, poems from this collection that focus on poets and the work they do. "The Poet Says" (Me: Poster 7), "Paper I" (Related Poems), and "If All the World Were Paper" (Related Poems) offer interesting perspectives regarding some writer's tools.

See Adding Music, page 180.

# Poets and Pigs

Poets and pigs,
Poets and pigs,
What is the difference, think?
Poets all have pen and ink.
Pigs all have a pen and oink!

*John Schaum*

# RESPONDING TO
# Railroad Reverie

BY E. R. YOUNG

## Recording The Poem

Children will enjoy learning to read this poem dramatically, first softly and then louder and louder until the train passes and its sound again grows faint. Once they have practiced and polished their reading, suggest that they tape-record the poem.

## Telling The Story Of The Poem

Ask children to tell the story in their own words. Ask, Where was the boy? What made him stop? What did he do? What do you think the boy might have done when he turned to "other business of the day"?

Talk about the boy's feelings and the words the poet uses to describe them. What do children think the boy would do when there was "joy in [his] feet?" You may want to point out that to a child of 50 or 100 years ago, a train was as exciting as a race car, a motorcycle, an 18-wheeler, or a rocket might be to today's youngster.

## Recognizing Onomatopoeia

Have children see how many words in the poem they can find that create a sound image: *rumble, rattle, clatter, clank, chugger, whoosh, catch-a-teacher, patch-his-britches*, and so forth. Teach them this verse about a train from "Toot! Toot!" (Related Poems), noting the onomatopoetic "Toot! Toot!":

A peanut sat on a railroad track,
His heart was all a-flutter;
The five-fifteen came rushing
by —
Toot! Toot! peanut butter!

While chanting the verse, children can line up and pretend to chug around the room like a train. On the last line, they will all fall down.

Children will have fun making up their own verses about things that could be crushed by a train, things like apples, crackers, or pickles:

A pickle sat on a railroad track,
Feeling mighty silly;
The train came roaring down the track,
Toot! Toot! piccalilli!

This would be a good time to look for onomatopoeia in two of Babs Bell Hadjusiewicz's poems: "From Mars to Safety" (Me and Others: Poster 2) and "Glug! Gurgle! Glug! (Word Play: Poster 2).

## Experimenting With Sound

Talk about hearing a faraway sound and ask children to think about how that sound changes and grows louder as it approaches. Have them imitate various sounds — sirens, cars, or airplanes — starting in the distance and then coming closer.

Challenge children to make up words for the sounds they make. Let them experiment with writing them first as separate words and then running the words together to suggest that the sound is getting louder or softer. You may also want to suggest that they try using different-size letters to indicate differences in loudness.

## Illustrating The Poem

Note that just as a faraway sound is softer and in some ways smaller than a nearby sound, so too a faraway object appears smaller than one that is nearby. Children can draw pictures of the train in the poem to illustrate this concept. The first picture would show the train far away down the track (you may want to show children how the lines of the track seem to converge in the distance); the next one would show the train going past the boy; the last would show the rear of the train as it disappears in the distance.

# Railroad Reverie

The little boy stopped in the middle of the hayfield
And cocked his head and listened for the sound.
It was there, it was coming, it was growing, it was coming.
Far away, but growing nearer, growing nearer, growing nearer,
Coming closer, coming closer, coming closer all the while;
Rumble-rumble, rattle-rattle, clatter-clatter, clank-clank.
Chugger-chugger, chugger-chugger, and it reached the final mile.

The little boy, rooted in the middle of the hayfield,
Cupped his eyes to shade them from the sun.
And heard the far-off whistle and the far-off rumble
And the far-off rattle of the railroad tracks
As the heavy giant train roared on.
Catch-a-teacher, catch-a-teacher, patch-his-britches,
Patch-his-britches, catch-a-teacher-patch-his-britches,
Catch-a-teacher Whoosh!

Chugger-chugger, chugger-chugger, smoke upon the hayfield,
Cinders in the boy's hair and soot upon his face;
Laughter in the boy's heart, joy in the boy's feet,
Laughter in the engineer's face.
Chuggerchugger growing fainter
Catchateacher patchhisbritches
Catchateacher patchhisbritches
Chuggerchugger sssssssssss

And the little boy turns to other business of the day
As the heavy giant rumble rumbles out and fades away.

*E. R. Young*

# RESPONDING TO
# Yellow Butter

BY MARY ANN HOBERMAN

## Having A Choral Reading

Once children are familiar with the words, have the class read alternating stanzas as you read the others. Then experiment with various groups and individuals reading the roles.

Children especially enjoy "living" the poem. Invite them to help provide the bread, jelly, jam, and butter. Divide children into two groups who take turns preparing and eating this special treat.

## Making Yellow Butter

To make butter in the classroom, fill a wide-mouth jar about half full of heavy cream. Screw the lid on tightly and have children take turns shaking it. After a while, the butter will separate from the clear liquid, or buttermilk.

Pour off the buttermilk, pressing the butter with a wooden spoon to remove all the liquid. Scrape the butter onto a plate and let children spread it on bread.

## Thinking About Colors Of Food

Ask what other colors jelly, jam, and bread might be. List the foods in three columns so children can compare the number of colors for each. Encourage children to tell the flavor or kind of food that is generally associated with each color. Have children tell about their favorite flavors and colors.

You may want to expand children's experiences by bringing in samples of different kinds of bread such as pumpernickel, sourdough, French, oatmeal, or rye.

## Recognizing Letters And Sounds

The poem is well-suited to a study of the *-er* suffix as well as letter and sound recognition of initial consonants *y, b, p, j,* and *r*. In addition, you may want to use this poem to introduce or review the blends and digraphs *spr, th, bl, br, wh,* and *qu,* or focus on different sounds of *ea* as in *repeat, eat, spread,* and *bread.*

## Enjoying Related Poems

Read and chant "Jelly on the Plate" by an anonymous poet:

Jelly on the plate,
Jelly on the plate,
Wibble wobble, wibble wobble,
Jelly on the plate.
Paper on the floor,
Paper on the floor,
Pick it up, pick it up,
Paper on the floor.

Model use of the poem's pattern by creating other versions.

Substitute words such as "Jelly on my face . . . wash it off . . ." or "Glue on the table . . . clean it off." You'll find that innovating on the text of this poem offers opportunities to remind children of some responsibilities without nagging.

Encourage children to brainstorm rhyming words for other ideas to create verses such as the following:

Bedtime at eight?
Bedtime at eight?
Surely not! Surely not!
Nine is not too late!

Homework tonight?
Homework tonight?
It's all done? It's all done!
And I did it right!

Children will also enjoy "Tiger," another poem by Mary Ann Hoberman (Related Poems), as well as "Toaster Time" (Related Poems), "Goops" (Me and Others: Poster 3), and "Rudes" (Me and Others: Poster 9).

# Yellow Butter

Yellow butter purple jelly red jam black bread

Spread it thick
Say it quick

Yellow butter purple jelly red jam black bread

Spread it thicker
Say it quicker

Yellow butter purple jelly red jam black bread

Now repeat it
While you eat it

Yellow butter purple jelly red jam black bread

Don't talk
With your mouth full!

*Mary Ann Hoberman*

# RESPONDING TO
# Yummy Humpty Dumpty

BY ANONYMOUS

### Reading Aloud

Prior to sharing the poem, children will enjoy finding in an anthology the traditional nursery rhyme this poem is based on. Reread the traditional rhyme for familiarity with the words, rhythm, and rhyme. Talk about Humpty Dumpty and the fact that he is an egg, and then tell children to listen as you read or recite a different "story" about Humpty Dumpty.

### Comparing Poem Versions

Ask children to tell how the two poems about Humpty Dumpty are similar and how they differ. Explain that the funny version is called a "parody" because it imitates or makes fun of the original poem. Ask what makes the parody funny.

### Talking About Breakfast

Help children identify the words that tell what the king's men ate. Write *scrambled eggs* and invite children to add to a list of breakfast foods as they talk about what they like to eat for breakfast.

### Listing, Writing, And Revising

Write headings such as "Who Ate" and "What They Ate" above "king's men" and "scrambled eggs" to begin two lists. Have each child name a food he or she ate for breakfast as you record the information. Model crossing out and condensing duplications after all children have named their foods.

Model a sentence such as "The king's men, Angela, and Ted ate scrambled eggs for breakfast." Encourage children to make up a sentence for each type of food in the list.

At another time, you may want to help children expand their sentences into an interesting paragraph.

### Thinking About Eggs

Discuss how the eggs we eat are laid by chickens, gathered, sorted, washed, crated, and taken to stores for people to buy to take home and cook.

Also, encourage children to think of the different ways the king's men could have prepared their eggs. Make a list of these and help children reread the poem for each item. As you read "If Humpty Dumpty Had a Great Fall" (Related Poems), tell children to listen for some other ways to cook Humpty Dumptys and some other ways to use eggs.

### Cooking And Eating

Children will enjoy thinking about foods such as "scrambled Humpty Dumptys," "deviled Humpty Dumpty," or "Humpty Dumpty McMuffin." Help children prepare Humpty Dumpty Salad:

Peel and dice 6 hard-boiled Humpty Dumptys. Dice 1 sweet pickle or use 1 teaspoon relish. Add 1/4 cup mayonnaise and mix well. Serve on crackers or bread.

Have children bring in simple recipes that call for one or more eggs and compile them to create a Humpty Dumpty cookbook.

### Thinking Critically

Ask children how the king's men were "making the most of a bad situation." Tell children about a time you "made the most of a bad situation" such as reading lots of good books when you were sick in bed or making applesauce with damaged apples. Encourage children to think of times when they have made the most of a bad situation.

### Writing Parodies

Children will enjoy writing their own last lines for the rhyme. Encourage children to read aloud to a friend before writing final drafts and drawing illustrations.

Extend the fun by rewriting and illustrating other nursery rhymes. You will also want to introduce "Alas!" (Me and Others: Poster 1) and "Mother Hubbard's Surprise" (Related Poems).

See Meet the Poet, page 192.

# Yummy Humpty Dumpty

Humpty Dumpty sat on a wall,
Humpty Dumpty had a great fall.
All the king's horses
And all the king's men
Had scrambled eggs for breakfast.

*Anonymous*

# Index to Related Poems

1. Bill and Jim and Joe and Zack..............page 199
2. I and My Echo.................................211
3. If All the World Were Paper...................214
4. If Humpty Dumpty Had a Great Fall.............215
5. I'll Always Wear You..........................213
6. Mother Hubbard's Surprise.....................223
7. Paper I......................................231
8. Pete and Repeat..............................232
9. Tiger........................................245
10. Toaster Time.................................246
11. Toot! Toot!..................................247
12. Trunk Skunk Stunk............................248
13. Who Is This Mouse?...........................253

# ADDING MUSIC

1. Cycles
2. Fog
3. Index
4. Old Grumbler
5. Poets and Pigs
6. The Purple People Eater

# Cycles
by John W. Schaum

Andante

One wheel makes a un-i-cy-cle. Two wheels make a bi-cy-cle.

Three wheels make a tri-cy-cle, But no wheels make an i-ci-cle.

Cir-cus clowns ride un-i-cy-cles. Boys and girls ride bi-cy-cles.

Young-er folks ride tri-cy-cles. But no one rides an i-ci-cle.

*Fine*

Composer: John W. Schaum. Copyright © 1945 by Belwin, Inc.
International copyright secured. Lithographed in the USA. From John W. Schaum's A, THE RED BOOK, EL00166, available from CPP/Belwin, Inc. at music stores for $5.00

# Fog
Words by Carl Sandburg
Music Anonymous

The fog comes on lit - tle cat feet.

It sits look - ing o - ver har - bor and ci - ty

on si - lent haun - ches and then moves on.

# Index
## Words by Babs Bell Hajdusiewicz
## Music by Susan Burkey

**Moderato**

# Old Grumbler

Anonymous

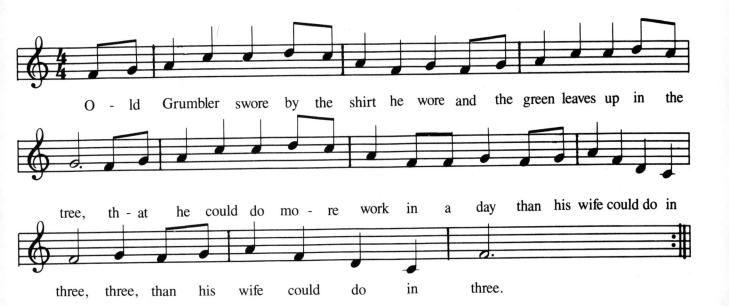

O - ld  Grumbler  swore  by  the  shirt  he  wore  and  the  green  leaves  up  in  the

tree,  th - at  he  could  do  mo - re  work  in  a  day  than  his  wife  could  do  in

three,  three,  than  his  wife  could  do  in  three.

# Poets and Pigs
## by John W. Schaum

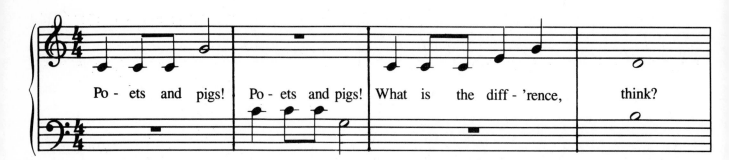

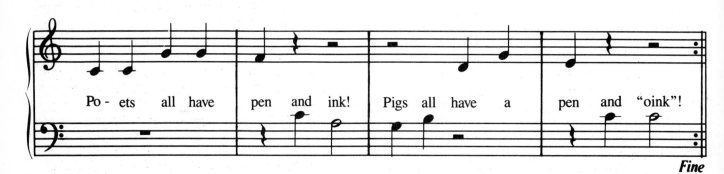

*Fine*

Composer: John W. Schaum. Copyright © 1945 by Belwin, Inc.
International copyright secured. Lithographed in the USA. From John W. Schaum's PRE-A, THE GREEN BOOK, EL00165, available from CPP/Belwin, Inc., at music stores for $4.50.

# The Purple People Eater
## words and music by Sheb Wooley

1. Well, I saw the thing — a-com-in' out of the sky, — It had
2. (Well, he) came down to earth— and he lit in a tree, — I said,

one long horn and one big eye. — I commenced to shakin' and I
"Mister Purple People Eater, don't eat me."— I heard him say in a

said, "Ooh-wee, — it looks like a pur-ple peo-ple eat-er to me."
voice so gruff,— "I wouldn't eat you 'cause you're— so tough." —

1. It was a one-eyed, one-horned, fly-in' pur-ple peo ple eat-er One-eyed, one-horned,
2. Well,— bless my soul, Rock 'n Roll, fly-in' pur-ple peo ple eat-er Pid geon toed, under growed,

fly-in' pur-ple peo-ple eat-er, One-eyed, one-horned, fly-in' pur-ple peo-ple eat-er,
fly-in' pur-ple peo-ple eat-er He wears short shorts, friendly lit-tle peo-ple eat-er,

Sure looked strange to me. — Well, he
What a sight to see. —

# MEET THE POETS

1. Gwendolyn Brooks
2. Tomie De Paola
3. Robert Frost
4. Babs Bell Hajdusiewicz
5. Carl Sandburg
6. William Shakespeare
7. Shel Silverstein
8. Judith Viorst
9. Deborah Vitello
10. Anonymous

# Gwendolyn Brooks (1917-    )

When Gwendolyn Brooks was growing up in Chicago, her parents always knew she would be a writer. At an early age, she began to "put rhymes together." Before she reached high school, she had published her first poem, and when she was 16 she was writing for the Chicago *Defender*, a black newspaper. So began a lifetime of writing. In 1950, Gwendolyn Brooks won the Pulitzer Prize for poetry. She was — and is — the only black ever to do so.

# Tomie De Paola (1934-      )

Tomie de Paola grew up in Meriden, Connecticut, where his mother spent long hours reading to him and his brother. As soon as he could write his name, he got a library card. By the time he reached the first grade door, he knew that he wanted to make picture books. Today Tomie de Paola has reached his goal, having written and illustrated dozens of children's books. He lives with his family in northern New England.

Photo: The Bettmann Archive, Inc.

# Robert Frost (1874-1963)

Robert Frost was born in San Francisco. When he was 11, his father died. His mother moved the family back to her New England home and Frost remained in the region for the rest of his life. His writings about its hills and farms made him the United States' most popular poet. People still read and enjoy "Stopping by Woods on a Snowy Evening," "Birches," and his many other poems. During his lifetime, Frost received many prizes. In 1961, he recited a poem at the inauguration of President John F. Kennedy.

# Babs Bell Hajdusiewicz (Hī'-dōō-shĕ'-vĭtz) (1944-    )

Babs Bell Hajdusiewicz attended a four-room schoolhouse in her hometown of Burrows, Indiana. Although she loved school, she always hated the poetry lessons. In fact, it was not until she started teaching that she discovered — along with her students — the joy of poetry. Since then, she has spent her working life teaching, writing and encouraging others to read. Hajdusiewicz lives in Texas with her husband and two children.

# Carl Sandburg (1878-1967)

Carl Sandburg was an American poet who liked to write about his country and its people. He was born in Galesburg, Illinois. When he was eighteen, he spent a year as a hobo, traveling around the country on trains.

Sandburg later moved to Chicago. There he began to write the first of six books about Abraham Lincoln. At the same time, he worked on funny books for children called *Rootabaga Stories* and wrote poems about the land he loved.

# William Shakespeare (1564-1616)

When William Shakespeare was born, Elizabeth I ruled England. Shakespeare grew up in Stratford-upon-Avon, a town in that country. At the Stratford Grammar School he attended classes from 7 A.M. to 5 P.M. He later married Anne Hathaway and they had three children. The family moved to London. There Shakespeare worked as an actor during the day and wrote at night. The plays and poems he created have been called the finest in the English language.

Photo: Larry Moyer

# Shel Silverstein (1932-        )

Shel Silverstein once said that when he was growing up in Chicago, he "would much rather have been a good baseball player" than a poet. "But," he continued, "I couldn't play ball . . . so I started to draw and to write." Today, Silverstein is best known for his children's books, *The Giving Tree* and *A Light in the Attic*. He also writes and sings folk songs and writes plays for the theater.

## Judith Viorst

When Judith Viorst was seven, she began to write poems.
She says they were "terrible poems about dead dogs,
mostly." It was not until many years later that her first work
was published. Much of Viorst's writing has been for and
about her own three children. Her book *I'll Fix Anthony* was
written to cheer up her son Nick. She wrote *Alexander and
the Terrible, Horrible, No Good, Very Bad Day* when her
son Alexander was having "a lot of them." Judith Viorst
lives in Washington, D.C.

## Deborah Vitello (1956-    )

Deborah Vitello enjoys many interests in addition to writing poems. She is a Girl Scout leader and trainer, plays piano and guitar, is an active member in the Southwestern Cherokee Confederacy, and creates latch hook and ceramic pottery crafts. Vitello wears hearing aids in both ears, but her hearing impairment hasn't even slowed her down. The idea for "Bubbles Popping" came to her as she watched her children playing with soap bubbles. They reminded her of how she felt about bubbles when she was a child.

## Anonymous

This frame has no picture. That's because we don't know the name of the person who wrote the poem. We say that the poem was written by an anonymous poet.

# RELATED POEMS

| TITLE | AUTHOR | PAGE |
|---|---|---|
| Adding | Babs Bell Hajdusiewicz | 194 |
| Adding 1 | Babs Bell Hajdusiewicz | 195 |
| Adding 2 | Babs Bell Hajdusiewicz | 196 |
| Antsy Pants | R. Gene McKenzie | 197 |
| Beehive | Anonymous | 198 |
| Bill and Jim and Joe and Zack | Babs Bell Hajdusiewicz | 199 |
| Book Search | Babs Bell Hajdusiewicz | 200 |
| Bubble Gum | Nina Payne | 201 |
| Bubbles | Babs Bell Hajdusiewicz | 202 |
| Choices | Babs Bell Hajdusiewicz | 203 |
| Circles | Babs Bell Hajdusiewicz | 204 |
| Counting to 12 | Babs Bell Hajdusiewicz | 205 |
| Crunchin' Luncheon | Heidi La Fiamma | 206 |
| Dinosaur Bones | Jean H. Marvin | 207 |
| Eensy Weensy Spider | Anonymous | 208 |
| Fractions Take the Cake | Heidi LaFiamma | 209 |
| Hamster | Alison Hajdusiewicz | 210 |
| I and My Echo | Anonymous | 211 |
| I Had a Little Pig | Anonymous | 212 |
| I'll Always Wear You | Babs Bell Hajdusiewicz | 213 |
| If All the World Were Paper | Anonymous | 214 |
| If Humpty Dumpty Had a Great Fall | Babs Bell Hajdusiewicz | 215 |
| Index | Babs Bell Hajdusiewicz | 216 |
| Jack and Jill | Anonymous | 217 |
| Jelly on the Plate | Anonymous | 218 |
| Just Like Me | Anonymous | 219 |
| Maybe Dats Youwr Pwoblem Too | Jim Hall | 220 |
| The Me Key | Biji Surber Malaker | 221 |
| Measurement Logic | Babs Bell Hajdusiewicz | 222 |
| Mother Hubbard's Surprise | Babs Bell Hajdusiewicz | 223 |
| My Organs | Babs Bell Hajdusiewicz | 224 |
| No Pronoun Problems | Babs Bell Hajdusiewicz | 225 |
| None | Babs Bell Hajdusiewicz | 226 |
| Old Man Moon | Aileen Fisher | 227 |
| One for Me | Babs Bell Hajdusiewicz | 228 |

| TITLE | AUTHOR | PAGE |
|---|---|---|
| Over in the Meadow | Anonymous | 229 |
| The Panther | Ogden Nash | 230 |
| Paper 1 | Carl Sandburg | 231 |
| Pete and Repeat | Anonymous | 232 |
| Poet Unknown | Babs Bell Hajdusiewicz | 233 |
| Poor Old Lady | Anonymous | 234 |
| Sad Bedtime | Babs Bell Hajdusiewicz | 235 |
| Shut Up | Babs Bell Hajdusiewicz | 236 |
| Song of the Witches | William Shakespeare | 237 |
| String to Remember, A | Babs Bell Hajdusiewicz | 238 |
| Summer | Frank Asch | 239 |
| Table of Contents | Babs Bell Hajdusiewicz | 240 |
| Tall and Small | Anonymous | 241 |
| There's a Hole in My Bucket | Anonymous | 242 |
| Things in Twos | Babs Bell Hajdusiewicz | 243 |
| This Tooth | Lee Bennett Hopkins | 244 |
| Tiger | Mary Ann Hoberman | 245 |
| Toaster Time | Eve Merriam | 246 |
| Toot! Toot! | Anonymous | 247 |
| Trunk Skunk Stunk | Babs Bell Hajdusiewicz | 248 |
| Way Down South | Anonymous | 249 |
| What Coin Do I Have? | Babs Bell Hajdusiewicz | 250 |
| Wheels Wheels Everywhere | Babs Bell Hajdusiewicz | 251 |
| Where's My Seat Belt? | Babs Bell Hajdusiewicz | 252 |
| Who Is This Mouse? | Babs Bell Hajdusiewicz | 253 |
| Who to Pet and Who Not to | X. J. Kennedy | 254 |
| Zero | Babs Bell Hajdusiewicz | 255 |

# Adding (Tune: Row, Row, Row Your Boat)

Guess what adding is —
It's making two groups one.
Lay out two groups of sticks and I
Will show you how it's done.

Two plus two is four;
Five plus one is six.
The trouble is, when you get done,
You still will have just sticks!

Sticks, sticks and then more sticks,
These sticks become a bore!
I want to learn to add my coins
To buy things at the store.

A nickel and a penny add
Together to make six.
Six cents has much more value than
A silly pile of sticks!

*Babs Bell Hajdusiewicz*

# Adding 1

Adding is a lot of fun
Especially when I'm adding 1,
'Cause all I do for 1 plus 1
Is count 1 more past 1 . . . I'm done!
Now how 'bout 2 plus 1? Let's see . . .
Count 2 . . . then 3; add easily.
For 3 plus 1. Count 3, then 4 . . .
Yes, 3 plus 1 is 4, no more.
Adding sure is lots of fun
Especially when I'm adding 1.

*Babs Bell Hajdusiewicz*

# Adding 2

Until today I never knew
How to add for 2 plus 2.
It's not so hard 'cause now I know
I start at 2 and then I go
To 3 and then I go 1 more
And 2 plus 2 will equal 4.
To start at 4 and add 2 more,
I simply start to count at 4.
Then 5 and 6, that's 4 plus 2
And counting's all I had to do.

*Babs Bell Hajdusiewicz*

# Antsy Pants

There was a young laddie from France
Who perched on a hill full of ants.
He laughed, I suppose,
When they tickled his nose,
But he cried when they crawled in his pants!

*R. Gene McKenzie*

# Beehive

Here is the beehive
But where are the bees?
Hiding away
Where nobody sees.
But now they are coming
Out of the hive —
One
   Two
      Three
        Four
          Five
Bzzzzzzzzzzzzzzzz!

*Anonymous*

# Bill and Jim and Joe and Zack

Bill and Jim and Joe and Zack
All wanted to sit way back in the back.
The driver said no, that could not be,
There were no seat belts there, you see.
The driver said they would have to sit,
In seats where seat belts would all fit.
So Bill and Jim and Joe and Zack
Rode safely in seat belts, NOT in the back.

*Babs Bell Hajdusiewicz*

# Book Search

Since I can't tell a book by its cover,
A page or two helps me discover:
Do I like what I see?
Can I read easily?
Or should I go search for another?

*Babs Bell Hajdusiewicz*

# Bubble Gum

I'm in trouble
made a bubble
peeled it off my nose

Felt a rock
inside my sock
got gum between my toes

Made another
told my brother
we could blow a pair

Give three cheers
now our ears
are sticking to our hair.

*Nina Payne*

# Bubbles

Bubbles, bubbles everywhere!
In the water, in the air.
Bubbly walls and bubbly floor,
Bubbly ceiling, bubbly door.

Bubbles, bubbles everywhere!
In the tub and in my hair.
Bubbly water, bubbly skin —
What a bubbly world I'm in!

*Babs Bell Hajdusiewicz*

# Choices

If the choice is one-half or one-third,
My answer depends on one word:
For COOKIE, one-half;
One-third if it's MATH;
And neither if SPINACH is heard.

*Babs Bell Hajdusiewicz*

# Circles <small>(Tune: Mulberry Bush)</small>

Circles can roll round and round,
Round and round,
Round and round.
Circles can roll round and round
But squares and triangles can't.

*Babs Bell Hajdusiewicz*

# Counting to 12 (Tune: Twinkle, Twinkle)

Zero, one, two, three, four, five,
Six, seven, eight, nine, sakes alive!
I have learned my numbers well
Next come ten, eleven, twelve.
I can sing a number song;
Won't you come and sing along?

*Babs Bell Hajdusiewicz*

# Crunchin' Luncheon

I like Stegosaurus a bunch,
But me he could easily crunch.
So I'll stay away
At least for today
So he won't digest me for lunch.

*Heidi La Fiamma*

# Dinosaur Bones

Dinosaurs don't rumble through the park
Or down my sidewalk after dark.
In museums, still as stones,
They stand in nothing but their bones.

*Jean H. Marvin*

# Eensy Weensy Spider

The eensy weensy spider went up the garden spout.
Down came the rain and washed the spider out.
Out came the sun and dried up all the rain,
And the eensy weensy spider went up the spout again.

*Anonymous*

# Fractions Take the Cake

I never cared for math that much,
But fractions I can take
'Cause without fractions, Mom would have
No recipes to bake.
I couldn't live without those pies
And cookies my mom makes.
So maybe some of math's OK,
Since fractions take the cake.

*Heidi LaFiamma*

# Hamster

You buy a hamster
All fuzzy and furry.
Gather supplies;
Take him home in a hurry.
You tend to his cage
And christen him Lou.
What thanks do you get?
He tries to bite you!

*Alison Hajdusiewicz*
*(written at age 9)*

# I and My Echo

I am a gold lock.
   Echo: I am a gold key.
I am a silver lock.
   Echo: I am a silver key.
I am a brass lock.
   Echo: I am a brass key.
I am a lead lock.
   Echo: I am a lead key.
I am a monk lock.
   Echo: I am a monk key (monkey).

*Anonymous*

# I Had a Little Pig

I had a little pig,
I fed him in a trough,
He got so fat
His tail dropped off.
So I got me a hammer,
And I got me a nail,
And I made my little pig
A brand-new tail.

*Anonymous*

# I'll Always Wear You

You've heard of seat belts
And car seats
And how we should use them,
Always and always
To keep us safe riding.
But do you believe
That you really must always wear them?

Seat belt, I love to wear you
When I'm riding in a car.
Seat belt, I'll always wear you
Whether going near or far.

One time I didn't wear you.
I didn't want to take the time.
I didn't hook myself up tightly
When I heard the warning chime.

It was on a sunny April day,
We were going for a treat.
The car stopped fast
When a dog ran past,
And I went f
                    l
                      y
                        i
                          n
                            g off my seat!

Now I can tell you, my friend,
What I will always do,
I'll ALWAYS wear my seat belt
And I hope that you will, too!

*Babs Bell Hajdusiewicz*

# If All the World Were Paper

If all the world were paper,
And all the sea were ink,
And all the trees were bread and cheese,
What should we do for drink?

*Anonymous*

# If Humpty Dumpty Had a Great Fall

If Humpty Dumpty had a great fall,
It wouldn't bother me at all.
I'd simply throw the shell away,
And eat the yolk and white some way . . .
Like fried
  or poached
    or scrambled
      or basted
or mixed in the yummiest cookies I've tasted.

If Humpty Dumpty had a great fall,
It wouldn't bother me at all.
I'd simply throw the shell away,
And use the yolk and white some way . . .
In pancakes
  or muffins
    or waffles
      or cake
Or whipped in a creamy banana milkshake.

No, if Humpty Dumpty had a great fall,
It wouldn't bother me at all.
I'd simply throw the shell away,
And use the yolk and white today!

*Babs Bell Hajdusiewicz*

# Index

If I don't know
On which page to look,
I'll use the Index
In the back of my book.

*Babs Bell Hajdusiewicz*

# Jack and Jill

Jack and Jill
Went up the hill
To fetch a pail of water.
Jack fell down
And broke his crown,
And Jill came tumbling after.

*Anonymous*

# Jelly on the Plate

Jelly on the plate,
Jelly on the plate,
Wibble wobble, wibble wobble,
Jelly on the plate.

Paper on the floor,
Paper on the floor,
Pick it up, pick it up,
Paper on the floor.

Piggy in the house,
Piggy in the house,
Kick him out, kick him out,
Piggy in the house.

*Anonymous*

# Just Like Me

I went up one pair of stairs.
  (Just like me)
I went up two pairs of stairs.
  (Just like me)
I went up three pairs of stairs.
  (Just like me)
I went into my bedroom
  (Just like me)
I looked out my window.
  (Just like me)
And there I saw a monkey
  (Just like me)

*Anonymous*

# Maybe Dats Youwr Pwoblem Too

All my pwoblems
who knows, maybe evwybody's pwoblems
is due to da fact, due to da awful twuth
dat I am SPIDERMAN.

I know, I know. All da dumb jokes:
No flies on you, ha ha,
and da one about what do I do wit all
doze extwa legs in bed. Well, dat's funny yeah.
But you twy being
SPIDERMAN for a month or two. Go ahead.

You get doze cwazy calls fwom da
Gubbener askin you to twap some boogler who's
only twying to wip off color T.V. sets.
Now, what do I cawre about T.V. sets?
But I pull on da suit, da stinkin suit,
wit da sucker cups on da fingers,
and I get my wopes and wittle bundle of
equiptment and den I go fwying like cwazy
acwoss da town fwom woof top to woof top.

Till der he is. Some poor dumb color T.V. slob
and I fall on him and we westle a widdle
until I get him all woped. So big deal.
You tink when you SPIDERMAN
der's sometin big going to happen to you.
Well, I tell you what. It don't happen dat way.
Nuttin happens. Gubbener calls, I go.
Bwing him to powice. Gubbener calls again,
like dat over and over.

I tink I twy sometin diffunt. I tink I twy
sometin exitin like wacing cawrs. Sometin to make
my heart beat a difwent wate.
But den you just can't quit being sometin like
SPIDERMAN.
You SPIDERMAN for life. Fowever. I can't even
buin my suit. It won't buin. It's fwame wesistent.
So maybe dat's youwr pwoblem too, who knows.
Maybe dat's da whole pwoblem wif everwytin.
Nobody can buin der suits, cuz day all fwame wesistent.
Who knows?

*Jim Hall*

# The Me Key

There's nothing much to it . . .
When I think I can do it . . .
Believing in me is the key.
I think I can do it —
I know I can do it —
I did it just now!
Look at me!

*Biji Surber Malaker*

# Measurement Logic

How far is it from me to you?
  To find out, all I have to do
Is measure, but I'll first decide
  What to use as a measuring guide.

Shall I use my feet? If so I'll find
  The distance by putting one foot behind
The other and count how many feet
  I use until we come to meet.

Or I could count the number of times
  An object is used — a penny or dime,
A paper clip, book, a pencil or pen,
  I lay the object from end to end.

But people's feet vary and pencils get used
  So the number depends on whose feet I choose.
And that's why an inch or centimeter's used,
  It's the same no matter whose ruler is whose.

*Babs Bell Hajdusiewicz*

POETRY WORKS! copyright © 1990 Modern Curriculum Press, Inc.

# Mother Hubbard's Surprise

Old Mother Hubbard
Went to the cupboard
To get her poor doggie a bone.
But when she got there,
The cupboard was bare,
'Cause her doggie had hosted a party.

*Babs Bell Hajdusiewicz*

# My Organs

My heart pumps my blood
From my head to my toes.
All over my body
My blood goes and goes.

My brain lets me think;
It explains what I see.
It stores all the facts
My teacher gives me.

My lungs breathe the air
That keeps me alive.
My heart, brain, and lungs
I need to survive.

And now that I know
What these organs are for,
I'll be wearing my seat belt
And locking my door.

Just in case that my car
Stops fast or is crashed;
Then my organs stay safe!
Not ripped apart! Not smashed!

*Babs Bell Hajdusiewicz*

# None

Give me some things
I'll hold every one.
Take them away
And I will have none.

*Babs Bell Hajdusiewicz*

# No Pronoun Problems

When telling a story of my friend and me,
I'm not always sure what the pronoun should be,
But I've made a plan that now helps me out
When pronouns are problems and I am in doubt.

Is it "Amy and I" or "Amy and me?"
Leave "Amy and" out, and it's easy to see
Which pronoun sounds best, so my little test
Tells me the right word, then I put back the rest.

*Babs Bell Hajdusiewicz*

POETRY WORKS! copyright © 1990 Modern Curriculum Press, Inc.

# Old Man Moon

The moon is very, very old.
The reason why is clear —
he gets a birthday once a month,
instead of once a year.

*Aileen Fisher*

# One For Me

We have five seat belts in our car.
One for Dad, one for Mom,
One for Grandpa, one for Grandma
And . . . one for me.

*Babs Bell Hajdusiewicz*

# Over in the Meadow

Over in the meadow, in the sand, in the sun,
Lived an old mother turtle and her little turtle one.
"Dig!" said the mother.
"I dig," said the one.
So he dug all day,
In the sand, in the sun.

Over in the meadow, where the stream runs blue,
Lived shiney mother fish and her little fishes two.
"Swim!" said the mother.
"We swim," said the two.
So they swam and they leaped,
Where the stream runs blue.

Over in the meadow, in a hole in a tree,
Lived an old mother bluebird and little birdies three.
"Sing!" said the mother.
"We sing," said the three.
So they sang and were glad,
In the hole in the tree.

Over in the meadow, in the reeds on the shore,
Lived a wet mother muskrat and her little muskies four.
"Dive!" said the mother.
"We dive," said the four.
So they dived and they burrowed,
In the reeds on the shore.

Over in the meadow, in a snug beehive,
Lived a mother honeybee and her little honeys five.
"Buzz!" said the mother.
"We buzz," said the five.
So they buzzed and they hummed,
Near the snug beehive.

Over in the meadow, in a nest built of sticks,
Lived black mother crow and her little crows six.
"Caw!" said the mother.
"We caw," said the six.
So they cawed and they cawed,
In their nest built of sticks.

Over in the meadow, where the grass is so even,
Lived a gay mother cricket and her little crickets seven.
"Chirp!" said the mother.
"We chirp," said the seven.
So they chirped cheery notes,
In the grass soft and even.

Over in the meadow, by the old mossy gate,
Lived a brown mother lizard and her lizards eight.
"Bask!" said the mother.
"We bask," said the eight.
So they basked in the sun,
By the old mossy gate.

Over in the meadow, where the clear pools shine,
Lived a green mother frog and her little froggies nine.
"Croak!" said the mother.
"We croak," said the nine.
So they croaked and they jumped,
Where the clear pools shine.

Over in the meadow, in a soft shady glen,
Lived a bright mother firefly and her little flies ten.
"Shine!" said the mother.
"We shine," said the ten.
So they shone like stars,
In the soft, shady glen.

*Anonymous*

# The Panther

The panther is like a leopard,
Except it hasn't been peppered.
Should you behold a panther crouch,
Prepare to say Ouch.
Better yet, if called by a panther,
Don't anther.

*Ogden Nash*

# Paper I

Paper is two kinds; to write on, to wrap with.
If you like to write, you write.
If you like to wrap, you wrap.
Some papers like writers, some like wrappers.
Are you a writer or a wrapper?

*Carl Sandburg*

# Pete and Repeat

If Pete and Repeat
Went out in a boat
And Pete fell out,
Who would be left?
(Repeat)

*Anonymous*

# Poet Unknown

Some poems are written
By poets who fail
To sign their names
At the end of their tale.

These poets remain
Unknown to us,
So we say their names
Are Anonymous.

*Babs Bell Hajdusiewicz*

# Poor Old Lady

Poor old lady, she swallowed a fly.
I don't know why she swallowed a fly.
Poor old lady, I think she'll die.

Poor old lady, she swallowed a spider.
It squirmed and wriggled and turned inside her.
She swallowed the spider to catch the fly.
I don't know why she swallowed a fly.
Poor old lady, I think she'll die.

Poor old lady, she swallowed a bird.
How absurd! She swallowed a bird.
She swallowed the bird to catch the spider,
She swallowed the spider to catch the fly,
I don't know why she swallowed a fly.
Poor old lady, I think she'll die.

Poor old lady, she swallowed a cat.
Think of that! She swallowed a cat.
She swallowed the cat to catch the bird.
She swallowed the bird to catch the spider.
She swallowed the spider to catch the fly,
I don't know why she swallowed a fly.
Poor old lady, I think she'll die.

Poor old lady, she swallowed a dog.
She went the whole hog when she swallowed the dog.
She swallowed the dog to catch the cat,
She swallowed the cat to catch the bird,
She swallowed the bird to catch the spider.
She swallowed the spider to catch the fly,
I don't know why she swallowed a fly.
Poor old lady, I think she'll die.

Poor old lady, she swallowed a cow.
I don't know how she swallowed the cow.
She swallowed the cow to catch the dog,
She swallowed the dog to catch the cat,
She swallowed the cat to catch the bird,
She swallowed the bird to catch the spider,
She swallowed the spider to catch the fly,
I don't know why she swallowed a fly.
Poor old lady, I think she'll die.

Poor old lady, she swallowed a horse.
She died, of course.

*Anonymous*

POETRY WORKS! copyright © 1990 Modern Curriculum Press, Inc.

# Sad Bedtime

Now that I have learned how to add,
My bedtime at 8 is quite sad!
It should be at 9,
One more hour'd be fine,
But now to convince Mom and Dad!

*Babs Bell Hajdusiewicz*

# Shut Up

We can shut up a box,
A window or door,
But when speaking to humans,
We need to think more.

A box is just paper.
A door has no ears.
A window is glass.
Not one can cry tears!

But a human's a person
With feelings and such,
And a "shut up" hurts feelings
So-o-o-o very much!

*Babs Bell Hajdusiewicz*

# Song of the Witches

Double, double toil and trouble;
Fire burn and caldron bubble.
Fillet of a fenny snake,
In the caldron boil and bake.

*William Shakespeare*

# A String to Remember

I'm trying to remember
To remember
To remember
To always remember
To never forget.
And that's why
You see this string
Tied around my finger.
It's to remind me that
I'm trying to remember
To remember
To remember
To always remember
To never forget.

*Babs Bell Hajdusiewicz*

# Summer

When it's hot
I take my shoes off,
I take my shirt off,
I take my pants off,
I take my underwear off,
I take my whole body off,
and throw it
in the river.

*Frank Asch*

# Table of Contents

If there is no Index
In the back of my book,
I'll turn to the front
And take a look.

The Table of Contents
Is where I will look
To find out what
Is in this book.

I'll find it in
The front of my book;
That's the Table of Contents,
And now, let's look!

*Babs Bell Hajdusiewicz*

# Tall and Small

Here is a giant
Who is tall, tall, tall;
Here is an elf
Who is small, small, small

The elf who is small
Will try, try, try
To reach to the giant
Who is high, high, high

*Anonymous*

# There's a Hole in My Bucket

1. There's a hole in my bucket, dear Liza, dear Liza,
There's a hole in my bucket, dear Liza, a hole.

2. Then mend it, dear Henry, dear Henry, dear Henry,
Then mend it, dear Henry, dear Henry, mend it.

3. With what shall I mend it, dear Liza, dear Liza,
With what shall I mend it, dear Liza, with what?

4. With straw, dear Henry, dear Henry, dear Henry,
With straw, dear Henry, dear Henry, with straw.

5. The straw is too long, dear Liza, dear Liza,
The straw is too long, dear Liza, too long.

6. Then cut it, dear Henry, dear Henry, dear Henry,
Then cut it, dear Henry, dear Henry, cut it.

7. With what shall I cut it, dear Liza, dear Liza,
With what shall I cut it, dear Liza, with what?

8. With a knife, dear Henry, dear Henry, dear Henry,
With a knife, dear Henry, dear Henry, a knife.

9. The knife is too blunt, dear Liza, dear Liza,
The knife is too blunt, dear Liza, too blunt.

10. Then sharpen it, dear Henry, dear Henry, dear Henry
Then sharpen it, dear Henry, dear Henry, sharpen it.

11. With what shall I sharpen it, dear Liza, dear Liza,
With what shall I sharpen it, dear Liza, with what?

12. With a stone, dear Henry, dear Henry, dear Henry,
With a stone, dear Henry, dear Henry, a stone.

13. But the stone is too dry, dear Liza, dear Liza,
But the stone is too dry, dear Liza, too dry.

14. Then wet it, dear Henry, dear Henry, dear Henry,
Then wet it, dear Henry, dear Henry, wet it.

15. With what shall I wet it, dear Liza, dear Liza,
With what shall I wet it, dear Liza, with what?

16. With water, dear Henry, dear Henry, dear Henry,
With water, dear Henry, dear Henry, with water.

17. In what shall I get it, dear Liza, dear Liza,
In what shall I get it, dear Liza, in what?

18. In a bucket, dear Henry, dear Henry, dear Henry,
In a bucket, dear Henry, dear Henry, in a bucket.

19. There's a hole in my bucket, dear Liza, dear Liza,
There's a hole in my bucket, dear Liza, a hole.

*Anonymous*

# Things in Twos

2 arms for reaching,
2 legs that walk,
2 nostrils for smelling,
2 lips to talk.

2 hands for holding,
To hug, or to touch.
2 ears for hearing
And washing too much.

*Babs Bell Hajdusiewicz*

# This Tooth

I jiggled it
  jaggled it
  jerked it.

I pushed
  and pulled
  and poked it.
But —

As soon as I stopped,
and left it alone,
This tooth came out
on its very own!

*Lee Bennett Hopkins*

POETRY WORKS! copyright © 1990 Modern Curriculum Press, Inc.

# Tiger

I'm a tiger
Striped with fur
Don't come near
Or I might Grrr
Don't come near
Or I might growl
Don't come near
Or I might
BITE!

*Mary Ann Hoberman*

# Toaster Time

Tick tick tick tick tick tick tick
Toast up a sandwich quick quick quick
Hamwich
Jamwich
Lick lick lick!

Tick tick tick tick tick tick- Stop!
POP!

*Eve Merriam*

# Toot! Toot!

A peanut sat on a railroad track,
His heart was all a-flutter;
The five-fifteen came rushing by —
Toot! toot! peanut butter!

A pickle sat on a railroad track,
Feeling mighty silly;
The train came roaring down the track,
Toot! Toot! piccalilli!

*Anonymous*

# Trunk Skunk Stunk

Do you know what I did when a skunk
Hitchhiked for a ride in my trunk?
I abandoned my car
And kept running far
So that you wouldn't smell how I stunk!

*Babs Bell Hajdusiewicz*

# Way Down South

Way down South where bananas grow,
A grasshopper stepped on an elephant's toe.
The elephant said, with tears in his eyes,
"Pick on somebody you own size."

*Anonymous*

# What Coin Do I Have?

I have a mystery coin in my hand
I have a mystery coin in my hand
I have a mystery coin in my hand
Now what coin do I have?

The coin I am hiding in my hand
Could be traded for ten pennies, in my hand
Could be traded for two nickels, in my hand
Now what coin do I have? (dime)

The coin I am hiding in my hand
Could be traded for five pennies, in my hand
Could buy a five-cent item, in my hand
Now what coin do I have? (nickel)

The coin I am hiding in my hand
Has the very smallest value, in my hand
Shows the head of Abraham Lincoln, in my hand
Now what coin do I have? (penny)

*Babs Bell Hajdusiewicz*

# Wheels Wheels Everywhere (Tune: Twinkle Twinkle Little Star)

Wheels, wheels, wheels, they're everywhere!
Under cars, trucks, bikes, trains, chairs.
Are wheels circles? Are they square?
Can triangles roll somewhere?
Oh, no, no, no, wheels have to be
Circles to roll easily.

*Babs Bell Hajdusiewicz*

# Where's My Seat Belt? (Tune: Are You Sleeping?)

Where's my seat belt?
Where's my seat belt?
Here it is!
Here it is!
Watch how I can hook it!
Watch how I can hook it!
Now I'm safe!
Now I'm safe!

*Babs Bell Hajdusiewicz*

# Who Is This Mouse?

Who is this tiny, little mouse
Who lives with me inside my house?
He always shares
His cheesy squares.
His name's (Good) Manners Mouse.

1) He asks for cheese
   But never says "please"!
   His name's (Poor) Manners Mouse.

2) He'd never burp;
   And doesn't slurp.
   His name's (Good) Manners Mouse.

3) He picks his nose
   So I suppose
   His name's (Poor) Manners Mouse.

4) He pulls my hair —
   I must beware!
   His name's (Poor) Manners Mouse.

5) He'll boast and brag
   And hit in "tag."
   His name's (Poor) Manners Mouse.

6) He doesn't peek
   In "hide-and-seek."
   His name's (Good) Manners Mouse.

*Babs Bell Hajdusiewicz*

# Who To Pet and Who Not To

Go pet a kitten, pet a dog,
Go pet a worm for practice,
But don't go pet a porcupine —

You want to be a cactus?

*X. J. Kennedy*

# Zero

How many is nothing?
How many is none?
How many's not any?
Is it one less than one?

Yes, zero's not any.
Zero is none.
It's nothing at all!
Zero's one less than one.

*Babs Bell Hajdusiewicz*

# Index - Author

| POET | POEM | PAGE | POET | POEM | PAGE |
|---|---|---|---|---|---|
| Anonymous | Beehive | 198 | dePaola, Tomie | Secret Place, The | 82 |
| | Dark House, The | 14 | Fisher, Aileen | Old Man Moon | 227 |
| | Eensy Weensy Spider | 208 | Frost, Robert | Last Word of a Bluebird | 122 |
| | Family of the Sun | 114 | | Pasture, The | 124 |
| | Hairy Toe | 16 | Greenfield, Eloise | Moochie | 102 |
| | Have You Ever Seen? | 158 | Hajdusiewicz, Alison | Hamster | 210 |
| | I and My Echo | 211 | Hajdusiewicz, Babs Bell | Adding | 194 |
| | I Had a Little Pig | 212 | | Adding 1 | 195 |
| | If All The Seas | 146 | | Adding 2 | 196 |
| | If All the World Were Paper | 214 | | Alas! | 92 |
| | If You Should Meet a Crocodile | 40 | | Arithmetic Pie | 136 |
| | Jack and Jill | 217 | | Bill and Jim and Joe and Zack | 199 |
| | Jelly on the Plate | 218 | | Book Search | 200 |
| | Just Like Me | 219 | | Bubbles | 202 |
| | Old Noah's Ark | 150 | | Bunny Rabbit's Predicament | 30 |
| | Over in the Meadow | 229 | | Calendar Rhyme | 138 |
| | Pete and Repeat | 232 | | Choices | 203 |
| | Poor Old Lady | 234 | | Circles | 204 |
| | Tall and Small | 241 | | Countdown to Recess | 140 |
| | There's a Hole in the Bucket | 242 | | Counting to 12 | 205 |
| | To Be or Not To Be | 62 | | Extraordinary Me | 70 |
| | Toot! Toot! | 247 | | From Mars to Safety | 94 |
| | Way Down South | 249 | | Glug! Gurgle! Glug! | 156 |
| | Yummy Humpty Dumpty | 172 | | I'll Always Wear You | 213 |
| Asch, Frank | Summer | 239 | | I've Figured It Out | 144 |
| Behn, Harry | Trees | 130 | | I, Myself, and Me | 72 |
| Benét, Stephen Vincent and Rosemary Carr | Nancy Hanks | 104 | | If Humpty Dumpty Had a Great Fall | 215 |
| Brand, Oscar | Old Grumbler | 106 | | If the Spider Could Talk | 38 |
| Brooks, Gwendolyn | Tommy | 128 | | In and Out | 160 |
| Brown, Beatrice Curtis | Jonathan Bing | 100 | | Index | 216 |
| Burgess, Gelett | Goops (Table Manners) | 96 | | It's Not Fair! | 50 |
| Carr, Rosemary and Stephen Vincent Benét | Nancy Hanks | 104 | | Lining up | 148 |
| Chute, Marchette | Drinking Fountain | 68 | | Me a Mess? | 74 |
| Conkling, Hilda | Dandelion | 112 | | Measurement Logic | 222 |
| de Regniers, Beatrice Schenk | Keep a Poem in Your Pocket | 162 | | Mother Hubbard's Surprise | 223 |
| | | | | Mr. Bear | 20 |
| | | | | My Organs | 224 |

| POET | POEM | PAGE |
|------|------|------|
| | My Turn to Talk | 54 |
| | No Pronoun Problems | 226 |
| | None | 225 |
| | One for Me | 228 |
| | Poet Says, The | 80 |
| | Poet Unknown | 233 |
| | Rudes | 108 |
| | Sad Bedtime | 235 |
| | Shut Up | 236 |
| | Silly Trees | 126 |
| | Sleepy Tiger | 44 |
| | Solo Sunday | 58 |
| | Statue on the Curb | 86 |
| | Stealing Feelings | 60 |
| | String to Remember, A | 238 |
| | Table of Contents | 240 |
| | Things in Twos | 243 |
| | Trunk Skunk Stunk | 248 |
| | What Coin Do I Have? | 250 |
| | Wheels Wheels Everywhere | 251 |
| | Where's My Seat Belt? | 252 |
| | Who is this Mouse? | 253 |
| | Zero | 255 |
| Hall, Jim | Maybe Dats Youwr Pwoblem Too | 220 |
| Hoberman, Mary Ann | Tiger | 245 |
| | Yellow Butter | 170 |
| Hoeft, Robert D. | One-Eyed Teddy | 56 |
| Hopkins, Lee Bennett | This Tooth | 244 |
| Hymes, Lucia and James L. | My Favorite Word | 164 |
| Jacobs, Leland B. | Bird Carpenter | 28 |
| Kanarek, Ruth | My Loose Tooth | 78 |
| Kennedy, X. J. | Who to Pet and Who Not to | 254 |
| Kinne, Bonnie | Mud Monster | 76 |
| LaFiamma, Heidi | Crunchin' Luncheon | 206 |
| | Fractions Take the Cake | 209 |
| Lonny, Alexander | Whose Face? | 88 |

| POET | POEM | PAGE |
|------|------|------|
| Malaker, Biji Surber | Me Key, The | 221 |
| Marvin, Jean H. | Dinosaur Bones | 207 |
| McCord, David | Frost Pane, The | 118 |
| McKenzie, R. Gene | Antsy Pants | 197 |
| Merriam, Eve | Toaster Time | 246 |
| Miller, Mary Britton | Cat | 32 |
| Moore, Lilian | Hey, Bug! | 98 |
| Morningstar, Teresa Lynn | Have You Seen Edgar? | 120 |
| Murphy, Eileen Ellen | Fourteen Cats | 36 |
| Nash, Ogden | Adventures of Isabel | 10 |
| | Panther, The | 230 |
| Payne, Nina | Bubble Gum | 201 |
| Resnikoff, Alexander | Bad and Good | 154 |
| Richards, Laura | Eletelephony | 34 |
| Roberts, Elizabeth Madox | Mumps | 52 |
| Sandburg, Carl | Fog | 116 |
| | Paper I | 231 |
| Schaum, John | Cycles | 142 |
| | Poets and Pigs | 166 |
| Segall, Pearl Bloch | Wishful Thinking | 64 |
| Shakespeare, William | Song of the Witches | 237 |
| | When Icicles Hang by the Wall | 132 |
| Silverstein, Shel | Hungry Mungry | 18 |
| | True Story | 24 |
| Smith, Helen C. | Silly Sleep Sheep | 84 |
| Stevenson, Robert Louis | Bed in Summer | 48 |
| Viorst, Judith | Mother Doesn't Want a Dog | 42 |
| Vitello, Deborah | Bubbles Popping | 12 |
| Wooley, Sheb | Purple People Eater | 22 |
| Young, E. R. | Railroad Reverie | 168 |

# Index - First Lines

| FIRST LINE | POEM | PAGE |
|---|---|---|
| A peanut sat on a railroad track | Toot! Toot! | 247 |
| A poem is a part of me | Poet Says, The | 80 |
| Adding is a lot of fun | Adding | 194 |
| All my pwoblems | Maybe Dats Youwr Pwoblem Too | 220 |
| Arithmetic pie is tasty and sweet | Arithmetic Pie | 136 |
| As I went out a Crow | Last Word of a Bluebird | 122 |
| Bill and Jim and Joe and Zack | Bill and Jim and Joe and Zack | 199 |
| Bubbles, bubbles everywhere! | Bubbles | 202 |
| Carpenters use nails and hammers, | Bird Carpenter | 28 |
| Circles can roll round and round, | Circles | 204 |
| Did you see | Have You Seen Edgar? | 120 |
| Dinosaurs don't rumble through the park | Dinosaur Bones | 207 |
| Do you know what I did when a skunk | Trunk Skunk Stunk | 248 |
| Do you know what is bad? | Bad and Good | 154 |
| Double, double toil and trouble; | Song of the Witches | 237 |
| Give me some things | None | 225 |
| Go pet a kitten, pet a dog, | Who to Pet and Who Not to | 254 |
| Guess what adding is | Adding 2 | 196 |
| Have you ever seen a sheet on a river bed? | Have You Ever Seen? | 120 |
| Here is a giant | Tall and Small | 241 |
| Here is the beehive | Beehive | 198 |
| Hey, bug, stay! | Hey, Bug! | 98 |
| How far is it from me to you? | Measurement Logic | 222 |
| How many is nothing? | Zero | 255 |
| Humpty Dumpty sat on a wall, | Yummy Humpty Dumpty | 172 |
| Hungry Mungry sat at supper, | Hungry Mungry | 18 |
| I am a gold lock. | I and My Echo | 211 |
| I had a feeling in my neck, | Mumps | 52 |
| I had a little pig, | I Had a Little Pig | 212 |
| I had a loose tooth, a wiggly, jiggly loose tooth. | My Loose Tooth | 78 |
| I have a mystery coin in my hand | What Coin Do I Have? | 250 |
| I jiggled it | This Tooth | 244 |
| I like Stegosaurus a bunch, | Crunchin' Luncheon | 206 |
| I never cared for math that much, | Fractions Take the Cake | 209 |
| I put a seed into the ground | Tommy | 128 |
| I sometimes think I'd rather crow | To Be or Not To Be | 62 |
| I think you'll never ever see | Extraordinary Me | 70 |
| I used to ask where I might go | I've Figured It Out | 144 |
| I was playing outside | From Mars to Safety | 94 |
| I went up one pair of stairs. | Just Like Me | 219 |
| I'll tell you a story of how old Mr. Bear | Mr. Bear | 20 |
| I'm a tiger | Tiger | 245 |
| I'm glad I'm me, and not a tree! | Silly Trees | 126 |
| I'm going out to clean the pasture spring; | Pasture, The | 124 |
| I'm in trouble | Bubble Gum | 201 |
| I'm trying to remember | String to Remember, A | 238 |
| If all the seas were one sea, | If All The Seas | 146 |
| If all the world were paper, | If All the World Were Paper | 214 |
| If Humpty Dumpty had a great fall, | If Humpty Dumpty had a Great Fall | 215 |
| If I am first, then you can't be | Lining Up | 148 |
| If I come in and no one's home, | I, Myself, and Me | 72 |
| If I don't know | Index | 216 |
| If Nancy Hanks | Nancy Hanks | 104 |
| If Pete and Repeat | Pete and Repeat | 232 |
| If the choice is one-half or one-third, | Choices | 203 |
| If the spider could talk, | If the Spider Could Talk | 38 |
| If there is no index | Table of Contents | 240 |
| If you should meet a Crocodile | If You Should Meet a Crocodile | 40 |
| In a dark, dark wood there was a dark, dark | Dark House, The | 14 |
| In winter I get up at night | Bed in Summer | 48 |
| Isabel met an enormous bear, | Adventures of Isabel | 10 |
| It was my secret place | Secret Place, The | 82 |
| It's not fair! It isn't! | It's Not Fair! | 50 |
| Jack and Jill | Alas! | 92 |
| Jack and Jill went up the hill | Jack and Jill | 217 |
| Jelly on the plate, | Jelly on the Plate | 218 |
| Keep a poem in your pocket | Keep a Poem in Your Pocket | 162 |
| Moochie likes to keep on playing | Moochie | 102 |
| Mother doesn't want a dog. | Mother Doesn't Want a Dog | 42 |

| FIRST LINE | POEM | PAGE |
|---|---|---|
| Momma Skunk had baby skunks, | In and Out | 160 |
| Mrs. Stairs owned fourteen chairs | Fourteen Cats | 36 |
| My hand goes up when I want to say | My Turn to Talk | 54 |
| My heart pumps my blood | My Organs | 224 |
| Now that I have learned how to add, | Sad Bedtime | 235 |
| O Little Soldier with the golden helmet, | Dandelion | 112 |
| Old Grumbler swore by the shirt he wore | Old Grumbler | 106 |
| Old Mother Hubbard went to her cupboard | Mother Hubbard's Surprise | 223 |
| Old Noah once he built an ark. | Old Noah's Ark | 150 |
| Once there was a woman went out to pick beans, | Hairy Toe | 16 |
| Once there was an elephant, | Eletelephony | 34 |
| One sheep, two sheep, three sheep, four . . . | Silly Sleep Sheep | 84 |
| One wheel makes a unicycle. | Cycles | 142 |
| Over in the meadow | Over in the Meadow | 229 |
| Paper is two kinds; to write on, to wrap with. | Paper I | 231 |
| Poets and pigs! | Poets and Pigs | 166 |
| Poor old Jonathan Bing | Jonathan Bing | 100 |
| Since I can't tell a book by its cover, | Book Search | 200 |
| Sister says it's just a button, | One-Eyed Teddy | 56 |
| Some days I just wish to sail out on the seas, | Wishful Thinking | 64 |
| Some poems are written | Poet Unknown | 233 |
| The black cat yawns, | Cat | 32 |
| The eensy weensy spider | Eensy Weensy Spider | 208 |
| The family of the sun, the family of the sun, | Family of the Sun, The | 114 |
| The fog comes | Fog | 116 |
| The gasoline goes into my car. | Glug! Gurgle! Glug! | 156 |
| The Goops they lick their fingers, | Goops (Table Manners) | 96 |
| The little boy stopped in the middle of the hayfield | Railroad Reverie | 168 |
| The moon is very, very old. | Old Man Moon | 227 |
| The mud monster | Mud Monster | 76 |
| The panther is like a leopard, | Panther, The | 230 |
| The Rudes don't know or even care | Rudes | 108 |
| The sleepy tiger in the zoo | Sleepy Tiger | 44 |

| FIRST LINE | POEM | PAGE |
|---|---|---|
| There is one word | My Favorite Word | 164 |
| There once was a little bunny rabbit | Bunny Rabbit's Predicament | 30 |
| There was a young laddie from France | Antsy Pants | 197 |
| There was an old lady | Poor Old Lady | 234 |
| There's a hole in my bucket, dear Liza | There's a Hole in My Bucket | 242 |
| There's nothing much to it . . . | Me Key, The | 221 |
| Thirty days are in September, | Calendar Rhyme | 138 |
| This morning I jumped on my horse | True Story | 24 |
| Tick tick tick tick tick tick tick | Toaster Time | 246 |
| Trees are the kindest things I know, | Trees | 130 |
| Two arms for reaching | Things in Twos | 243 |
| Unclean and unbuckled, | Me a Mess? | 74 |
| Until today I never knew | Adding 1 | 195 |
| Way down South | Way Down South | 249 |
| We can shut up a box, | Shut Up | 236 |
| We have five seat belts in our car. | One for Me | 228 |
| Well, I saw the thing | Purple People Eater | 22 |
| What's the good of breathing | Frost Pane, The | 118 |
| Wheels, wheels, wheels, | Wheels Wheels Everywhere | 251 |
| When crossing the street, | Statue on the Curb | 86 |
| When I climb up | Drinking Fountain | 68 |
| When I'm feeling lonely | Stealing Feelings | 60 |
| When icicles hang by the wall, | When Icicles Hang by the Wall | 132 |
| When it's hot | Summer | 239 |
| When telling a story of my friend and me, | No Pronoun Problems | 226 |
| Where's my seat belt? | Where's My Seat Belt? | 252 |
| Who is this tiny, little mouse | Who is This Mouse? | 253 |
| Whose is that funny, stringbean face | Whose Face? | 88 |
| Why don't bubbles ever last? | Bubbles Popping | 12 |
| Yellow butter purple jelly red jam black bread | Yellow Butter | 170 |
| You buy a hamster | Hamster | 210 |
| You know the Sunday paper, | Solo Sunday | 58 |
| You've heard of seat belts | I'll Always Wear You | 213 |
| Zero's the number we say when there's one; | Countdown to Recess | 140 |
| Zero, one, two, three, four, five, | Counting to 12 | 205 |

# Index - Title

| POEM | POET | PAGE |
|---|---|---|
| Adding | Hajdusiewicz, Babs Bell | 194 |
| Adding 1 | Hajdusiewicz, Babs Bell | 195 |
| Adding 2 | Hajdusiewicz, Babs Bell | 196 |
| Adventures of Isabel | Nash, Ogden | 10 |
| Alas! | Hajdusiewicz, Babs Bell | 92 |
| Antsy Pants | McKenzie, R. Gene | 197 |
| Arithmetic Pie | Hajdusiewicz, Babs Bell | 136 |
| Bad and Good | Resnikoff, Alexander | 154 |
| Bed in Summer | Stevenson, Robert Louis | 48 |
| Beehive | Anonymous | 198 |
| Bill and Jim and Joe and Zack | Hajdusiewicz, Babs Bell | 199 |
| Bird Carpenter | Jacobs, Leland B | 28 |
| Book Search | Hajdusiewicz, Babs Bell | 200 |
| Bubble Gum | Payne, Nina | 201 |
| Bubbles | Hajdusiewicz, Babs Bell | 202 |
| Bubbles Popping | Vitello, Deborah | 12 |
| Bunny Rabbit's Predicament | Hajdusiewicz, Babs Bell | 30 |
| Calendar Rhyme | Hajdusiewicz, Babs Bell | 138 |
| Cat | Miller, Mary Britton | 32 |
| Choices | Hajdusiewicz, Babs Bell | 203 |
| Circles | Hajdusiewicz, Babs Bell | 204 |
| Countdown to Recess | Hajdusiewicz, Babs Bell | 140 |
| Counting to 12 | Hajdusiewicz, Babs Bell | 205 |
| Crunchin' Luncheon | LaFiamma, Heidi | 206 |
| Cycles | Schaum, John | 142 |
| Dandelion | Conkling, Hilda | 112 |
| Dark House, The | Anonymous | 14 |
| Dinosaur Bones | Marvin, Jean H. | 207 |
| Drinking Fountain | Chute, Marchette | 68 |
| Eensy Weensy Spider | Anonymous | 208 |
| Eletelephony | Richards, Laura | 34 |
| Extraordinary Me | Hajdusiewicz, Babs Bell | 70 |
| Family of the Sun, The | Anonymous | 114 |
| Fog | Sandburg, Carl | 116 |
| Fourteen Cats | Murphy, Eileen Ellen | 36 |
| Fractions Take the Cake | LaFiamma, Heidi | 209 |
| From Mars to Safety | Hajdusiewicz, Babs Bell | 94 |

| POEM | POET | PAGE |
|---|---|---|
| Frost Pane, The | McCord, David | 118 |
| Glug! Gurgle! Glug! | Hajdusiewicz, Babs Bell | 156 |
| Goops (Table Manners) | Burgess, Gelett | 96 |
| Hairy Toe | Anonymous | 16 |
| Hamster | Hajdusiewicz, Alison | 210 |
| Have You Ever Seen? | Anonymous | 158 |
| Have You Seen Edgar? | Morningstar, Teresa Lynn | 120 |
| Hey, Bug! | Moore, Lilian | 98 |
| Hungry Mungry | Silverstein, Shel | 18 |
| I and My Echo | Anonymous | 211 |
| I Had a Little Pig | Anonymous | 212 |
| I'll Always Wear You | Hajdusiewicz, Babs Bell | 213 |
| I've Figured It Out | Hajdusiewicz, Babs Bell | 144 |
| I, Myself, and Me | Hajdusiewicz, Babs Bell | 72 |
| If All The Seas | Anonymous | 146 |
| If All the World Were Paper | Anonymous | 214 |
| If Humpty Dumpty Had a Great Fall | Hajdusiewicz, Babs Bell | 215 |
| If the Spider Could Talk | Hajdusiewicz, Babs Bell | 38 |
| If You Should Meet a Crocodile | Anonymous | 40 |
| In and Out | Hajdusiewicz, Babs Bell | 160 |
| Index | Hajdusiewicz, Babs Bell | 216 |
| It's Not Fair! | Hajdusiewicz, Babs Bell | 50 |
| Jack and Jill | Anonymous | 217 |
| Jelly on the Plate | Anonymous | 218 |
| Jonathan Bing | Beatrice Curtis Brown | 100 |
| Just Like Me | Anonymous | 219 |
| Keep a Poem in Your Pocket | De Regniers, Beatrice Schenk | 162 |
| Last Word of a Bluebird | Frost, Robert | 122 |
| Lining Up | Hajdusiewicz, Babs Bell | 148 |
| Maybe Dats Youwr Pwoblem Too | Hall, Jim | 220 |
| Me a Mess? | Hajdusiewicz, Babs Bell | 74 |
| Me Key, The | Malaker, Biji Surber | 221 |
| Measurement Logic | Hajdusiewicz, Babs Bell | 222 |
| Moochie | Greenfield, Eloise | 102 |
| Mother Doesn't Want a Dog | Viorst, Judith | 42 |

| POEM | POET | PAGE |
|------|------|------|
| Mother Hubbard's Surprise | Hajdusiewicz, Babs Bell | 223 |
| Mr. Bear | Hajdusiewicz, Babs Bell | 20 |
| Mud Monster | Kinne, Bonnie | 76 |
| Mumps | Roberts, Elizabeth Madox | 52 |
| My Favorite Word | Hymes, Lucia and James L. | 174 |
| My Loose Tooth | Kanarek, Ruth | 78 |
| My Organs | Hajdusiewicz, Babs Bell | 224 |
| My Turn to Talk | Hajdusiewicz, Babs Bell | 54 |
| Nancy Hanks | Benét, Stephen Vincent and Rosemary Carr | 104 |
| No Pronoun Problems | Hajdusiewicz, Babs Bell | 226 |
| None | Hajdusiewicz, Babs Bell | 225 |
| Old Grumbler | Brand, Oscar | 106 |
| Old Man Moon | Fisher, Aileen | 227 |
| Old Noah's Ark | Anonymous | 150 |
| One for Me | Hajdusiewicz, Babs Bell | 228 |
| One-Eyed Teddy | Hoeft, Robert D. | 56 |
| Over in the Meadow | Anonymous | 229 |
| Panther, The | Nash, Ogden | 230 |
| Paper I | Sandburg, Carl | 231 |
| Pasture, The | Frost, Robert | 124 |
| Pete and Repeat | Anonymous | 232 |
| Poet Says, The | Hajdusiewicz, Babs Bell | 80 |
| Poet Unknown | Hajdusiewicz, Babs Bell | 233 |
| Poets and Pigs | Schaum, John | 166 |
| Poor Old Lady | Anonymous | 234 |
| Purple People Eater | Wooley, Sheb | 22 |
| Railroad Reverie | Young, E. R. | 168 |
| Rudes | Hajdusiewicz, Babs Bell | 108 |
| Sad Bedtime | Hajdusiewicz, Babs Bell | 235 |
| Secret Place, The | dePaola, Tomie | 82 |
| Shut Up | Hajdusiewicz, Babs Bell | 236 |
| Silly Sleep Sheep | Smith, Helen C. | 84 |
| Silly Trees | Hajdusiewicz, Babs Bell | 126 |
| Sleepy Tiger | Hajdusiewicz, Babs Bell | 44 |
| Solo Sunday | Hajdusiewicz, Babs Bell | 58 |
| Song of the Witches | Shakespeare, William | 237 |
| Statue on the Curb | Hajdusiewicz, Babs Bell | 86 |

| POEM | POET | PAGE |
|------|------|------|
| Stealing Feelings | Hajdusiewicz, Babs Bell | 60 |
| String to Remember, A | Hajdusiewicz, Babs Bell | 238 |
| Summer | Asch, Frank | 239 |
| Table of Contents | Hajdusiewicz, Babs Bell | 240 |
| Tall and Small | Anonymous | 241 |
| There's a Hole in the Bucket | Anonymous | 242 |
| Things in Twos | Hajdusiewicz, Babs Bell | 243 |
| This Tooth | Hopkins, Lee Bennett | 244 |
| Tiger | Hoberman, Mary Ann | 245 |
| To Be or Not To Be | Anonymous | 62 |
| Toaster Time | Merriam, Eve | 246 |
| Tommy | Brooks, Gwendolyn | 128 |
| Toot! Toot! | Anonymous | 247 |
| Trees | Behn, Harry | 130 |
| True Story | Silverstein, Shel | 24 |
| Trunk Skunk Stunk | Hajdusiewicz, Babs Bell | 248 |
| Way Down South | Anonymous | 249 |
| What Coin Do I Have? | Hajdusiewicz, Babs Bell | 250 |
| Wheels Wheels Everywhere | Hajdusiewicz, Babs Bell | 251 |
| When Icicles Hang by the Wall | Shakespeare, William | 132 |
| Where's My Seat Belt? | Hajdusiewicz, Babs Bell | 252 |
| Who is This Mouse? | Hajdusiewicz, Babs Bell | 253 |
| Who to Pet and Who Not to | Kennedy, X. J. | 254 |
| Whose Face? | Lonny Alexander | 88 |
| Wishful Thinking | Segall, Pearl Bloch | 64 |
| Yellow Butter | Hoberman, Mary Ann | 170 |
| Yummy Humpty Dumpty | Anonymous | 172 |
| Zero | Hajdusiewicz, Babs Bell | 255 |

# Index - Curriculum Connections

### THE PAGE NUMBERS INDICATE WHERE ACTIVITIES RELATED TO VARIOUS PARTS OF THE CURRICULUM ARE LOCATED

## Art

| | |
|---|---|
| Capturing Facial Expressions | 20 |
| Categorizing Clothing | 20 |
| Colors | |
| Blowing Bubbles | 12 |
| Thinking about Colors of Food | 170 |
| Comparing Illustrations | 10, 34, 116 |
| Creating a Cartoon | 22 |
| Creating a Model of the Solar System | 114 |
| Demonstrating Word Meanings | 56 |
| Drawing Events in Sequence | 156 |
| Enjoying Other Artistic Expression | 132 |
| Expanding the Poem | 102 |
| Exploring Bubble Shapes | 12 |
| Illustrating the Poem | 10, 158, 168 |
| Illustrating to Show Sequence | 144 |
| Learning about Statues | 86 |
| Looking at Fine Art | 162 |
| Making a Made-for-TV Movie | 14 |
| Making Arithmetic Pizza | 136 |
| Making Mobiles | |
| Giving Examples of Other Prefixes | 74 |
| Making Sound Mobiles | 36 |
| Making Murals | |
| Creating a Mural | 122 |
| Relating the Poem to Social Studies | 126 |
| Making Puppets | |
| Dramatizing the Poem | 44, 84 |
| Making Signs and Posters | |
| Looking for Safety Signs | 86 |
| Using Special Cues When Reading and Writing | 16 |
| Making Snowflakes | 120 |
| Making Spiders | 38 |
| Mapping Locations | 18 |
| Naming Opposites | 96 |
| Observing Shapes | |
| Exploring Bubble Shapes | 12 |
| Noticing Shapes and Patterns | 44 |
| Painting in the Impressionist Style | 112 |
| Painting Word Pictures | 130 |
| Picturing Poems | 162 |
| Rereading to Create in Detail | 70 |
| Sorting Out Feelings | 54 |
| Using Imagery to Create | 74 |

## Health and Safety

| | |
|---|---|
| Analyzing the Poem | 40 |
| Becoming Safety Conscious | 92 |
| Building Background | 52 |
| Clothing | |
| Categorizing Clothing | 20 |
| Linking Uniforms to Occupations | 100 |
| Conducting a Survey, | 52 |
| Discovering the Truth about Losing Teeth | 78 |
| Enjoying a Related Poem | 44, 154 |
| Enjoying More Poetry | 92 |

## Feelings

| | |
|---|---|
| Being "Glad I'm Me" | 126 |
| Conducting an Experiment in Perception | 68 |
| Discussing Peer Pressure | 108 |
| Dramatizing to Talk about Feelings | 120 |
| Enjoying Other Poetry | 98 |
| Exploring Self Image | 88 |
| Identifying Feelings | 62 |
| Personalizing the Poem | 70 |
| Relating the Poem to Other Literature | 68 |
| Responding to the Poem | 68 |
| Sharing Common Experiences | 68 |
| Sharing Fears | 38 |
| Sharing Feelings | 48, 72, 84 |
| Sorting Out Feelings | 54 |
| Talking about Feelings | 10, 124 |
| Talking and Writing about Feelings | 52 |
| Thinking about Cause and Effect | 62 |
| Writing about Feelings | 146 |
| Writing about Friendship | 68 |
| Food | |
| Cooking | |
| Cooking and Eating | 172 |
| Cooking with Fractions | 136 |
| Having a Choral Reading | 170 |
| Making Yellow Butter | 170 |
| Talking about Breakfast | 172 |
| Thinking about Colors of Food | 170 |
| Thinking about Eggs | 172 |
| Interviewing Others | 52 |
| Learning from the Poem | 74 |
| Looking for Safety Signs | 86 |
| Manners | |
| Analyzing Rude Behavior | 108 |
| Categorizing Behaviors | 96, 154 |
| Creating a Book | 96 |
| Naming Opposites | 96 |
| Thinking about Behaviors | 154 |
| Thinking Seriously | 154 |
| Meeting a Traffic-Safety Expert | 86 |
| Relating to Other Literature | 74 |
| Surveying Hiccup Cures | 102 |

## Language Arts

### Listening

| | |
|---|---|
| Enjoying a Poem with a New Twist | 92 |
| Enjoying Suspense | 14 |
| Expanding Vocabulary | 86 |
| Identifying the Problem | 58 |
| Identifying Words for Sounds | 94, 156 |
| Listening Critically | 24 |
| Listening for Enjoyment | 132 |
| Listening for Numbers | 142 |
| Listening for Rhyming Words | 166 |
| Listening for Specific Information | 14 |
| Listening Purposefully | 38 |
| Listening to Recall Information | 96 |
| Thinking about Sounds | 156 |

## Reading

| | |
|---|---|
| Adjectives | |
| Using Adjectives | 100 |
| Using Synonyms to Describe | 144 |
| Writing with Adjectives | 88 |
| Antonyms | |
| Exploring Antonyms | 74 |
| Identifying Words for Opposites | 154 |
| Naming Opposites | 96 |
| Rewriting to Say the Opposite | 60 |
| Thinking about Words with Opposite Meanings | 60 |
| Building Sight Vocabulary | 14 |
| Capitalization and Punctuation | |
| Discussing and Using Hyphenated Words | 118 |
| Talking about Questions | 164 |
| Using Asking Sentences | 104 |
| Using Commas | 14 |
| Using Context to Gain Meaning | 160 |
| Using Parentheses | 144 |
| Using Quotations | 164 |
| Using Special Cues When Reading and Writing | 16 |
| Cloze | |
| Completing the Lines | 56 |
| Reciting with the Teacher | 74 |
| Comprehension | |
| Examining Mood | 22 |
| Exploring the Meaning | 12 |
| Identifying Feelings | 60 |
| Identifying with the Characters | 36 |
| Sequencing | 18, 32 |
| Using Figures of Speech | 54 |
| Using Language Literally and Figuratively | 52 |
| Contractions | |
| Looking at Contractions | 12 |
| Recognizing and Using Contractions | 68 |
| Using Contractions | 48, 126 |
| Decoding | |
| Alliteration | |
| Exploring Alliteration | 162 |
| Talking to Write | 58 |
| Using Alliteration | 84 |
| Compound Words | |
| Examining Compound Words | 88 |
| Using Position Words and Compound Words | 156 |
| Letter Sounds | |
| Analyzing Words (aw) | 32 |
| Identifying Letters and their Sounds | 166 |
| Making Sound Mobiles | 36 |
| Recognizing Initial Consonant Blends | 68 |
| Recognizing Letters and Sounds | 170 |
| Recognizing Spellings of a Sound | 60 |
| Writing a Poem . . . and a Song (final y as long e) | 76 |

Prefixes and Suffixes
  Decoding Words 142
  Expanding Vocabulary 74
  Giving Examples of Other Prefixes 74
  Reciting with the Teacher 74
  Recognizing Letters and Sounds 170
  Using Position Words and
    Compound Words 156
  Using Suffixes to Make
    Comparisons 144
Syllabication
  Enjoying Related Literature 118
  Extending the Poem 150
  Using the Poet's Model 34
Figurative Language
  Literal and Figurative Expressions 78
  Thinking Critically 172
  Understanding Figures of Speech 70
  Understanding the Use of Slang 62
  Using Figurative Language 104
  Using Language Literally and
    Figuratively 48
  Using Other Resources 62
Holding a Fast Reading Contest 160
Homonyms and Homographs
  Comparing the Poem to Other
    Literature 158
  Using Homographs 28
  Writing with Homonyms 158
Literature
  Comparing Poems 38
  Comparing the Poem to Other Literature
    10, 30, 56, 84, 86, 100, 104, 106, 128, 158
  Discussing Related Poems 60
  Enjoying Other Literature 38, 108
  Finding Other Non-Rhyming Poems 58
  Finding Other Poems by Anonymous
    Poets 40
  Learning about the Poet 122
  Nursery Rhymes
    Comparing Poems 38
    Counting to Twelve 140
    Enjoying a Poem with a New Twist 92
    Enjoying Other Poetry 98
    Enjoying Other Related Poems 140
    Exploring Alliteration 162
    Reading Aloud 172
    Singing the Poem's Words 114
    Studying the Poem's Structure 144
    Thinking about Wheels 142
    Using New Words 124
    Writing Parodies 172
  Personalizing the Poem 68
  Reading More by and about the Author 24
  Reading Other Works by Judith Viorst 42
  Reading Related Books 24, 132
  Relating the Poem to Other
    Literature 44, 64, 102, 130, 150
  Responding to the Poem 120
  Talking about Famous Crocodiles 40
Onomatopoeia
  Creating New Words 94

Identifying Words for Sounds 94, 156
Recognizing Onomotopoeia 168
Parodies
  Comparing Poem Versions 172
  Enjoying a Poem with a New Twist 92
  Identifying Humor 92
  Thinking to Write 92
Personification
  Understanding Personification 130
  Using Personification 120
Poem Structure
  Analyzing the Poem's Form 44
  Appreciating the Poem's Structure 60
  Identifying Couplets 12
  Learning How to Identify a Rhyming
    Pattern 108
  Narrative
    Dramatizing the Story 160
    Viewing a Poem as a Story 20
  Observing the Structure of the Poem 82
  Studying the Poem's Structure 144
Reading Rate
  Holding a Fast Reading Contest 160
  Locating Rhyming Words (scanning) 108
Remembering
  Making a List 100
  Remembering Lines 128
  Remembering the Planets in Order 114
  Using a Mnemonic Device 138
  Using Pronouns 72
Rhyming Words
  Analyzing Rhyming Words in Context 20
  Discovering Internal Rhyme 36
  Enjoying Related Poems 170
  Enjoying Rhyme 122
  Extending the Poem 150
  Finding Other Non-Rhyming Poems 58
  Identifying Couplets 12
  Identifying Rhyming Words 70
  Introducing the Poem 130
  Learning How to Identify a Rhyming
    Pattern 108
  Listening for Rhyming Words 166
  Locating Rhyming Words 108
  Making Sound Mobiles 36
  Playing a Rhyming Game 36
  Recognizing Rhyming Words 20
  Thinking with the Poet 24
  Writing Couplets 12
Spelling
  Decoding Words 142
  Fun with Order in Words: Palindromes 148
  Identifying Rhyming Words 70
  Making Sound Mobiles 36
  Noticing a Word's Spelling 154
  Playing with Words 160
  Recognizing Spellings of a Sound 60
  Understanding the Use of Slang 62
Synonyms
  Finding Synonyms 164
  Giving Meaning to Words 40
  Learning the Meaning of Words 36

Sorting Out Feelings 54
Using Synonyms to Describe 144
Using Metaphors 86, 112, 126
Using Pronouns 72
Using the Context
  Comparing Poems about Strange
    Creatures 22
  Examining Mood 22
  Exploring Word Meanings 106
  Listening Critically 24
  Listening for Enjoyment 132
  Making Inferences 106
  Using Context to Gain Meaning 160
Verbs
  Exploring the Power of Colorful Verbs 32
  Exploring Word Meanings 106
  Understanding Personification 16
  Using Colorful Words 18
Vocabulary
  Conducting an Experiment in Perception 68
  Demonstrating Word Meanings 56
  Dictionary Use
    Creating New Words 94
    Giving Meaning to Words 40
    Learning the Meaning of Words 36
    Using the Dictionary 92, 126
  Examining Mood 22
  Expanding Vocabulary 74, 86, 100, 128
  Exploring Word Meanings 106
  Learning Scientific Names 112
  Listening for Specific Information
    (number words) 14
  Making Words and Ideas Meaningful 126
  Multiple-Meaning Words
    Introducing the Poem 166
    Using Words with Multiple Meanings 166
  Using Words Meaningfully 10, 30
Writing the Way People Talk 22

Speaking

Adding Details 124
Choral Reading
  Enjoying the Poem 62
  Giving a Choral Reading 50
  Giving a Dramatic Reading 28
  Having a Choral Reading 172
  Memorizing Lines 128
  Reading and Reciting 78
  Reciting with the Teacher 74
  Tracking the Words 166
Cloze
  Categorizing Behaviors 96
  Completing the Lines 56
  Dramatizing the Poem 102
  Enjoying the Poem 100
  Introducing the Poem 130
Debating
  Comparing Poems about Strange
    Creatures 22
  Considering Pros and Cons 144
Discussing the Details 82

Dramatizing    14, 16, 18, 30, 32, 44, 84, 86, 100, 102, 120, 128, 148, 150, 156, 160, 162

Acting Out One-to-One Correspondence  28
Acting Out the Poem  122, 126
Capturing Facial Expressions  20
Enjoying Dramatic Nonsense  154
Fingerplay
  Dramatizing the Poem  22
  Enjoying Other Poetry  98
Pantomiming
  Dramatizing  20
  Dramatizing the Poem  94
  Exploring Antonyms  74
Recording the Poem  168
Singing It Out; Acting It Out  106
Staging a Skit  136
Staging Tableaux Vivants  24
Using New Words  124
Using Props to Act Out the Poem  72
Expanding the Idea of Communication  122
Experimenting with Sound  168
Giving Oral Reports  42
Holding a Poetry Reading  80
Interviewing
  Conducting a Yes/No Survey  164
  Gathering Oral History  78
  Interviewing Others  52
Learning about the Author  132
Personalizing the Poem  102
Playing "What Am I?"  128
Putting on a Teddy Bear Fair  56
Recording
  Giving a Dramatic Reading  70
  Recording the Poem  168
  Remembering Rock 'n Roll  22
  Tape Recording the Poem  86
Sharing Personal Experiences  42
Singing (see Music)
Talking about Breakfast  172
Talking about Talking  34
Telling a Story
  Imagining the Action  122
  Paraphrasing the Poem  160
  Telling a Circle Story  158
  Telling the Story in Sequence  106
  Telling the Story of the Poem  168
  Thinking Critically  94
Tongue Twisters
Exploring Alliteration  162
Using Alliteration  84
Turning Statements into Questions  164

## Thinking

Analyzing Characters  10
Analyzing the Poem  40
Appreciating Brevity  116
Be Inventive  68
Becoming Safety Conscious  92
Cause and Effect
  Identifying Cause and Effect  106
  Thinking about Cause and Effect  30, 60

Comparing and Contrasting
  Comparing Characters  76
  Comparing and Contrasting as a Detail  10
  Comparing Poem Versions  172
  Comparing Poems  162
  Comparing the Poem to Other Literature  100
  Enjoying Related Poems  96
  Singing the Words  166
  Using Suffixes to Make Comparisons  144
Considering Point of View  98
Decision Making
  Considering Pros and Cons  144
  Introducing the Poem  72
  Making Decisions  62
  Examining Motivation  98
  Experimenting with Motion  92
  Figuring It Out  146
  Identifying Humor  84, 92
  Identifying Silly and Serious Ideas  126
  Identifying with the Character  146, 164
  Making a List  100
  Making Inferences  56, 102, 106, 136
  Personalizing the Poem  54
  Reading for Details  76
Real and Make Believe
  Identifying Real and Make Believe  20
  Talking about Dreams  94
Recognizing Different Interpretations  72
Relating Poetic Images to the Actual Object  112
Relating to the Poem  76
Responding to an Opinion  48
Responding to the Poem  50
Sequencing (see Social Studies)
Sorting out an Issue  50
Stating and Supporting an Opinion  50
Talking about and Writing Opinions  118
Talking about Dreams  94
Talking about Predicaments  30
Thinking about Paper  80
Thinking Critically  80, 94, 172
Thinking Critically to Write  42
Thinking Seriously  154
Thinking to Prevent  54
Thinking to Write  92
Understanding Personification  16
Viewing Things from Another Perspective  44
Weighing the Problem  58
Writing a New Ending  100

## Writing

Analyzing Rude Behavior  108
Capitalization and Punctuation (see Reading)
Conducting a Survey  52
Describing
  Using Synonyms to Describe  144
  Writing to Describe  74
  Writing with Adjectives  88

Encoding (See Spelling)
Experimenting with Sound  168
Exploring and Creating a Newspaper  58
Extending Text
  Expanding on the Theme  88
  Extending the Ideas  12
  Extending the Poem  150
  Writing a New Ending  16, 100
Having a Reason to Write  80
Innovating on Text
  Creating a New Metaphor  112
  Extending the Poem  80
  Innovating on the Text  14
  Parodies
    Thinking to Write  92
    Writing Parodies  172
  Thinking of Pets Mother Definitely Doesn't Want  42
  Using Analogies to Innovate on Text  156
  Using Metaphors  88
  Using the Poet's Model  34
  Writing Couplets  12
  Writing Tall Tales  24
Letter Writing
  Meeting a Traffic-Safety Expert  86
  Writing a Letter  104
Making a List/Sharing Solutions  58
Making an Outline  114
Making Books
  Categorizing Behaviors  154
  Creating a Book  96
  Making a Walking Book  98
  Thinking about Wheels  142
  Writing Creatively  164
Mimicking the Style of the Poem  50
Revising
  Listing, Writing, and Revising  172
  Rewriting  116
  Rewriting and Revising  154
  Rewriting to Say the Opposite  60
Speech Bubbles
  Capturing Facial Expressions  20
  Illustrating the Poem  10
Making Cartoons  108
Spelling
Talking about and Writing Opinions  118
Talking about Writing by Children  112
Talking and Writing about Feelings  48
Thinking Critically to Write  42
Using Alliteration
  Talking to Write  58
  Writing Examples of Alliteration  124
Using Commas  14
Using Quotation Marks  164
Writing a Sequence of Events  76
Writing about Friendship  64
Writing about Trees  130
Writing Poems
  Being "Glad I'm Me"  126
  Considering Point of View  98
  Creating a New Mataphor  112
  Recognizing Onomotopoeia  168
  Using Knowledge to Write and Illustrate  126

Writing a Poem . . . and a Song 76
Writing Verses 40
Writing with a Partner 104
Writing Reasons and Opinions
  Exploring the Meaning 12
  Responding to an Opinion 48
  Stating and Supporting an Opinion 50, 58
Writing Stories
  Comparing the Poem to
    Other Literature 106
  Expanding a Line into a Story 158
  Learning About Statues 86
  Paraphrasing the Poem 160
  Stretching the Imagination by Writing 150
  Using Special Cues When Reading
    and Writing 16
  Viewing a Poem as a Story 20
  Writing about Feelings 146
  Writing about Losing Teeth 78
  Writing Tall Tales 24
Writing the Way People Talk 22
Writing with Homonyms 158
Writing Without Paper 108

# Math

Adding
  Enjoying Other Related Poems 140
  Recognizing Counting as Adding 9, 140
Charts, Graphs, and Diagrams
  Making a Bar Graph 118
  Making Diagrams and Charts 114
  Using Another Meaning of "Cycles" 142
Counting
  Acting Out One-To-One
    Correspondence 36
  Appreciating Brevity 116
  Counting Objects 140
  Counting to Twelve 140
  Identifying "All the Rest" 138
  Making Number Comparisons 38
  Recognizing Counting as Adding 1 140
Fractions
  Cooking with Fractions 136
  Exploring the Principles of the Whole
    and Its Parts 56
  Identifying and Comparing Fractional
    Parts 136
  Making Arithmetic Pizza 136
  Making Inferences 136
  Using Fractions 56, 136
Grouping
  Arranging and Rearranging by Numbers 150
  Extending the Poem 150
  Relating to Math 150
Measurement
  Making Size Comparisons 14
  Measuring for Size Relationships 146
  Weighing the Problem 58
Money
  Enjoying Other Related Poems 140
  Gathering Oral History 78

Numbers and Number Words
  Experimenting with Motion (tallying) 92
  Introducing the Poem 140
  Listening for Numbers 142
  Making Number Comparisons 48
  Telling the Story in Sequence 106
  Using Numbers 70
Ordinal Numbers
  Introducing and Dramatizing the Poem 148
  Recognizing Ordinal Number Words 148
  Writing about Feelings 148
Shapes
  Exploring Bubble Shapes 12
  Noticing Shapes and Patterns 44
  Studying Shapes 70
  Thinking about Wheels 142
Time
  Discussing Leap Years 138
  Exploring Seasonal Changes 48
  Identifying "All the Rest" 138
  Introducing the Poem 138
  Placing the Poem in Time 48, 100
  Using a Clock 48

# Music

Acting Out One-to-One Correspondence 36
Counting to Twelve 140
Enjoying Other Artistic Expression 132
Enjoying Other Related Poems 140
Looking at Fine Art 162
Singing It Out; Acting It Out 106
Singing the Poem 22, 114, 116, 140, 166
Staging a Musical 114
Studying the Poem's Structure 144
Thinking about Wheels 142

# Science

Animals
  Classifying Animals 150
  Classifying Cats 32
  Discussing Talking Birds 122
  Doing Research 40
  Doing Research about Animals 50
  Dramatizing the Poem 150
  Enjoying a Related Poem 44
  Examining Motivation 98
  Exploring Animal Ownership 146
  Finding Out More about Birds 122
  Giving Oral Reports 42
  Learning about Dinosaurs 146
  Learning about Instincts 160
  Learning about Spiders 38
  Measuring for Size Relationships 146
  Talking about Seasonal Changes and
    Animals' Responses 122
  Thinking about Eggs 172
  Viewing Animals as Workers 28
Appreciating Our Earth 114

Experiments
  Blowing Bubbles 12
  Conducting an Experiment in Perception 68
  Conducting and Recording an
    Experiment 118
  Experimenting with Motion 92
  Experimenting with Sound 168
  Experimenting with Suction 76
  Exploring Relativity and Perspective 146
  Learning about Snow 120
  Making Butter 162
  Performing an Experiment 30, 116
  Recording Observations 126
Learning Scientific Names 112
Space
  Creating a Model of the Solar System 114
  Learning about a Planet 94
  Making an Outline 114
  Making Diagrams and Charts 114
  Remembering the Planets in Order 114
Thinking about Sounds 156
Trees and Plants
  Categorizing Trees 126
  Comparing the Poem to Other
    Literature 128
  Creating a Mural 128
  Examining Real Trees 130
  Listing Products That Come From
    Trees 130
  Planting Seeds 128
  Playing "What Am I?" 128
  Relating the Poem to Other Literature 130
Weather and Seasons
  Exploring Seasonal Changes 48
  Learning about Snow 120
  Naming Summer and Winter Activities 118
  Talking about and Writing Opinions 118
  Talking about Seasonal Changes and
    Animals' Responses 122
  Understanding Personification 16
  Using Comparison/Creative Writing 116

# Social Studies

Career Education
  Extending the Poem 80
  Identifying Tools and Their Uses 28
  Learning about a Carpenter's Work 28
  Linking Uniforms to Occupations 100
  Singing the Poem 22
  Thinking of Other Occupations and
    Their Tools 28
Critical Thinking (see Language
  Arts, Thinking)
Feelings (see Health and Safety)
Learning about Statues 86
Maps and Globes
  Mapping Locations 18
  Thinking about Cooperative Efforts 144
  Using Directions 70
  Using the Globe 144
Placing the Poem in Time 48, 100

Real and Make-Believe (see Language
Arts, Thinking)
Relating the Poem to History     104
Relating the Poem to Social Studies     116
Sequencing
    Drawing Events in Sequence     156
    Illustrating to Show Sequence     144
    Recognizing Ordinal Number Words     148
    Sequencing (addresses)     18
    Telling the Story in Sequence     106
Transportation
    Becoming Safety Conscious     92
    Placing the Poem in Time     100
    Thinking about Wheels     142
    Using the Dictionary     92

# Modeling Opportunities

Identifying Real and Make-Believe (using
quotations)     20
Making Decisions     62
Reading Aloud
    Dramatizing     20
    Reading Dramatically     98
    Using Special Cues When Reading and
    Writing     16
Telling Stories
    Talking about Predicaments     30
    Thinking Critically     172
Using Anthologies     34
Using Pronouns     62
Using Vocabulary
Personalizing the Poem     108
Using Figures of Speech     54
Using Literal and Figurative Expressions     78
Using Meaningful Words and Phrases     68
Using Words Meaningfully     10, 30
Writing
    Creating a New Metaphor     112
    Enjoying Related Poems     170
    Listing, Writing, and Revising     172
    Rewriting and Revising     154
    Rewriting to Say the Opposite     60
    Writing a Poem . . . and a Song     76

# Parental Involvement

Conducting a Yes/No Survey     164
Gathering Oral Information     78
Having a Reason to Write     78
Interviewing Others     52
Making Words and Ideas Meaningful     126
Measuring for Size Relationships     144
Recognizing Different Interpretations     70

# Index of Literature Connections

**The page numbers indicate where you can find the Literature Connections in the Idea Book.**

## Biographies

Bains, Rae. *Abraham Lincoln*. Mahwah, New Jersey: Troll Associates, 1985.  104

Faber, Doris. *Robert Frost, America's Poet*. Englewood Cliffs, New Jersey: Prentice Hall, 1964.  122

Lee, Susan Dye. *Abraham Lincoln*. Chicago: Children's Press, 1978.  104

Smith, Katie B. *Abraham Lincoln*. Englewood Cliffs, New Jersey: Jullian Messner, 1987  104

## Books

Alexander, Martha. *Nobody Asked Me If I Wanted a Baby Sister*. New York: Dial Books for Young Readers, 1971.  102

Allard, Harry and Marshall, James. *Miss Nelson Is Missing*! Boston: Houghton Mifflin Co., 1977.  108

Anno, Mitsumasa. *Anno's Peekaboo*. New York: The Putnam Publishing Group, 1988.  102

Barrie, James M. *Peter Pan*. New York: Charles Scribner's Sons, 1972.  40

Basil, Cynthia. *How Ships Play Cards: A Beginning Book of Homonyms*. New York: William Morrow and Co., Inc., 1980.  158

Basil, Cynthia. *Nailheads and Potato Eyes: A Beginning Word Book*. New York: William Morrow and Co., Inc., 1976.  158

Bentley, W. A. & Humphreys, W. J. *Snow Crystals*. New York: Dover Publications, Inc., 1931.  120

Birdseye, Tom *Airmail to the Moon*. New York: Holiday House, Inc., 1988.  78

Bourgeois, Paulette. *Franklin in the Dark*. New York: Scholastic, Inc., 1987.  84

Burton, Virginia L. *Katy and the Big Snow*. Boston: Houghton Mifflin Co., 1974.  120

Carr, Jan. *Felix the Cat*. New York: Scholastic, Inc., 1986.  32

Coates, Laura J. *The Oak Tree*. New York: Macmillan Publishing Co., Inc., 1987.  130

Craig, Helen. *The Night of the Paper Bag Monsters*. New York: Alfred A. Knopf, Inc., 1985.  64

Davis, Jim. *The Garfield Treasury*. New York: Ballantine Books, Inc., 1984.  32

Dr. Seuss. *The Cat in the Hat*. New York: Random House, Inc., 1987.  32

Dr. Seuss. *The Five Hundred Hats of Bartholomew Cubbins*. New York: Vanguard Press, Inc., 1938.  100

Edelman, Elaine. *I Love My Baby Sister (Most of the Time)*. New York: Penguin Books, Inc., 1984.  102

Freeman, Don. *Corduroy*. New York: Viking Penguin, Inc., 1968,  56

Goor, Ron and Nancy. *Signs*. New York: Thomas Y. Crowell Company, 1983.  86

Hall, Rich. *Sniglets (Snig' lit) — Any Word That Doesn't Appear in the Dictionary, but Should*. New York: Macmillan Publishing Co., Inc., 1984.  30

Hall, Rich. *More Sniglets: Any Word That Doesn't Appear in the Dictionary, but Should*. New York: Macmillan Publishing Co., Inc., 1985.  30

Hoban, Lillian. *Arthur's Loose Tooth*. New York: Harper and Row Junior Books Group, 1987.  78

Hoban, Russell. *A Baby Sister for Frances*. New York: Harper and Row Junior Books Group, 1976.  102

Hoban, Russell. *Best Friends for Frances*. New York: Harper and Row Junior Books Group, 1976.  64

Hoban, Tana. *Look Again!* New York: Macmillan Publishing Co., Inc., 1971.  102

Hoff, Syd. *Danny and the Dinosaur*. New York: Harper and Row Junior Books Group, 1978.  146

Janson, H. W. & Janson, D. J. *The Story of Painting for Young People, from Cave Painting to Modern Times*. New York: Harry N. Abrams, Inc., 1966.  132

Johnson, Crockett. *Harold and the Purple Crayon*. New York: Harper and Row Junior Books Group, 1981.  82

Johnson, Crockett. *A Picture for Harold's Room*. New York: Harper and Row Junior Books Group, 1960  82

Karlin, Nurit. *The Tooth Witch*. New York: Harper and Row Junior Books Group, 1985.  78

Keats, Ezra Jack. *The Snowy Day*. New York: Viking Penguin, Inc., 1962.  120

Kelider, D. *The Great Book of French Impressionism*. New York: Outlet Book Co., 1984.  132

Keller, Holly. *Ten Sleepy Sheep*. New York: Greenwillow Books, 1983.  84

Krauss, Ruth. *The Carrot Seed*. New York: Harper and Row Junior Books Group, 1945.  128

Lobel, Arnold. *Frog and Toad Are Friends*. New York: Harper and Row Junior Books Group, 1970.  64

Lobel, Arnold. *Frog and Toad Together*. New York: Harper & Row Junior Books Group, 1972.  128

MacLachlan, Patricia. *Sarah, Plain and Tall*. New York: Harper and Row Junior Books Group, 1987.  104

Marshall, James. *George and Martha*. Boston: Houghton Mifflin Company, 1972.  64

Minarik, Else H. *No Fighting, No Biting*! New York: Harper and Row Junior Books Group, 1958.  108

Munsch, Robert N. *Mud Puddle*. Toronto: Gage Educational Publishing Company, 1984.  76

Ormerod, Jan. *One Hundred One Things to Do with a Baby*. New York: Lothrop, Lee and Shepard Books. 1984.  102

Peterson, Roger Tory. *A Field Guide to the Birds: A Completely New Guide to All the Birds of Eastern and Central North America*. Boston Houghton Mifflin Company, 1980.  122

Pomerantz, Charlotte. *The Mango Tooth*. New York: Greenwillow Books, 1977.  78

Sharmat, Marjorie W. *Go to Sleep, Nicholas Joe*. New York: Harper and Row Junior Books Group, 1988.  48

Sharmat, Marjorie W. *Mooch the Messy*. New York: Harper and Row Junior Books Group, 1976.  74

Silverstein, Shel. *The Giving Tree*. New York: Harper and Row Junior Books Group, 1964.  130

Silverstein, Shel. *Lafcadio, the Lion Who Shot Back*. New York: Harper and Row Junior Books Group, 1963.  24

Stevenson, James. *No Friends*. New York: Greenwillow Books, 1986.  64

Stevenson, James. *We Can't Sleep*. New York: Greenwillow Books, 1982.  24

Terban, Marvin. *In a Pickle and other Funny Idioms*. New York: Ticknor and Fields, 1983.  62

Terban, Marvin. *Too Hot to Hoot: Funny Palindrome Riddles*. New York: Ticknor and Fields, 1985.  148

Viorst, Judith. *Alexander and the Terrible, Horrible, No Good, Very Bad Day*. New York: Atheneum, 1972.  42, 68

Viorst, Judith. *Try It Again, Sam; Safety When You Walk*. New York: Lothrop, Lee and Shepard Books, 1970.  86

Viorst, Judith. *I'll Fix Anthony*. New York: Macmillan Publishing Co., Inc., 1988.  42

Waber, Bernard. *Lyle, Lyle Crocodile*. Boston: Houghton Mifflin Company, 1973.  40

Weiss, Harvey. *Shelters: From Tepee to Igloo*. New York: Harper and Row Junior Books Group, 1988.  28

White, E. B. *Charlotte's Web*. New York: Harper and Row Junior Books Group, 1988.

Zolotow, Charlotte. *The Hating Book*. New York: Harper and Row Junior Books Group, 1969.  64

## Collections of Poetry

Burgess, Gelett. *Goops and How to Be Them*. New York: Dover Publications, Inc., 1968.  96

Burgess, Gelett. *More Goops and How Not to Be Them: A Manual of Manners for Impolite Infants*. New York: Dover Publications, Inc., 1968.  96

*Childcraft Volume 1: Poems and Rhymes.* Chicago: World Book, Inc., current edition. 34

Cole, Joanna. *A New Treasury of Children's Poetry*. New York: Doubleday and Co., Inc., 1984. 34

De Regniers, Beatrice Schenk, Eva Moore, Mary Michaels White, & Jan Carr. *Sing a Song of Popcorn*. New York: Scholastic, Inc., 1988. 10

Prelutsky, Jack. *The Random House Book of Poetry for Children*. New York: Random House, Inc., 1983. 10

Royds, Caroline. *Poems for Young Children*. New York: Doubleday and Co., Inc., 1986. 34

Viorst, Judith. *If I were in Charge of the World and Other Worries*. New York: Antheneum Children's Books, 1981. 42

## Magazines

*Highlights for Children*. Highlights for Children, Inc., Box 269, Columbus, Ohio 43272-0002. 112

Humpty Dumpty's Magazine. Benjamin Franklin Literary and Medical Society, Inc., Box 567, 1100 Waterway Blvd., Indianapolis, IN 46206. 86

*National Geographic World*. National Geographic Society, 17th and M Sts., N.W., Washington, DC 20036. 56

*Stone Soup*. Children's Art Foundation, Box 83, Santa Cruz, CA 95063. 112

## Nursery Rhymes

Lobel, Arnold. "Little Miss Muffet." *The Random House Book of Mother Goose*. New York: Random House, Inc., 1986. 38

Peppe, Rodney, Illus. *Humpty Dumpty*. New York: Viking Kestrel, 1976. 172

Stevens, Janet, illus. *The House That Jack Built: A Mother Goose Nursery Rhyme*. New York: Holiday House, Inc., 1985. 144

## Reference Books

*Guinness Book of World Records, 1989*. Ed. by David A. Boehm et al. New York: Sterling Publishing Co., Inc., 1988, 144

*World Almanac and Book of Facts, 1989*. Mark S. Hoffman. New York: Pharos Books, 1988. 144

## Stories & Folktales

Dasent, George W. "The Husband Who Was to Mind the House," *Popular Tales from the Norse: With an Introductory Essay on the Origin and Diffusion of Popular Tales*. Los Angeles, CA: Hoyt Rodney Gale, 1971. 106

de Paola, Tomie, illus. *David and Goliath.* San Francisco: Winston Press, Inc. 10

Galdone, Paul. *Jack and the Beanstalk*. New York: Ticknor & Fields, 1982. 32

Galdone, Paul. *Puss In Boots*. New York: Ticknor and Fields, 1976. 32

Keats, Ezra Jack. *John Henry: An American Legend*. New York: Alfred A. Knopf, Inc., 1987. 24

Kellogg, Steven. *Paul Bunyan*. New York: William Morrow and Company, Inc., ND. 16. 144

Rockwell, Anne. *The Emperor's New Clothes*. New York: Harper and Row Junior Books Group. 100

Sherlock, Philip M. *Anansi, the Spider Man: Jamaican Folk Tales*. New York: Thomas Y. Crowell Company, 1954. 44

Spier, Peter. *Noah's Ark*. New York: Doubleday and Co., Inc., 1981. 150

Steel, Flora A. "The Tiger, the Brahman and the Jackal," *Tales of the Punjab*. Lawrence, KS: A M S Publishing, ND. 44

# ACKNOWLEDGEMENTS

1. "Hey Bug!" reprinted with permission of Atheneum Publishers, an imprint of Macmillan Publishing Company, from I FEEL THE SAME WAY by Lilian Moore. Copyright © 1967 by Lilian Moore. 2. "Mother Doesn't Want a Dog" reprinted with permission of Atheneum Publishers, an imprint of Macmillan Publishing Company, from IF I WERE IN CHARGE OF THE WORLD AND OTHER WORRIES by Judith Viorst. Copyright © 1981 by Judith Viorst. 3. "Nancy Hanks" by Rosemary Carr Benet from A BOOK OF AMERICANS by Rosemary and Stephen Vincent Benet. Copyright © 1933 by Rosemary and Stephen Vincent Benet, © renewed 1961 by Rosemary Carr Benet. Reprinted by permission of Brandt & Brandt Literary Agents, Inc. 4. "Tommy" from BRONZEVILLE BOYS AND GIRLS by Gwendolyn Brooks. Copyright © 1956 by Gwendolyn Brooks. Reprinted by permission of the author. 5. "Drinking Fountain" From AROUND AND ABOUT by Marchette Chute. Copyright © 1957 by E.P. Dutton, Inc. Copyright renewed © 1985 by Marchette Chute. Reprinted by permission of the author. 6. "Cycles" Composer: John W. Schaum. Copyright © 1945 by Belwin, Inc. International copyright secured. Lithographed in the USA. From John W. Schaum's A, THE RED BOOK, EL00166, available from CPP/Belwin, Inc. at music stores for $5.00. 7. "Poets and Pigs" Composer: John W. Schaum. Copyright © 1945 by Belwin, Inc. International copyright secured. Lithographed in the USA. From John W. Schaum's PRE-A, THE GREEN BOOK, EL00165, available from CPP/Belwin, Inc., at music stores for $4.50. 8. "Whose Face?" From JOY, POEMS FOR CHILDREN by Mrs. Lonny Alexander. Copyright © 1976, 1988. Reprinted by permission of Gazelle Publications. 9. "One-Eyed Teddy" reprinted by permission of the author, Robert D. Hoeft. 10. "Mud Monster" Reprinted by permission of the author, Bonnie Kinne. 11. "Dandelion" from POEMS BY A LITTLE GIRL by Hilda Conkling, originally published by J.B. Lippincott. 12. "Have You Seen Edgar?" reprinted by permission of the author, Teresa Lynn Morningstar. 13. "Fourteen Cats" reprinted by permission of the author, Eileen Murphy. 14. "Trees" from THE LITTLE HILL, Poems and Pictures by Harry Behn. Copyright © 1949 by Harry Behn; copyright © renewed 1977 by Alice L. Behn. Reprinted by permission of Marian Reiner. 15. "Keep a Poem in Your Pocket" by Beatrice Schenk de Regniers, from SOMETHING SPECIAL by Beatrice Schenk de Regniers. Copyright © 1958, 1986 by Beatrice Schenk de Regniers. Reprinted by permission of the author. 16. "Wishful Thinking" reprinted by permission of the author, Pearl Bloch Segall. Originally published in BUBBLES by Gazelle Publications, Copyright © 1987. 17. "Silly Sleep Sheep" reprinted by permission of the author, Helen C. Smith. 18. "Bubbles Popping" reprinted by permission of the author, Deborah Vitello. 19. "Mumps" from UNDER THE TREE by Elizabeth Maddox Roberts. Copyright 1922 by B. W. Huebsch, Inc. Copyright renewed 1950 by Ivor S. Roberts. Copyright 1930 by The Viking Press, Inc. Copyright renewed 1958 by Ivor S. Roberts and The Viking PRess, Inc. All rights reserved. Reprinted by permission of Viking Penguin, a division of Penguin Books USA, Inc. 20. "The Secret Place" by Tomie de Paola, © 1986 by G.P. Putnam's Sons. Illustration from TOMIE de PAOLA'S BOOK OF POEMS, © 1988 by Tomie de Paola. Reprinted by permission. 21. "The Frost Pane" from ONE AT A TIME by David McCord. Copyright © 1925 by David McCord. First appeared in The Saturday Review. By permission of Little, Brown and Company. 22. "Jonathan Bing" by permission of Curtis Brown Ltd. 23. "The Pasture" copyright 1939, © 1967, 1969 by Holt, Rinehart and Winston. Reprinted from THE POETRY OF ROBERT FROST edited by Edward Connery Lathem. Reprinted by permission of Henry Holt and Company, Inc. 24. "The Last Word of a Bluebird" copyright 1916 by Holt, Rinehart and Winston and renewed 1944 by Robert Frost. Reprinted from THE POETRY OF ROBERT FROST edited by Edward Connery Latham, by permission of Henry Holt and Company, Inc. 25. "Fog" from CHICAGO POEMS by Carl Sandburg, copyright 1916 by Holt, Rinehart and Winston, Inc. and renewed 1944 by Carl Sandburg. Reprinted by permission of Harcourt Brace Jovanovich, Inc. 26. "True Story" from WHERE THE SIDEWALK ENDS by Shel Silverstein. Copyright © 1974 by Evil Eye Music, Inc. Reprinted by permission of Harper & Row, Publishers Inc. 27. "Moochie" from HONEY I LOVE by Eloise Greenfield. (Thomas Y. Crowell) Text copyright © 1978 by Eloise Greenfield. Reprinted by permission of Harper & Row, Publishers Inc. 28. "Hungry Mungry" from WHERE THE SIDEWALK ENDS by Shel Silverstein. Copyright © 1974 by Evil Eye Music, Inc. Reprinted by permission of Harper & Row, Publishers Inc. 29. "Adventures of Isabel" from THE BAD PARENTS' GARDEN OF VERSE by Ogden Nash. Copyright 1936 by Ogden Nash. By permission of Little, Brown and Company. 30. "Bird Carpenter" by permission of Instructor Magazine. 31. "Cat" by permission of